Rewiring Your Self to Break Addictions and Habits

Rewiring Your Self to Break Addictions and Habits

Overcoming Problem Patterns

ANGELA BROWNE-MILLER

PRAEGER
An Imprint of ABC-CLIO, LLC

Santa Barbara, California • Denver, Colorado • Oxford, England

Library of Congress Cataloging-in-Publication Data

Browne Miller, Angela, 1952–
    Rewiring your self to break addictions and habits : overcoming problem patterns / Angela Browne-Miller.
        p. cm.
    Includes bibliographical references and index.
    ISBN 978–0–313–35388–8 (hbk. : alk. paper) — ISBN 978–0–313–35389–5 (ebook : alk. paper)
1. Compulsive behavior—Treatment. 2. Habit breaking. 3. Substance abuse—Treatment. I. Title.
RC533.B758   2010
    616.85'84—dc22   2009034151

14 13 12 11 10   1 2 3 4 5

This book is also available on the World Wide Web as an eBook.
Visit www.abc-clio.com for details.

ABC-CLIO, LLC
130 Cremona Drive, P.O. Box 1911
Santa Barbara, California 93116-1911

This book is printed on acid-free paper ∞

Manufactured in the United States of America

To all of us.

Addiction, Slaves to Programming?

(Illustration by and courtesy of Angela Browne-Miller.)

Contents

List of Figures   xiii

Preface: It Is Never Too Late   xv

Acknowledgments   xvii

Introduction to Overcoming Problem Patterns   1

PART ONE: RECOGNIZING POWERFUL PATTERN   5
ADDICTIONS AROUND AND WITHIN US

1. Survival and Counter-Survival   7
   Survival?   8
   Gratification?   8

2. The Problem of the Problem Addiction Industry   11
   Example: The Matter of Stimulants Such As Cocaine   12
      and Meth
   Example: Legal and Illegal Opioids   12
   Example: The Question of Right Use As Per Cannabis   13
   Age at First Use   13
   Always Emerging Addictions   14
   Altered States of Consciousness (ASCs)   14
   Example: Addiction to Legal Drugs Such As Smoking and   15
      Coffee Drinking
   Are There Levels of Acceptable Use?   15
   Example: Prescription Drugs and Even Household Substances   16

Nondrug Addictions   17
The Problem Addiction Industry   17

3. Overarching Problem Conditions: Chemicalization and   19
    Mechanization
    Overarching Addiction Condition One: Chemicalization   19
    Overarching Addiction Condition Two: Mechanization   20

4. Problem States of Mind: Addictive Materialism and   23
    Addictive Inadequacy
    Addictive Materialism   23
    Addictive Inadequacy   24
    These Addictions Apply to All of Us   25

5. Creatures of Habitual Addiction   27
    Automatic Behavior All Around and Within   27
    Parallels between Drug and Nondrug Addictions   28
    Example: Food Addiction   30
    Example: Shopping/Spending Addiction   31
    Example: Work Addiction   32
    Key Realities   33

6. Creatures of Pleasure and Stimulation   39
    The Compelling Pleasure Pathway   39
    Example: Alcohol and Beta-Endorphine Craving   40
    Pleasure and Relief from Pain and Discomfort As Pleasure   41
    Example: Consider Heroin and Morphine Withdrawals   42
    Tolerance and Diminishing Returns   42
    Example: Commonplace Caffeine Addiction   43
    Example: The Smoking Gun of Nicotine Addiction   45
    Nondrug Addiction Stimulation of Pleasure Pathways   46
    Example: Food, Sex, and Runaway Dimensions of   46
      Our Coding
    Continued Use and Engagement   47

7. When Good Judgment Falls by the Wayside   49
    When Good Judgment Is Not Working   50
    Wise and Right Use of Decision-Making Ability   50
    Decision Making Is Central   52
    Making a Good Decision Is a Process   53
    Decision Making and Problem Solving: The *How*   54
      Matters Here

With Maturity Can Come Better Decision-Making Processes,   55
    But When Is Maturity?
The Greater Good   55

8. Addiction and Excessive Consumption   57
    In Excess   57
    Several Types of Excess   58
    The Consumption Trap   59

PART TWO: RECOGNIZING OUR POWERFUL   63
INNER CODING TO BE PATTERN-ADDICTED

9. Our Rigid Yet Paradoxical Addictions to What We See   65
    As Reality
    We Can Even Resist Healing Change   65
    Our Rigid Yet Paradoxical Addiction to the Patterned   66
      State Itself
    The Tug of Choice   67
    Explicit and Implicit Addictions   68
    Hidden Implicit Patterning   69
    Underlying Source Patterning to be Addicted to a Reality 70

10. Underlying Source Patterning Driving All Addictions   73
    Survival Relies on This Programming   73
    Risk and Stimulation As Triggers for Gambling and   74
      Gambling with Life

11. Slaves to Attentional Bias   77
    Attentional Bias Programming   78
    Conscious Attention to Triggers   80
    Bad Learnings   81
    Triggers Themselves May Induce Highs   82

12. Degraded Decision-Making Functioning   83
    Go and No-Go   83
    Action Selecting and Inhibiting   84

13. Compromised Thinking and Situation Responsivity   87
    Situations, Situations, Situations   87
    Executive Control   88
    Action Selection Decisions Respond to Situations   89

PART THREE: THE IMPORTANCE OF   91
PROMOTING SITUATIONAL TRANSCENDENCE

14. The Case for Situational Transcendence   93
    Situation Dependence and Situation Restriction   94
    Addiction-Specific Situations   95

15. Patterns of Progression into Problem Addiction Situations 97
    Casual to Regular   98
    Regular to Troubled   99
    Troubled to Addicted   100
    Descent into Detrimental Pattern Addiction   101
    The Freeing and Right Use of Our Energy   101

16. Achieving Situational Transcendence   117
    Condition One: Commitment   118
    Condition Two: Attention   121
    Condition Three: Fortitude   124
    Condition Four: Faith   125
    Conditions for Situational Transcendence   126

17. Phases of Situational Transcendence   129
    Phase Characteristics   129
    Phase 1: Struggle   130
    Phase 2: Paradox   131
    Phase 3: Insight   133
    Phase 4: Elevation   134
    Life Phases and Patterns   136
    No One's Life Pattern Is Written in Stone   138

18. Foundations of Situational Transcendence of Addiction   139
    Idea One   139
    Idea Two   140
    Idea Three   140
    Idea Four   140
    Idea Five   140
    Idea Six   141
    Idea Seven   141

PART FOUR: CONDUCTING LIFESTYLE   143
SURGERY

19. Lifestyle Surgery: Breaking Addiction   145
    The Reaching Hand   146

Overcoming Programming   148
Doing Something New   148
Elements of Addictive Patterning Cycle   149
Overcoming Resistance to Change   149

20. Dictionary of Triggers   151
Problem Area One: Practical Triggers   152
Problem Area Two: Temporal Triggers   152
Problem Area Three: Environmental Triggers   153
Problem Area Four: Media Triggers   153
Problem Area Five: Emotional Triggers   154
Problem Area Six: Spiritual Triggers   155
Problem Area Seven: Social Triggers   155
Problem Area Eight: Physical Triggers   156
Problem Area Nine: Nutritional Triggers   156
Problem Area Ten: Chemical Triggers   157

21. Trigger Charting: Seeing the Addiction Process   159
Mapping Addiction   159
Ongoing Charting   164

22. Life Management Planning   167
A Life Management Plan   168

PART FIVE: KNOWING ADDICTION   183

23. Addiction As a Family and Social System Affair   185
Chemical Dependence   186
Haven in a Heartless World?   187
The Symptoms and Effects of Family Drug Problems   188
Lies   189
Communication Breakdowns   191
Grudge Developments   192
Hurts   193
Familial Co-Addictions   194
Practical Difficulties And Simple Catastrophes   195

24. Protecting the Children of Our Patterns   197
Carriers of Patterns?   197
Teaching Denial   198
Harsh and Painful Reality   198
Children Have a Right to This Information   199

Conflict of Interests   200
Fading Heart   200

25. When "Love" or What Appears As Love Is Too Much   203
Why "Love" Is Relevant to Drug and Other Addictions—   204
    Which We Also Think We Love
Checkpoints along the Path to Violence   206
Tolerance Can Be Dangerous   206
Conflicting Experience   207
Establishing and Maintaining Healthy Patterns   208
Love?   209
Habits Sneak Up on Us   210
Running into Someone's Arms, Anyone's   210
Emotional Sadomasochism   210
Like Is Too Simple a Word for Love or Drug Addictions   212
When Relationships Like Drugs Kill   213

26. Rethinking Recovery As Discovery   215
Limitations in Our Thinking   215
Rethinking Addiction   218
Suggesting the Discovery Model   219

27. A Note About Synaptic Rights   223
The Synapse   223
Mental Chemistry   224
Addicting the Brain   225
The Other Face   227

28. Epilogue: Calling for Complete Overhaul   229
Substance Addiction As an Example   231
The Choicepoint   231
Overhaul Is Key to Healing Pattern Affliction   233

Bibliography   235
Index   267

List of Figures

Fronticepiece: Addiction, Slaves to Programming?   vi

Part One: Problem Addictions Around and Within   5

   2.1: Philosophical Addictivity, Addictivity Harm, and Addictivity   16
     Tolerance Continuums

   5.1: Example of Categories for Substances of Abuse/Addiction   34

   5.2: Example of Categories for Nondrug Activity Abuse/Addiction   36

   7.1: General Decision-Making Questions   56

   8.1: Consumption to Excess to Consumption to Excess Again Cycle   60

   8.2: No Way Out Trap or Paradox   60

Part Two: No Thanks, I'm an Addict and You Will Kill Me   63

   9.1: Basic Cycle of Addiction   69

   9.2: Full Patterning Addiction Hierarchy   71

Part Three: The Journey Starts Here   91

   14.1: Release from the Paradox of No Exit Addiction Situation   95

   15.1: Cocaine Addicted Person's Trigger Chart: All Triggers   103
     Leading to One Point

   15.2: Trigger Chart of Individual Who Has Chronic Headaches   104
     and Painkiller Addiction: All Triggers Leading to One Sensation

   15.3: Alcohol, Tobacco and Stimulant Dependent Individual's   105
     Triggers: All Triggers Feeding Addiction

   15.4: Alcohol Addicted Person's Trigger Chart: All Roads Leading   106
     to the Same Place

   15.5: Alcohol and Pain Killer Addicted Person's Trigger Chart: 107
     The Compounded Trigger Trap

15.6: Troubled Relationship (to Person or Drug or Activity)   108
Pattern #1: Common Addictive Discomfort-Comfort Cycle
or Pattern

15.7: Troubled Relationship (to Person or Drug or Activity)   109
Pattern #2: Common Addictive Longing for Contact Cycle
or Pattern

15.8: Sample Positive Relationship (to Person or Drug or Activity)   110
Progression Pattern: Common Anatomy of a Positive Bond
Progression

15.9: Sample Troubled Relationship (to Person or Drug or Activity)   111
Progression Pattern: Common Anatomy of a Negative Bond
Progression

15.10: Sample Mixed Positive and Negative Bond (to Person or   112
Drug or Activity) Progression: Pattern with Reversals

15.11: Sample Patterns of Cyclic Emotional and Sexual Patterns of   113
Relationship (to Person or Drug or Activity) Behaviors:
With Pleasure and Pain Driving the Cycles or Patterns

15.12: Emotional and Sexual Pleasure-Pain Cycles or Patterns: 114
Patterns Can Interlink and Compound

15.13: Sample Pain-Pleasure Confusion Mini-Cycles or Subloops: 115
Pleasure, Pain and the Illusion of Escape from the Patterns

16.1: Four Basic States of Mind, Mental Conditions, for   127
Transcendence

17.1: Phase 1: Struggle Pattern   131

17.2: Phase 2: Paradox Pattern   132

17.3: Phase 3: Insight Pattern   134

17.4: Phase 4: Elevation, a Situational and Spiritual Pattern for   135
Transcendence

17.5: Four Basic Phases of Situational Transcendence: Model Pattern 136

17.6: Life Map: Ongoing Process of Situational Transcendence: 137
Ideal Pattern of Progression

17.7: Variation on Life Map: Ongoing Struggle to Paradox to   138
Struggle: Common Pattern

Part Four: Time to Overcome Addictions   143

21.1: Sample Trigger Chart #1: Seeing the Internal Map or   165
Pattern for Change

21.2: Sample Trigger Chart #2: Mapping the Problem Addiction   166
Pattern

Part Five: Addiction Troubles on the Mind   183

Epilogue: Answer Problem Addiction with Complete Overhaul   229

Preface: It Is Never Too Late

It is never, never, too late.

You find yourself struggling in the rubble of broken dreams. You have been there a moment, a month, a decade—however long. You may feel your pain, your tears, your sense of loss and hopelessness, or you may just feel confusion, or you may just feel nothing at all. You say please, please some one fix this. Please please show me a way out. Please please God, if you are out there, help me.

The bits and pieces of the life you wanted to lead lie around you, shattered. You may weep or you may scream or you may sit in numb silence. You tread carefully through the fragments of your fractured dreams because you hurt when you walk on them, as if they are broken glass and your feet are bare. Everywhere you see wasteland, your own personal wasteland.

But these bits are the ingredients of something new. Put them together, like pieces of a jigsaw puzzle, and you will solve the mystery of the new you. There is a secret there among those ruins, there is something new waiting for you to see: There is always time to begin again . . . .

A hand reaches out from somewhere, a hand you can almost see. Is it your imagination or it there someone there? Look again, the hand you see is your own. Yes, there may be others trying to help. Or you may be all alone in this. But the hand you see is your own. You are calling yourself back to life. Listen. You want to be heard. You want to come back.

The view from this rock bottom place is the best view ever. Open your eyes. From here you can truly see. The possibilities are endless. Believe that you can resurrect yourself—believe—and you can.

Acknowledgments

Such a long journey it has been to this moment when a few of my thoughts regarding addiction can make their way from my mind and soul to these pages. Every stop along the way, every bend in the road, every hurdle, I have found my friends and colleagues standing by me, waving the flag of hope. To have such special people around me is a blessing, and gratitude for this washes through me in indescribable waves. Words of thanks just will not suffice.

Each and every one of these special persons deserves at least a book length if not an encyclopedic note of appreciation, and where I fall short of this, it speaks only to my being at a loss for words here. Let me at least say a few words of humble and heartfelt thanks to my dear friends and colleagues: the insightful and talented writer, Lee Brazil, who was there shining the light on the darkest of nights; David Parker, the greatest orator I have ever known, and one with heart, who I have known since childhood at that; Marty Kendrick Ketmer, who I have admired since the day we met in Washington, D.C. and who was and still is a fabulous mentor and role model; Gregory Bateson, the father of the double bind theory and perhaps the greatest teacher I have ever had—Gregory I wish you could be here in person now to see how you have influenced my life and work; and so many others including the thousands of persons struggling to break their problem addictions who have come to me for assistance—you know this journey, you have walked this path, you show us the way and the meaning of addiction itself.

And I wish to acknowledge and thank my amazing, talented, and incredible daughter, a superb editor and writer in her own right, Ms.

Evacheska deAngelis. Evacheska lived most of her childhood in addiction treatment. From the time she was ten days old, she was a guest at the table of addiction treatment, accompanying me in my work week after week, watching so many persons crawl in almost dead and, as she once said, "Hurting their lives," and then emerging later, looking whole and hopeful, as if finally the future was making itself an option to these people. To watch my child watch the addiction treatment process, and to know how deep and long lasting these impressions run, is to know she has walked a not so beaten track insofar as childhoods go. I thank you, Evacheska, for standing by me and being there to learn what we all were learning with you.

Angela Browne-Miller

Introduction to Overcoming Problem Patterns

The work of overcoming detrimental habits and addictions is, in essence, dialoging with the magnificent although perhaps archaic human brain. Behavioral change, especially the "breaking" (as it is called) of habits and addictions, involves change at the micro and at the macro levels of being, in fact on all levels of being. And virtually all these levels are directed by the mind and the brain which organizes it, drives it, and, for the most part, houses it. Where we—as addicted or co-addicted persons (which as I explain herein is all of us in some way), or addiction treatment or other health professionals, or those who research or legislate addiction—strive to encourage such profound behavioral change, we speak to the human brain virtually every day, virtually every moment of every day.

This book is written with this speaking to the mind-brain in mind. The wording of this material, especially in parts three and four of this book, is such that persons in all walks of life, lay and or professional, can access and share the ideas and the presentation of these ideas with others, including persons who are addicted and co-addicted. Think of my words as a simple dialog with the mind-brain, an attempt to befriend the mind-brain, to coax it, to inspire it, into prompting within itself profound behavioral change. After all, communicating in a manner that will be heard is already adjusting the communication process in the direction of increased accessibility. (Note that for those seeking the research into the mechanisms of substance as well as process addiction out of which I have developed the approach I set forth in this book, I have included an extensive research bibliography.)

My goal herein is to gently interject into the field of addiction a slight yet serious reformulating of itself, to add a meta-level overlay, a widening perspective, and based on this widened perspective to offer some tools for thinking about and for utilizing this perspective. In working with several thousand persons who are addicted and co-addicted, whether it be to substances or to behaviors—to drugs, alcohol, food, on-ground and online gambling and gaming, online and on-ground sex, relationships themselves, spending and shopping, television, work, violence, and or hundreds of other materials and activities, I have seen the addict and I know the addict to be us. I see that:

- habits and addictions themselves can be seen as a natural part of life, with many habits and addictions being positive, healthy and necessary behaviors;
- detrimental habits and addictions can be identified as such, clearly seen as behavior for which we are coded gone awry;
- troubled and dangerous addictions can be overcome **situationally**; and,
- overcoming detrimental habits and addictions requires a rewiring of ourselves—a rewiring of the *self and of its perceptions of its situation*—a rewiring of our minds and brains, and of our spirits, to change our behaviors.

Stepping back for a moment, let's turn to another aspect of our functioning, the heart beat. Here is something, a pattern, not only natural to our biological functioning, but essential. And when there is a troubled heart beat, one that may be either mildly troubling or seriously dangerous, we identify this heart beat and where required treat it. However, we do not call the beating of the heart itself a sickness, a disease. And we do not say that heart should not beat.

Hence where we find patterning behavior which brings about addictions and habits, we do not seek to remove that very essential to life patterning behavior. Instead we want to heal problem patterns. We do not call the patterning behavior itself a sickness, a disease. And we do not say that we, the organism, should not become patterned or addicted to good patterns such as stopping at red lights, putting on seat belts, brushing teeth, riding a bicycle, (perhaps to even deeper biological patterns and directives such as basic breathing and digesting), and so on. Now, while all this is quite obvious to some, I do find it quite necessary to clarify my perspective here as, you see, we are *all* creatures reliant upon our ability to grow patterned, *all* even addicted to both positive and likely also negative behaviors. Where we run into problems, very serious problems, is when this patterning capability within us seriously malfunctions either because of internal or external factors—directives, susceptibilities and or pressures on us.

This book is a contribution to the evolution of our understanding of addiction. I am calling for a slight reformulation of our thinking here, a rewiring of the philosophical perspective from which we address addictions. The *situation* in which problem addiction is taking place and is running awry must be understood for its power to send the natural coding messages and programming we carry within us down the wrong neuropsychological path (or down the right neuropsychological path for the wrong reasons, or too frequently). To formulate this rewiring of the SELF approach for my clients and colleagues, I have laid out my general thinking in parts one and two of this book. And then in parts three and four, I have set forth actual concepts and steps we can apply in helping the mind-brains of ourselves and others in the process of overcoming problem addictions. I call the heart of this process **Situational Transcendence**, a process and way of thinking I have devised and suggest we bring into our thinking processes, and into our daily lives, as well as into addiction treatment and research settings. (See especially Chapters 14 and 16.)

So we are all addicted to many things and to many behaviors, as we are all coded to be so. Perhaps even most of what we as individuals, families and societies do in our lives is driven by some form of pattern addiction. We are born with this capacity to be addicted and even need it. No one is exempt. Addiction to patterns is common to all of us. Addiction to situations in which we can play out our patterns is also common to all of us. We even favor—exhibit attentional biases toward—triggers for these patterns, as I will discuss in the coming chapters. (See Chapters 11, 12, and 13.)

Note that this book is an effort to reach beyond, to add to, the wonderful wealth of literature presently available regarding breaking addictions, to bring together and build upon current neuroscience, biological, psychological, social and spiritual perspectives on the workings of addiction and recovery from addiction. Here, I want to bring the SELF fully into focus, to say that getting to truly know oneself, to really know oneself, is to delineate between the true **self** and the problem pattern addiction that appears to be the self or part of the self. We are not our problem patterns, these are not our identities, although it is easy to err and think these are one in the same.

Now, as the addict, which is all of us, we can reposition ever so slightly our approach to overcoming problem addiction patterns, which is going to also be repositioning rather profoundly. We can test the waters, expand the scope of addiction itself, and see where this view might take us. Let's give this a try here on the following pages . . . .

PART ONE

Recognizing Powerful Pattern Addictions Around and Within Us

Problem Addictions Around and Within

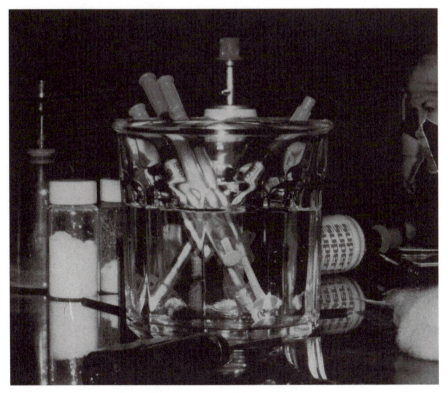

(Photograph by and courtesy of Angela Browne-Miller.)

1

Survival and Counter-Survival

We are all about survival. Or are we? Survival is why we live. Or is it? We have to wonder. Although our personal experiences in our daily lives may not tell us this directly, survival of the species appears to be what most of our behavior is about. After all, we sense, on some deep level, that without the survival of the species, we as individuals have no future and will cease to exist. Yet, the human brain, and the behaviors it conducts, do not always work toward survival. Sure, the human brain does its best. Yet, this human brain of ours is not coping as well as, nor evolving as rapidly as, we may need it to.

At the center of this quagmire is the matter of the environment which is changing at an ever faster pace than is the brain which directs us as we live in the environment. This conflict in the rate of change between the environment and the brain may be resulting in a diminishing of the brain's ability to read essential feedback coming from the environment to the brain. The brain therefore cannot rely entirely on the modern environment to set limits. As a result, behaviors directed by the brain frequently slip into runaway mode. While the older environment regulated these behaviors (via danger, pain, fear, and famine for example) and thereby placed greater limits on runaway behaviors driven by the brain, the modern environment, especially in the so-called "developed" world, offers far less in the way of these very external controls the brain evolved itself to respond to.

SURVIVAL?

We have arrived in these times, apparently far less able to regulate our behaviors just when we need to be far more able to regulate our behaviors. Here we are, in the modern world, in the face of opportunities for *endless excess*—excess in consumption of refined sugar, low quality carbohydrates, alcohol, drugs, gambling, spending, and a host of other compelling substances and activities. We feel the pull of excess, we are even drawn to it. We are confused by yet recognize this sensation. We want to turn away but too often cannot. We feel this tug of war on some very deep level. Too often we find that neither our environments nor our brains can stop us from slipping into detrimental patterns of excess and of addiction to detrimental excess.

Excess, runaway excess, is a mounting and potentially devastating problem loaded with the tragic flaws of hypocrisy and the failing of the human brain to set limits. Most excess has lost its purpose in modern times and in the modernized world, rarely now appearing again in new versions of more legitimate survival oriented forms such as the layer of excess fat found on an animal storing up for winter hibernation. Modern people almost entirely miss the point, the survival value, of excess, yet consume to the level of excess whenever possible. While entire populations in some areas of the planet cannot get enough food, water, medicine and shelter to live, entire modernized populations (even in times of what they perceive as economic hardship) are driven to seek, to constantly seek, immediate gratification. In fact, in modern times, immediate gratification has become an expectation.

GRATIFICATION?

Yet, in the all out no-holds-barred drive for immediate gratification can also be found the seeking of relief from suffering, rather than from only the direct pleasure or gratification sensation seeking behavior we associate with it. For example, those who have suffered from severe migraines know what it feels like to have that intense pain finally recede—it feels good! Relief from extreme suffering is surely a form of pleasure, perhaps the greatest pleasure there is. This problem of the drive for desire gratification is an equal opportunity, a malady affecting people of all ages, in all walks of life, in all economic situations, in all levels of "well" being, everywhere. Hence, this monster we call problem addiction rears its ugly head everywhere we look. And it reaches to great and seemingly unlikely extremes, for example to street children in Bolivia who use cocaine paste to relieve their hunger pains, to street children in Nepal who sniff glue to push back the cold and their hunger pains, to masses of children around the world, in all walks of life, exposed to drugs and alcohol prior to birth and during childhood.

Here we must force ourselves to witness (even when we may choose to deny) this reality, the modern problem addictions seizing the human population worldwide. The objects of these addictions move to the forefront—these are substances and activities many of which powerfully stimulate the pleasure and reward (reinforcement) centers of the brain to generate direct pleasure as well as the pleasure of relief from displeasure, discomfort, and suffering. The objects of these addictions can now regulate the human behavior more powerfully than can the environment the brain needs to have helping it control itself.

We know this, we are sensing this disturbing development. And we also know that in nature, immediate gratification is rare. Instead, nature takes its time. A primary exception to this taking of time in nature is the instance of immediate response to danger when the "fight or flight" syndrome kicks in. Fortunately, some of this mechanism remains functional in our brains today. When instinct kicks in, we instinctively respond to danger by either taking flight or fighting back. Unfortunately, many drugs and activities to which we can become addicted stimulate parts of the brain involved in this fight or flight reflex.

Furthermore, the fight or flight reflex is confused now. When the modern brain senses an actual shortage of something, or even the threat of a pause in the flow of needed resources and security, it responds to the perceived as well as actual famine (of supplies and resources, of opportunity, of power, of safety) by consuming, even consuming dangerously at times, and or expressing *addictively* whatever it can—no matter how counter-survival this expression may be.

2

The Problem of the Problem Addiction Industry

Addiction is clearly a global issue touching every population, every nation, and every age group, people from all walks of life everywhere, directly or indirectly. Indeed, we are talking about an affliction of epic and epidemic proportions. We cannot look away. This is the health of the human species we are talking about.

The World Health Organization tells us that psychoactive substance use poses a serious threat to families, communities and nations. In fact, there are, worldwide, at least billions of alcohol users, over a billion smokers and billions of legal and illegal drug users; and, of these there are a minimum of nearly a billion persons with alcohol use disorders, and a minimum of a billion others with drug (legal and illegal drug) use disorders. Alcohol use and abuse as well as the use and abuse of other psychoactive substances contributes to substantial individual and public health costs. Alcohol is but one substance playing a major role in this global addiction epidemic, and clearly there are many others, despite efforts to prevent new addictions and addicts, and to contain world drug, alcohol, gambling, gaming, sex, pornography, and other addiction-related markets and industries, both on-ground and online. While substance—drug and alcohol—addiction is most obvious, other behavioral—nondrug or "process"—addictions are at least as prevalent and insidious.

We are all impacted by the far reach of these troubling addictions and the legal and illegal industries that market, push, and sell these to us. I offer a few examples below. Keep in mind that, whether or not you are personally addicted to any one of these substances or activities, you are, we all are, carrying deep within us biochemical programming, deeply embedded prewired templates, for such or similar addictions. (Also note that readers who are seeking in-depth discussion of specific addictions and their mechanisms are referred to the extensive bibliography at the end of this book and are also to the vast array of already extensive, and therefore not reiterated herein, literature on the basics of addiction available to us.)

EXAMPLE: THE MATTER OF STIMULANTS SUCH AS COCAINE AND METH

Cocaine and crack cocaine have shared the stage with other abused drugs for quite some time. It was not until the 1980s that modern awareness gelled regarding the potent addiction that popular neurostimulants such as cocaine can trigger within us. We are a self-stimulating species largely in love with the stimulation we provide ourselves—in love, that is, until we are in danger (and sometimes even past that point). The prevalence of cocaine (and coca and crack) use is especially serious in developing countries, with severe medical, psychological, social, and economic consequences including, but not limited to, the spread of infectious diseases (e.g., AIDS, hepatitis, and tuberculosis), plus crime, violence, and neonatal drug exposure.

Additionally, amphetamine-type stimulant (ATP) abuse is more widespread than cocaine abuse in at least 20 countries, or some ten percent of all the countries in the world. Methamphetamine is presumed to lead in ATP addiction rates, with massive meth epidemics affecting several whole countries and entire regions of others. Social and public health costs of methamphetamine production and use via smoking, sniffing, inhaling, and injecting are staggering and growing in many regions.

EXAMPLE: LEGAL AND ILLEGAL OPIOIDS

Cocaine and meth and are just one piece of the global drug use and addiction picture. There has been a global increase in the production, transportation, and use of opioids, including but not limited to codeine, oxycodone, morphine, and also heroin, the latter being one of the strongest opioids. Worldwide heroin production has been doubling or even tripling since the mid-1980s. Global estimates are that there are millions of persons who have tried and or regularly consume opioids, with many millions of these being regular heroin users who face health risks including hepatitis, HIV, and death.

EXAMPLE: THE QUESTION OF RIGHT USE AS PER CANNABIS

Now let's shift gears to consider what is generally viewed as one of the more innocuous drug problems. The hotly debated drug cannabis—the cannabis family of drugs with the euphoria-inducing tetrahydrocannabinols, or THCs, including marijuana, THC tinctures, and hashish-related preparations—is said to be the most widely used as well as abused drug. Critics of widespread cannabis use suggest the risk for significant health effects in long-term, chronic cannabis use, including potential impairment of cognitive development, learning, memory, recall, attention, and coordination. This is *long term* chronic use. Certainly, the presence and extent of long-term effects of casual, regular and even of chronic use itself are as yet not entirely ascertained. Both casual use of marijuana and medical use of forms of what is termed medical marijuana (e.g., dronabinol sold as Marinol, the cannabidiols, or CBDs) are subsets of all forms of cannabis use. There are legitimate therapeutic uses of this substance, and these uses make it all the more difficult to regulate marijuana drugs fairly and effectively. And with the ongoing criminalization of cannibis use, we see the fueling of crimes related to its misuse, smuggling and underground production and distribution.

We have here, and in the use of any psychoactive medication for therapeutic purposes, a gray area in which illicit and licit use overlap and can confuse many adult and youth drug consumers, researchers, and policy makers, among others. In the emergence (or reemergence in history, some will argue) of cannabis as medicine, we have a model for asking which, if any, abused substances may, and perhaps should, be repurposed for medicinal or treatment purposes, and how this is best done against the backdrop of the global addiction epidemic.

AGE AT FIRST USE

In marijuana, we are confronted with a good example of the age-at-first-use issue, which suggests that early onset of regular cannabis use may affect not only the academic and social performance of children and teens, but also their future susceptibility to addictions. It was in the 1960s (when available marijuana was not as potent as it is today) that the hotly debated label "gateway drug" was applied to marijuana, perhaps to scare off its use. Only in the decades since have we understood better what this might actually mean to us. It may not be that marijuana surely provides the training wheels for drug addiction, but rather that it may serve as an *indicator of future use* of the same or other drugs. Of course, today, with so many young people having access, and taking advantage of their access, to the whole range of psychoactive substances, the question of which drug might be a gateway to which other drug dissolves into the fury of the countless addiction conundrums of our constantly changing times.

ALWAYS EMERGING ADDICTIONS

There is always a new, or rediscovery of an old, addiction on the horizon. There is also always a new (or rediscovered) psychoactive substance for recreational, exploratory, research and perhaps even treatment purposes emerging (or reemerging). Labeling all of these substances as addictive (or problematically addictive) right out the gate may or may not serve science or even humanity itself. How can we be certain the approach we take will be a constructive one? With new legal (where licensed for development and experimentation) and illegal (where not being utilized under protection of law) so-called designer drugs emerging at a staggering rate, we must admit that we cannot know what is coming, nor whether the new compound will be harmfully addictive, or popular, or of medicinal value, or even accessible. We can only imagine what the brave new worlds of chemistry and its offshooting psychopharmacology will continue to bring and whether any benefits can be made available without accompanying risks and detriments.

ALTERED STATES OF CONSCIOUSNESS (ASCs)

Moreover, the desire to explore and achieve various altered states of consciousness, in personal, religious, spiritual, ritual and perhaps even treatment settings, is unfolding into debates about both addiction risks and personal rights. The question emerges: When there is no demonstrated risk to self or others, should this right should be protected, especially in circumstances of traditional uses for religious purposes? (Refer to Chapter 27 for further comment on this matter.) Again, this dilemma arises against the backdrop of the global and runaway epidemic of substance addiction. How do we balance pressures in opposite directions (freedom protecting right to use versus control to stop injury, social costs of using, and addiction itself), when these pressures are not balancing themselves? And how do we define "demonstrated risks" to self or others?

EXAMPLE: ADDICTION TO LEGAL DRUGS SUCH AS SMOKING AND COFFEE DRINKING

Also against the backdrop of global addiction levels, is the massive level of addiction to legal drugs, many of which are heavily marketed to consumers. The legal drug tobacco is said to be the substance causing the most damage globally, with at least one-third of the global population smoking. While smoking rates may register as dropping in some countries, the reverse is true globally. Even now, after its vast and apparently successful anti-smoking campaigns, tobacco use is overwhelmingly viewed as being the single most avoidable cause of disease, disability and death in the United States. As just one of its numerous detrimental effects, smoking accounts worldwide for the large majority of all lung cancer in both men and women. (We return to nicotine in Chapter 6, Creatures of Pleasure and Stimulation.)

And perhaps nothing here has touched so many lives around the world as the regularly consumed, legal drug caffeine, perhaps because coffee drinking is not only tolerated, it is considered very normal and acceptable, even necessary, in everyday life. However, we must ask whether there is a level of caffeine use that is abuse—or perhaps self-abuse. Do we not want to put caffeine use onto this list of substance abuses and addictions? Or do we want to ignore the pervasive worldwide use of and addiction to caffeine? (We return to the complex matter of the all popular drug caffeine, also in Chapter 6.)

ARE THERE LEVELS OF ACCEPTABLE USE?

While this is not necessarily to cause readers who drink such a common drug as coffee to feel alarmed about the direction of this

Figure 2.1. Philosophical Addictivity, Addictivity Harm, and Addictivity Tolerance Continuums

(examples) **CAFFEINE ↔ ALCOHOL ↔ METHAMPHETAMINE**

low level of perceived addictivity ↔ high level of perceived addictivity

highly acceptable addiction ↔ low or no acceptable addiction

low degree of distinguishable harm ↔ high degree of distinguishable harm

highly acceptable harm ↔ low or no acceptable harm

high tolerance for a particular addiction ↔ low or no tolerance for a
particular addiction

(Diagram by and courtesy of Angela Browne-Miller.)

commentary, this is meant to ask: How do we select which addictions we support, advertise, or perhaps simply chose to look away from? And what does the question of looking away actually ask? Could it be that we accept, even invite, some problem addictions, while labeling others as truly harmful? Perhaps there are degrees of *addictivity* and degrees of *distinguishable harm* we accept, along hidden philosophical continuums such as those listed in Figure 2.1.

We, as a society, as all our societies in all our nations, tend to tolerate, even prefer, some problem addictions over others. Generally speaking, societal tolerance of an addiction is based on that particular addiction being seen as: not very addictive, while somewhat or even highly socially acceptable; not very harmful, while any harm there is is viewed as acceptable, and most harm there is is not distinguishable. All this results in a high degree of tolerance for, and even a conscious and subconscious looking away from, an addiction.

EXAMPLE: PRESCRIPTION DRUGS AND EVEN HOUSEHOLD SUBSTANCES

And then there are also the addictions to prescription drugs (such as legally and also illegally obtained Vicodin, Percocet, OxyContin, and Darvon), which we find ever increasing and a worldwide phenomenon, with the most commonly abused prescription drugs being opiates. The U.S. National Institute of Mental Health characterizes prescription drug addiction as the second most common illegal use of drugs in the United States, second only to marijuana. Worldwide prescription drug abuse is reaching phenomenal proportions, with virtually every addictive prescription drug being available illegally as well as legally.

We must also note that unusual, virtually invisible, psychoactive substances are working their way into our everyday lives. Household and workplace products contain many volatile substances, exposure to which can be not only damaging, but also intoxicating, and in many instances even dangerously addicting. We must acknowledge the severe and perhaps largely unmeasured effects of this domain of even routine, legal substance use as well as its unintentional and intentional abuse and addictions.

NONDRUG ADDICTIONS

So as not to exclude the all important and highly relevant nonsub-stance—nondrug—process—behavioral—addictions in this discussion, we must include work, television, shopping, relationship, food (with its particularly difficult-to-call-addiction nature), sex, pornography, violence, gambling, and Internet addictions in our understanding of troubled patterning, as these too make their addiction-related marks in all our lives, either indirectly or directly. These behavioral, nondrug addictions, which occur alone and co-occur with each other, also do co-occur with substance uses, abuses, and addictions. Every human being is indeed in some way affected by the prevalence of behavioral addictions. (Refer to Chapter 5.) The study of behavioral addictions teaches us a great deal about addiction itself. We are looking at ourselves here, all of us, as members of an addiction-prone and largely chemically- and addictive activity-dependent human species.

THE PROBLEM ADDICTION INDUSTRY

Calling to us, shouting to us, from all around and deep within is the reality that we have generated entire cultures and even whole national and multinational industries around our problem addictions. The doggedly determined investment in our problem addiction industry is therefore not only biological and the cause of an addicted brain, but also a major economic (and likely even cultural) force. Entire regions of the world are virtually dependent upon income from gambling, prostitution, alcohol consumption, and the sale of many of the substances and activities of addiction. If we were actually able to abruptly halt all profits being made on various drug, alcohol, gambling and pornography addictions, entire economies would wobble if not be devastated. Moreover, we cannot even begin to estimate the "losses" that we would see were we to add in shopping and spending addictions—were we to bring about the abrupt halting of economies' fueling and feeding on their people's shopping and spending addictions. Ultimately, there are whole industries dependent upon keeping people addicted. We are a species who has addicted itself to, and has a great investment in, its problem addictions.

3

Overarching Problem Conditions: Chemicalization and Mechanization

Why are problem addictions seizing the human species? Why is a major proportion of humanity, even a critical mass of humanity, falling prey to patterns of problem addiction? While we as individuals struggle with the effects and pulls of troubled and dangerous drug and nondrug addictions, our species as a whole is ailing. Overarching trends threaten to engulf us all, entire subpopulations are succumbing, and all this is making the struggle for the individual all the more profound. Problem addiction in a problem addicted world is part of the program, intrinsic to our realities now, part of overarching trends almost too massive for us to recognize.

OVERARCHING ADDICTION CONDITION ONE: CHEMICALIZATION

Reaching beyond the boundaries of individual bodies and psyches, is our broad and inescapable modern-day species-wide dependence on chemicals. Let's call this overarching addiction condition *chemicalization*. Slowly, man-made chemicals are filling our air, our water, our food, our bodies, and our minds. Our homes are cleaned with detergents. Plastics are everywhere—we wear them, we play with them, we may ingest them even if trying not to, we even drive them. Medicine says it offers chemical solutions to many of our health problems. A reliance on manufactured chemicals has become a way of life in our modern world. As a result, we are all to a great degree chemically dependent. We are all pattern-addicted to the chemical world. We are in a can't live without it, cant live with it position. What a trap! What a paradox! Substance-addicted people, singled out as the only chemically dependent ones among us, are actually making the reality of everyone's increasing dependence on chemicals more apparent. Yet, they represent just the tip of the iceberg. They represent us, our ailing species.

OVERARCHING ADDICTION CONDITION TWO: MECHANIZATION

Also reaching beyond the boundaries of individual bodies and minds is the overarching addiction condition we can call *mechanization*. Not only does the increasing mechanization of everything we do affect our lives, but it also affects our definitions of ourselves. Every day we feel either indirectly or directly the increasing mechanization of our realities. And slowly, almost invisibly, we are surrendering our individual identities. We are acquiescing to the reality of what we can call *numbership*—a reality in which we identify ourselves as a series of numbers (telephone, social security, drivers license, tax identification, et cetera) and mechanical processes (checking in and checking out, logging on and logging off, signing in and signing out, as well as functions such as registering, paying, driving, et cetera).

Without even seeing it happen, we are beginning to treat ourselves as numbers, machines, items, THINGS. The effect of mechanization on our perceptions of ourselves reaches into the deepest recesses of our psyches largely unbeknownst to our consciousnesses. It is ironic that contained in the word for our being numbered that I like to use, *numbership*, is the word *numb*. As we become more like numbers, more like machines, more this way not only biophysically, but psychologically and socially, we may actually be becoming *numb to our humanity*. We slip into mechanical on-off, turn me on turn me off, states of mind.

And here is the alarm going off: many problem addicted individuals claim that they want to "numb the pain" and or anxiety of their existences by using drugs or other substances or activities to "turn off." Others want to feel more, to stop being turned off and be "turned on." We are learning more about our *behavioral switches* and our use of these. We know that some of us are addicted to the chemical switches we call "drugs" and others to foods or activities that numb us, distract us, give us an escape, at least temporarily, from pain and stress. Yet this is more than just some of us. We all treat ourselves like machines with on-off buttons.

Just about everyone has turned to painkillers to dim or switch off headaches, body aches, and injuries. Check the inside of your medicine chest. Can you toss out its contents without hesitation? We turn ourselves on and off like machines whenever we can. We mechanize ourselves without even realizing it. What switches do you use? *How frequently do you treat yourself like a machine?*

Chemical switches are part of our modern (and even our ancient) lives. And so are electrical switches (such as television) and emotional switches (activities and events we rely upon to change our feelings, such as parties for energy or happiness, music for sexual arousal or general fun or relaxation, disagreements for neurologically-registered anger or righteousness, full blown arguments for adrenaline-driven violence or other tension release). As you can see from this partial list, turning to switches is not, in itself, bad for us. What is problematic is the way we use switches on ourselves plus the tendency we have to rely on them—*to run on automatic like machines* —rather than to *pay attention* to how we are turning events, emotions, objects, and chemicals into switches and ourselves into things which can be switched on and off.

This matter of treating ourselves like machines runs quite deep. As later chapters will say, even the micro level workings of our brains are mechanized—or perhaps better stated—*biomechanized.* We function like fleshy biocomputers, fully loaded with biochemical chips driven by genetic codes, codings with our response to most if not all triggers, and with most if not all our addictions predictable on a biochemical level. In a biological but nevertheless mechanical way, our behaviors and even our tendencies to pattern addiction are virtually preordained. Where the environment plays a part in the play of pattern addiction is where we are coded to allow the environment to do so, and where we are coded to affect the environment in such a way that we will chose to allow it to play a role in our pattern addiction. Again, this is a no exit circular maze where cause and effect look or at least feel alike. This no exit trap is the paradox, the SITUATION, from which we need to, (and hopefully want to) spring.

4
Problem States of Mind: Addictive Materialism and Addictive Inadequacy

The human condition carries within it natural addiction functions, complete with built in lures serving as bait, to pull us in to addiction cycles and trigger-hypersensitivties, to bring us back again and again to addictive patterns. Sure, the brain is not entirely at fault, as the physical, social and economic environments call us to addiction, even demand we become addicted. We are perhaps subjecting ourselves to a multiply-compounded condition, an entangled network of genetic, environmental, age old societal and now modern societal, triggers for addicted patterning and repatterning, and reinforcement of this patterning.

ADDICTIVE MATERIALISM

One way to look at modern addictions is to see our **SELVES** as object-addicted, and object-addicted people as materialistic. (Note: The emphasis on the word SELF [and SELVES] herein is intentional. As the following chapters will show, we must be able and willing to differentiate between the problem addiction *pattern* and the SELF, in order to separate, to disentangle, the identity of the SELF and its own behaviors from the problem addiction patterns that can overtake it.) The object-addicted within us reach outside our **selves** for a material thing or experience—exercise a sort of *addictive materialism* —going for a purchase, a car, a house, someone's body, a food, a drug, a game or gamble—or a relationship, a job, a shopping trip, a television show—as a way of working with, soothing, calming, massaging, feeding, our psyches. For example, if we feel depressed, we may take a "drink," a "hit," or a "line." We depend upon an externally provided (or at least externally originated) material item or sensation to rescue us from an undesired internal state of mind, and to provide us with the biochemical shift we seek, even crave. Of course our state of mind may reflect external predicaments—things going on in the world around us—but our ability to cope with those predicaments is weakened. Instead this ability is naively based on a concrete external item, object, or sensation usually to be taken or experienced physically, as in a "hit" or "drink" or a nondrug fix, perhaps a sexual or gambling or eating or shopping or other interlude.

The addicted individual's preoccupation with something, such as a chemical substance or brain chemistry-altering activity, is an escape from the more arduous task of really dealing with feelings and situations. Addictions have become the quick fix "answer" for so many of us. In a materialistic society, we are conditioned to depend on a material substance or material experience in order to avoid the pain of actually living through and learning from a crisis.

ADDICTIVE INADEQUACY

This addictive materialism also reflects a state of inadequacy. The addicted individual has come to regularly rely on relationships, or food, or shopping, or gambling, or drugs (including alcohol) or some other addictive activity to take the more jagged edges off the harsh realities of life. In this picture of drug and other forms of addiction, individuals use drugs or engage in their addictions because they feel they cannot cope. These persons sense that their own psychological coping mechanisms may be insufficient and inadequate in the face of the pressures of life.

Most of us are taught adequate coping skills as we grow up in this society. We believe we are "able to handle" whatever or most of whatever comes along. But if chemically or behaviorally addicted individuals have learned these coping skills, they lose these through disuse when these skills are blocked and disabled by the artificial coping mechanisms of problem addictive behaviors. In this way, the illusion of coping addictively through chemicals—addiction to drugs, or through the brain chemistry of problem nondrug addiction patterns, is powerful. This illusion is the problem pattern addiction telling the brain—telling the SELF—that this problem pattern is needed for coping, that it helps make life livable—and ultimately that this problem pattern addiction is the SELF itself.

THESE ADDICTIONS APPLY TO ALL OF US

These two explanations point to the global nature of addiction. The problems of addictive materialism (dependence on outer means for solving inner problems) and of addictive inadequacy (a habitual response driven by a sense of not having or being enough to cope or of just not being able to cope) are common to a greater portion of society than the mere population of those addicted to drugs and alcohol. How many of us end up overeating or overspending, overdoing something, anything, whatever it is, when we are bored, lonely, stressed, depressed or faced with a crisis? How many of us have trouble dealing with the realities of life and are forced to depend on externalities? Not all of us are formally and explicitly addicted to dangerous chemicals or activities, but we all exhibit signs of addictive materialism and addictive inadequacy. Each of us regularly seeks to compensate for these source level addictive characteristics within ourselves. This means that the addicted individual is not alone, and not unlike the seemingly non-addicted person. We all have a great deal in common. If we are honest with ourselves we will admit again that we have seen the pattern addict. And he, or she, is us.

5

Creatures of Habitual Addiction

We frequently describe ourselves and each other as "creatures of habit." We know we are such creatures, we know we can fall into patterns of living, patterns of behaving, even patterns of thinking. Indeed, we are quite readily patterned—programmed into living and behaving and thinking close to the same way again and again. And why not? Using a pattern already burned into our brain-space means we do not need more brain-space or more brain time to respond to the same old thing again and again; we can just go onto automatic. We can just have our brains go to the record of how whatever it is we are responding to or doing was done before, and before that, and before that and before, and so on.

AUTOMATIC BEHAVIOR ALL AROUND AND WITHIN

This automatic behavior is an unsettlingly mechanical function. We do not like to say so, yet we can indeed describe ourselves as fleshy robots—nice, soft cuddly ones maybe, but nevertheless, programmable biological and biochemical machines. In fact, the genetic programming tendencies, capabilities, susceptibilities, we are born with, and all the programming we absorb, acquire—burn into our brains and nervous systems as we live in our environments and societies—determines a great deal of who we are. We even tend to wrap our identities into our patterns, so much so that we confuse ourselves with our patterns. The SELF thus submerges itself into the problem pattern.

Such a heavy influence upon us has the neural programming we inherit plus accumulate during our physical lifetimes that it can be immensely difficult to erase, especially when the programming is that of detrimental habits and addictions. Where we are gripped by the hand of the deep, unrelentingly ongoing and doggedly reinforcing addictive programming of detrimental, even dangerous, damaging and destructive biochemical, behavioral, and thought pattern habits and addictions, we face enormous challenges. Yet, as difficult as habitual patterning is to erase, it can be modulated and addressed when we see the situation for what it is, and learn to transcend this situation. When I use the word transcendence here, I am not speaking about something vague and otherworldly, but rather the rather practical process I use in my work, the process of what I call **Situational Transcendence** (as will be detailed in Part Three of this book).

So, while some will say that the most certain erasure of deep neural programming may be the death of the physical body and its brain and physical nervous system, I have come to see that **Situational Transcendence** is another path to overcoming this programming. Some things—some situations and patterns—have to die out or, better stated, be transcended, or at least overridden, for new things to begin. Problem situations and their problem patterns must be overridden.

PARALLELS BETWEEN DRUG AND NONDRUG ADDICTIONS

We know that troubled addictions have besieged us throughout our history, for many thousands of years. And throughout time, troubled addictions have made deep and frequently lasting changes in brain function, some quite difficult to reverse. And at this time in our modern history, we are beginning to recognize that problem addiction has become a global matter, with virtually no population or region untouched by either its direct or indirect effects. With drug and alcohol use themselves reaching all time highs around the world, and other nondrug addictions (which we are now learning to call addictions as well) also spiraling in numbers everywhere, we can see, we can almost feel, the ubiquitous nature of troubled addiction patterns.

Drugs of use, abuse and addiction have been categorized in several ways, including according to their various legalities, mechanisms and effects. Frequently drugs (substances of addiction) are categorized into three general groups: stimulants, depressants and hallucinogens.

Even these very general categories can be blurred as the characteristics of some drugs differ according to character or dose. For example, marijuana or cannabis is frequently labeled as a depressant, however, at higher doses, it may be a hallucinogen, and may perhaps require its own category. A perhaps more complete categorization is that identified by the Substance Abuse and Mental Health Services Administration of the United States Department of Health and Human Services. In this schema, there are seven basic categories: narcotics, depressants, stimulants/inhalants, hallucinogens, cannabis, alcohol, and steroids, as listed in Figure 5.1.

Again, substance (drug) addiction tells us a great deal about nonsubstance (nondrug) addiction. We are increasingly aware of the marked, even biochemical, parallels among the various problem addictions. We might add at least the following to the list we see in Figure 5.1: gambling and online gambling, gaming and online gaming, shopping and online shopping, spending and online spending, sex and online sex, pornography and online pornography, relationships and online relationships, violence and online violence, and so on, as suggested in Figure 5.2.

Although there is ongoing debate regarding clinical diagnosis of drug and alcohol addiction, there is general agreement. According to the Diagnostic and Statistical Manual of Mental Disorders, 1994 4th edition, DSM-IV, (of the American Psychiatric Association), symptoms of addiction include: persistent desire to engage in, or unsuccessful efforts to cut down or control, substance use; and continued substance use despite knowledge of having a persistent or recurrent physical or psychological problem that is likely to have been caused or exacerbated by the substance; with the probability of increase in tolerance, and of withdrawal symptoms. The American Psychiatric Association (APA) also suggests that substance abuse refers to a pattern of substance use leading to significant impairment in functioning. We will return to this significant impairment in functioning in Part Two of this book. (More recently, responding to widening appreciation of diversity, there have been calls for adding cultural, ethnic, gender, age, and even religious orientation, and also possible disability factors, to definitions of addiction and its symptoms.)

General definitions of substance addiction can be and are applied to nonsubstance addiction as well. While there is some debate regarding the use of the word addiction in addressing nondrug but related behaviors, there is a growing understanding that similar brain actions and functions are involved in addiction-type behavior whether the object of addiction is a substance or an activity such as gambling. As is indicated in Chapters 11, 12 and 13, the brain functions to addict us to activities in much the same way it does to addict us to drugs and alcohol. Basically, we are chained to the biochemistries of our pleasure and cognitive pathways, (among others).

EXAMPLE: FOOD ADDICTION

Consider for a moment the unpopular and too often cruel label: foodaholic. While debate continues regarding whether food addiction is addiction, and whether all compulsive food related behaviors are addictions, the relationship between some eating disorders and substance addiction is being increasingly acknowledged. There are three basic forms of eating disorders: anorexia nervosa, bulimia, and compulsive eating. Each of these involves excessive behaviors and or excessive emotions. Food may be consumed too much, or too little, or be too frequently rejected (regurgitated for example). Extreme distress in general, or extreme distress regarding weight or food consumption are common with eating disorders, as are emotional and biophysical roller coaster rides that parallel the drug addiction experience: highs then lows, and triggers, urges then responses (as in the basic cycle of addiction patterning explained in Chapter 9 and diagrammed in Figure 9.1 on page 69). Compulsive overeating is perhaps the most readily paralleled to drug addiction.

All eating disorders are on the rise, with the rate of these disorders in the United States steadily rising, especially during the past thirty to forty years. Proper nutrition is essential in maintaining proper weight and warding off many chronic diseases. Age at first experience of improper nutrition determines significant effect on well being, achievement and health in adulthood, as well as during childhood and adolescence. While lack of protein and other forms of malnutrition in early childhood and later childhood years are not the focus of this discussion, these too warrant attention regarding their potential for impact on the development of problem substance and nondrug addictions. (Recall the examples in Chapter 1 of hungry children in Bolivia and Nepal turning to drug use—cocaine and glue—to ward off hunger pains and the cold.)

Here we consider more pointedly the parallel between drug addiction and compulsive over eating and under eating (the former also

sometimes cruelly called "gluttony" and the latter also known as
"stringent fasting"). Generally speaking, the reward circuitry—the
pleasure pathway—of the brain is involved in both drug highs and
food highs. The neurotransmitter dopamine (detailed in the following
chapter), known to relate to the drug high, even directly relates here:
the level of dopamine released into the system directly parallels the
drug high. Compulsive over and under eating patterns both affect
and reflect dopamine levels, and share many characteristics with compulsive drug use patterns. The significant similarities between the
neurotransmitters involved signify the same or related parts of the
brain involved. Additionally, it is being observed that several key treat-
ments for substance addiction can be and are being successfully
applied to eating addiction, with significant and parallel results. While
deep nutritional needs, and storage of nutritional gains and losses, are
working around food consumption in ways that make eating addictions even more complex than substance addictions, the parallels are
marked enough to warrant inclusion in this discussion. All in all, we
see that hunger, what the brain tells us is hunger for something, food
in this case, is a driving force. Yes, satisfying one's hunger is a good
idea, however the hunger function all to frequently runs far awry.
Here we see again the drive for gratification, for the satisfaction of a
longing or a hunger, running awry.

EXAMPLE: SHOPPING/SPENDING ADDICTION

There are other hungers that we may respond to in excess. Consider
the popular and too often cruel label: shopaholic. Amidst ongoing
debate regarding what truly qualifies as an addiction from a traditional
drug and alcohol related standpoint, recognition of the troubled shopping and spending **pattern** has become painfully apparent worldwide.
(Whether we want to ignore or deny the addictive nature of this
behavior, we cannot ignore or deny the pattern-addicting nature of
this behavior.) Shoppers (at all socioeconomic levels) who continue
to shop in the face of adverse financial, psychological, social and other
adverse consequences to themselves and to their families do exhibit
characteristics of, and their behavior does meet the definition of,
addiction. Moreover, in the shopping-spending pattern addict, the
role of the brain's pleasure and relief from discomfort experience (further discussed in the following chapter) so common to drug addicted

persons, is obvious. Persons addicted to shopping and spending are driven to shop and spend to satisfy a hunger, to address cravings, and to satisfy this hunger and address these cravings in excess. How often have you watched some one buying more and enjoying it less? What about entire societies doing the same? Persons of all walks of life around the world are affected by the virtually universal affliction, even encouraged by massive advertising to be afflicted this way. Think of the grand profits made by the pushers of shopping addicions.

EXAMPLE: WORK ADDICTION

A brief excursion into a sacred territory: work. We have many times heard persons called, or call themselves, workaholics. What might this mean? We all need work, paying jobs make survival in a money driven economy possible (perhaps barely possible in times of economic downturn of course). Many positive and even survival oriented characteristics can be confused with, or mix with, workaholism. Being goal-oriented, motivated, even hard working, is not considered undesirable and is actually considered admirable. And many employers may unwittingly or even purposefully favor the workaholic over others. (Consider the finca owners of the 1400s in Spain who brought indigenous workers back from South America, and worked them to death while administering coca to them, a drug which they also brought back from South America.) Addiction to work or to what makes hard work happen was and is too often courted and even encouraged by employers of both yesteryear and of today. Yet it is where the continued working, past the point of "bare" (rather than perceived) necessity (yes, difficult to define as necessity may be), in the face of harm to self or others takes place, that addiction to work, a troubling and difficult to ferret out individual and or corporate-societal pattern addiction, reveals itself. Some report that where the highly motivated employee experiences pleasure in her or his work, the employee who works just as hard but does not experience such pleasure in so doing is perhaps more the workaholic. What a simple matter this would be were this the case. Unfortunately many persons "working themselves to the bone" are doing so in the face of no choice. For some, becoming a workaholic may be what it takes to survive the pressure. Making oneself like, even love and crave, work may be the only way to keep going.

KEY REALITIES

These and several other nondrug addictions actually serve to clarify for us a few key realities. The brain and the body can grow addicted to behavioral patterns other than drug addiction patterns, as if these were drug addiction patterns. The brain experiences highs and lows, roller coaster rides particular to particular addictions, but parallel to all addictions. We are coded to grow addicted to that which we must do to survive. We are not coded to prevent ourselves from having this addiction run awry on us. We can be drawn to a behavior such as eating or acquiring resources (shopping) or working (making a living) because it is intrinsic to our survival. We can fall into a tight and tough to escape pattern of addiction to this behavior because of the very nature of this behavior—do this or you may not survive, do this in excess or your pattern addiction to this may not survive. And you need your pattern addiction here, or so the message says.

Figure 5.1.   Example of Categories for Substances of Abuse/Addiction

DRUG CATEGORIES (examples of)	SPECIFIC DRUGS (examples of)
Narcotics	Alfentanil
	Cocaine
	Codeine
	Crack Cocaine
	Fentanyl
	Heroin
	Hydromorphone
	Ice
	Meperidine
	Methadone
	Morphine
	Nalorphine
	Opium
	Oxycodone
	Propoxyphene
Depressants	Benzodiazepine
	Chloral Hydrate
	Chlordiazepoxide
	Diazepam
	Glutethimide
	Meprobamate
	Methaqualone
	Nitrous Oxide
	Pentobarbital
	Secobarbital
Alcohol	Ethyl Alcohol
Ethyl Alcohol	Amphetamine
	Benzedrine

DRUG CATEGORIES (examples of)	SPECIFIC DRUGS (examples of)
	Benzphetamine
	Butyl Nitrite
	Dextroamphetamine
	Methamphetamine
	Methylphenidate
	Phenmetrazine
Hallucinogens	Bufotenine
	LSD
	MDA
	MDEA
	MDMA
	Mescaline
	MMDA
	Phencyclidine
	Psilocybin
Cannabis	Marijuana
	Tetrahydrocannabinol
Steroids	Dianabol
	Nandrolone

(Material adapted from information found at http://ncadi.samhsa.gov/govpubs/rpo926/.)

Figure 5.2.   Example of Categories for Nondrug Activity Abuse/ Addiction

"DRUG" CATEGORIES (examples of)	SPECIFIC "DRUGS" (examples of)
Gambling Addiction	On-Ground, Direct
	Telephone
	Online, Internet
	Other
Gaming Addiction	On-Ground, Direct
	Telephone
	Online, Internet
	Other
Sex Addiction	On-Ground, Direct
	Telephone
	Online, Internet
	Other
Pornography Addiction	On-Ground, Direct
	Telephone
	Online, Internet
	Other
Relationship Addiction	On-Ground, Direct
	Telephone
	Online, Internet
	Other
Eating	Compulsive Eating, All Foods
	Compulsive Eating, Carbohydrates
	Compulsive Eating, Other Specific Food Groups
	Overeating
	Undereating, Anorexia

"DRUG" CATEGORIES (examples of)	SPECIFIC "DRUGS" (examples of)
	Bulemia
	Other
Self-Mutilation	Cutting
	Burning
	Other
Work Addiction	Long Work Hours
	Large Workloads
	Other
Television Addiction	Long Viewing Hours
	Other
Abuse and Violence against Others	Abuse, Forms of
	Violence, Forms of

(Chart by and courtesy of Angela Browne-Miller.)

6

Creatures of Pleasure and Stimulation

We are creatures of, even slaves to, our built-in drives to experience pleasure and stimulation. What a marvelous innovation is the pleasure function. We are programmed to find pleasure in pleasure. It is fortunate that we take pleasure in mating, eating and winning competitions for resources, as these are linked to survival. We need to procreate, we need to nourish ourselves, and we need to have sufficient resources, to even win these resources when we sense that these resources are scarce or could grow scarce. How splendid that this has worked its way into our coding long ago. It may be that this very function is what has kept us alive across time. Yet this same function may be harming us, even killing us. What has gone wrong?

THE COMPELLING PLEASURE PATHWAY

Even the drive to experience pleasure can run awry. Many addictions to substances, drugs and tobacco (which for all intents and purposes is also a drug) stimulate—or act in some way upon—the pleasure pathway in the brain. This pathway is also described as the pleasure circuit (or the mesolimbic-cortical system) and involves several areas of the brain (these areas being known as the ventral tegmental area—a group of neurons close to the midline of the floor of the midbrain; the prefrontal cortex—the anterior part of the frontal lobes of the brain; the amygdala—located deep within the medial temporal lobes of the brain; and the accumbens nucleus—a collection of neurons in the forebrain). These areas of the brain speak to each other by means of our biochemical neurotransmitters, particularly the important neurotransmitter, dopamine, which is active here in terms of its reinforcing action linked to addictive responses. Playing a role in this system's functioning is what is called the opioid system, as beta-endorphins (endogenous opioids) can be liberated by the hypothalamus area of the brain to indirectly free up dopamine. (Note that drugs do act on the opioid system in numerous other ways not being addressed here.) Our bodies produce their own opioids, which are molecules derived from some of the amino acids found in our cells. Let's look at a few drugs and activities of choice among problem addicted persons, to see how our brain chemistries control us.

EXAMPLE: ALCOHOL AND BETA-ENDORPHINE CRAVING

Let's briefly consider alcohol (ethanol), perhaps the number one drug of choice around the globe. Alcohol depresses the central nervous system and generates a series of biochemical actions within the body of the person drinking it. Among the biological actions of or responses to alcohol is the freeing up or liberation of beta-endorphins (the endogenous opioids referred to above) by the hypothalamus. As it has been found that many alcoholic persons show a (likely natural) deficiency of beta-endorphins, it appears to be so that this release of wonderful beta-endorphins generates a *more pleasant effect* in these people than it does in those who do not show this deficiency. This pleasant effect includes a relief from the conscious and subconscious sensations that accompany such a beta-endorphin deficiency. And through this release of beta-endorphins other effects occur, further reinforcing the alcohol addiction pattern or cycle in those who may have the biochemical setup for this addiction. Ultimately, in those wired to seek fulfillment of their beta-endorphin need, the drive to drink is fueled by the drive to experience the pleasure of this fulfillment and the drive to experience the accompanying relief from discomfort.

As alcohol is such a large part of our lives and of human history, we know that the human brain has been dealing with alcohol consumption almost as long as it can remember (or is recorded in history, that is). Alcohol consumption and addiction is clearly not a new event. Alcohol abuse itself has likely been with us throughout the history of mankind, at least since we learned to turn barley and corn into mead.

Even today, African villagers in rural areas brew maise, producing 80 percent proof alcoholic beverages. Alcohol was and still is used as medicine as well as for ritual and recreational purposes. Alcohol was and in many areas still is a standard item in the family medicine chest; and, until recently in history, alcohol was commonly used as an anesthetic in surgical procedures. Today, we are facing a worldwide alcohol consumption and abuse epidemic. The classification of "heavy alcohol user" is becoming more common, with the rate of heavy alcohol use in all age groups in almost all nations increasing at virtually epidemic proportions.

At an alarming rate, human brain biochemistries everywhere are being affected directly and indirectly by massive alcohol abuse and addiction. Note that alcohol intake in small doses from time to time can be flushed out of the body via the natural action of a catalytic enzyme (alcohol dehydrogenese) that metabolizes this alcohol, thus reducing any toxic effects. Yet, excessive drinking, particularly *rapid excessive drinking* (a growing and disturbing trend), overburdens the body and its systems. Rather than being metabolized and flushed out, the rapidly and excessively consumed alcohol floods the blood stream and moves into the brain where the alcohol is literally toxic to the neurons there. In instances of excessive drinking, the more alcohol consumed, the greater the occurrence of permanent brain damage, especially to the frontal lobe and the cerebellum. (The frontal lobe is key to a range of important brain functions including emotion regulation and executive functioning such as abstract reasoning, organization, planning, self-monitoring, and other behavior governing functions.)

PLEASURE AND RELIEF FROM PAIN AND DISCOMFORT AS PLEASURE

It is important to note here that the same type of opioid referred to above is active in what may at first sound to be a drive opposing the drive for pleasure; this opposing drive being the drive for *relief from pain and or other discomfort*. This is the case as the reduction of pain and discomfort can be just as pleasurable as—register in the brain as just as pleasurable as if not more pleasurable than—the presence of pleasure. This is an important factor in a wide range of problem addictions, both substance type addictions and behavioral or process addictions. (Chapter 15 presents several relief from discomfort cycles, see Figures 15.6. and 15.7.)

EXAMPLE: CONSIDER HEROIN AND MORPHINE WITHDRAWALS

Take drug withdrawals for example. Among commonly abused drugs which act on the opioid system are heroin and morphine, providing two powerful examples of the pleasure of pain relief pull to return to a cycle of addiction, (to any cycle, of any addiction). Halting addicted use of these drugs can bring on a severe withdrawal, or what is also called an abstinence syndrome. What surfaces again and again is the question regarding whether the person who is addicted to these drugs is craving, driven to reexperience, the pleasure associated with use, or is craving, is driven to reexperience, the relief from the terribly uncomfortable even extremely painful withdrawal. Both can be and are likely to be true. This does fit with the pleasure plus pleasure in relief from pain model, a powerful duality when desired together.

Both our own experiences (whether or not struggling with problem addictions) and science tell us that eliminating such an unpleasant stimulus as a withdrawal symptom can be as much a driving factor in behavior as can be enjoying a positive stimulus. Withdrawal or abstinence syndromes for heroin and morphine addiction can offer pointed examples here, and include two intense phases. Phase one is characterized by behaviors such as sweating, irritability, trembling, agitation, anorexia, tearing at the skin, and *cravings for the drug itself*. Phase two is characterized by behaviors such as nausea, vomiting, diarrhea, blood pressure and heart rate increases, muscle spasms, dehydration, depression, a tendency to convulsive events, and *craving for relief from these withdrawal or abstinence symptoms, a relief from discomfort*.

TOLERANCE AND DIMINISHING RETURNS

There are numerous "popular" drugs of addiction that stimulate the central nervous system (CNS), beyond the most recognized as CNS addicting, the big addicters—amphetamine, methamphetamine, and cocaine. Although not taken nearly so seriously as the big addicters, there are many "every day" drugs which are also stimulants, such as caffeine. The varying effects of these stimulant-type drugs reflect differences in their chemical structures. However, similar brain functions are at work where problem addiction to many of these substances takes place.

Characteristic of many addictive processes is the development of *tolerance* to the drug (or object or activity of the addiction). Generally speaking, tolerance in addiction processes refers to diminishing "returns" when taking the same medication or drug (or engaging in the same addictive activity) over time, meaning that the same "dose" of the same "drug" produces lower and lower "highs" or "desired effects" over time. An ever increasing dose or increasing frequency of use eventually results in the same effect ever decreasing. (The highs get lower and the lows get lower, until there are no further highs, then the lows get lower and lower.) Yet the *investment* in the pattern addiction is already in place. Once its returns begin diminishing, the stubborn problem pattern itself continues to live on as long as it can, no matter how dangerous. The thrill may be going or gone, but the problem addiction is not. The pattern is going to maintain itself, keep itself alive, until the body and brain which hosts it wears out, is too run down to even host a problem pattern addiction, or simply dies.

EXAMPLE: COMMONPLACE CAFFEINE ADDICTION

Some drugs do not bring on distinctly diminishing returns. We must pause to look at caffeine here. So common is caffeine addiction that we tend not to think it exists. Yet this condition is age old and only growing over time. Caffeine is perhaps the best example of how insidious and pervasive the addicted state can be. So let's dig into the workings of this everyday addiction.

As early as 3000 BC in ancient China, if not prior to that, caffeine was a popular drug. Early cultures discovered that the chewing and ingestion of caffeine-containing plants and seeds resulted in desirable mood-altering and stimulatory effects. The stimulation itself was recognized for its value in general in awakeness and alertness, in lovemaking, in work and in many activities of human life. Worldwide trade of caffeine grew. Today, we see enormous worldwide demands for caffeine that make it a major commodity virtually everywhere. So prevalent is this caffeine industry that we rarely think of it as an addiction industry, however perhaps we might want to, at least for the sake of this discussion. (Note that it is safe to read on without fearing finding oneself compelled to stop drinking coffee, as this discussion is not arguing for either the cessation or initialization of caffeine's use. Rather, I am inferring that we are all addicts in some way, quite frequently unbeknownst or unacknowledged to ourselves. Refer again to Figure 2.1 on page 16.

Today, caffeine is indeed the most commonly used psychoactive drug in the world, a daily drug for the majority of adults and many young people. Its most common sources are coffee, tea, soft drinks, and chocolate. The average cup of coffee contains approximately 100 mg. of caffeine, while average servings of tea, soft drinks, and chocolate are slightly lower, 50 mg., 40 mg., and 20 mg., respectively. Caffeine tablets of 50–200 mg. are available virtually everywhere without a prescription. Numerous over-the-counter pain relievers, migraine medications, and antihistamines also contain caffeine.

Following absorption, caffeine is distributed freely throughout the body and the brain. The half-life of caffeine at modest levels of intake is approximately 4–6 hours in most adults. This period increases with higher levels of intake. At low to moderate daily doses (50–300 mg.), commonly reported subjective effects include arousal, increased concentration, elevated mood, increased motivation to work, and decreased sleepiness. The most typical mood altering effects include increases in energy, alertness, and feelings of well-being.

Caffeine withdrawal can include headache, fatigue, decreased energy/activity, decreased alertness, drowsiness, decreased contentment, depressed mood, difficulty concentrating, irritability, and fogginess or cloudiness of mind. Flu-like symptoms, including nausea, vomiting, tremors, and muscle pain and stiffness are often reported. The most commonly reported symptom in caffeine withdrawal is headache. Withdrawal symptoms generally begin within 12–24 hours following cessation of caffeine, and reach peak intensity at approximately 20–48 hours with an overall duration of 2–7 days. Severity and occurrence of symptoms appear to relate to increases in dosage. However, withdrawal symptoms have been exhibited in those consuming as little as 100 mg./day (approximately one cup of coffee). Many persons drinking coffee only at work on Monday through Friday experience at least minor withdrawals every weekend, and then find themselves craving returning to work on Monday not realizing this is, at least in part, to drink caffeine. They may not realize this, but their bodies do.

We tend to downplay the dangers of caffeine addiction, perhaps because we do not see these, or do not recognize the more subtle diminishing returns in the face of prolonged use. Or perhaps we do not see caffeine as dangerous. Or perhaps we do not choose to see any of this. We do love our primary stimulant, coffee, and after all, when all is said and done, caffeine addiction is in the main innocuous. The diagnosis of caffeine intoxication reflects daily consumption generally exceeding 250 mg. (more than 2–3 cups of coffee), plus anxiety, restlessness, excitement, insomnia, rambling flow of thought and speech, irritability, tremor, diuresis, flushed face, gastrointestinal disturbance, psychomotor agitation, and irregular or rapid heartbeat. In highly elevated dosages, symptoms such as fever, hallucinations, delusions, and loss of consciousness have occurred. Caffeine intoxication resolves rather quickly with cessation of consumption and supportive care. However doses exceeding 5–10 g taken within a limited time frame are generally considered a significant risk. Such a sizeable dose is difficult to achieve under conventional methods (50–100 average cups of coffee), but can be more readily administered with the ingestion of caffeine tablets. In cases of lethal overdose, the typical cause of death is generally listed as ventricular fibrillation. Generally speaking, we have a high social and biological acceptance of the risks we see or sense in caffeine.

EXAMPLE: THE SMOKING GUN OF NICOTINE ADDICTION

Returning to the earlier comment regarding nicotine in Chapter 2, a further word about smoking here. In many parts of the world, the risk of, and problem of, nicotine addiction tends to be downplayed or entirely ignored. Concurrently, in some nations such as the United States, the addictive and dangerous characteristics of nicotine and the tobacco which carries it are being taken quite seriously, the health effects are being increasingly acknowledged as serious and oft fatal. (Although there is clearly more work to do even in the United States, as the far reaching and permanent positive effects of this campaign are being debated.)

Nicotine addiction is a worldwide problem, reaching virtually epidemic proportions. Although smoking is an age old practice, nicotine was first isolated from tobacco leaves in 1828. The nicotine content of a modern cigarette normally ranges from 1 to 2 percent. Nicotine is absorbed through the mucus membranes, skin and lungs. From there, it spreads through the bloodstream in just a few seconds. Like many other molecules, nicotine requires receptors to produce its biological action. These receptors are proteins that can be found in the cell membrane, the cytosol or the cell nucleus. The nicotine receptors, called nicotinic, found in the cell membrane joined to ionic channels, can be activated by a transmitter of nerve impulses, acetylcholine, or by nicotine. Once the ligand, in this case nicotine, binds to the receptor, it generally produces excitability in the cell. In the central nervous system, nicotine acts on several regions where there are nicotinic receptors; and, it acts upon nicotinic receptors in the mesolimbic-cortical system that affect reinforcing mechanisms. Again, the pleasure pathway is directing much of this addiction.

NONDRUG ADDICTION STIMULATION OF PLEASURE PATHWAYS

To reemphasize, nonsubstance—behavioral or process—addictions (what in my terminology can also be called troubled behavioral *pattern* addictions) such as online and on-ground gambling and gaming, Internet and on-ground pornography, excessive spending and shopping, and other excessive behaviors, also tend to involve stimulation of pleasure pathways in the brain. Moreover, just as is true in substance use, abuse and addiction, while some persons can be exposed to particular activities without becoming addicted to these, many others cannot be. Exposure to painkillers offers an example of this variable response to exposure. Many of us have taken painkillers for physical pain, as this is a common treatment. Yet the rate of addiction to painkillers does not equal the rate of their use. Again, some (but always we have to ask who, as it could be any one of many of us) are more likely to fall into patterns of troubled addiction to painkillers than others—(although this "who" may not be entirely predictable to the health care professional recommending or prescribing their use). Similarly, it appears that many of us can be exposed to activities such as gambling, gaming, spending, even eating, and only some will fall prey to their addictive hooks; however, we cannot know who or whether only some for sure, as the circumstances of exposure also matter.

EXAMPLE: FOOD, SEX, AND RUNAWAY DIMENSIONS OF OUR CODING

We respond to exposure to potentially addictive activities much the way we do to addictive drugs. Exposure to food provides a good

example. Some can be exposed to food (actually all of us must consume food so we are all of course exposed to food) without becoming
addicted, while others cannot. I want to further qualify (beyond what
has been said in Chapter 5) the matter of eating addiction here, as this
is a complex biochemical, nutritional, and psychological problem:
Many persons who are not addicted to food are actually being labeled
as addicted, while many others who have developed a problem addiction to an eating behavior or to eating some things in particular are
not being viewed as addicted. Therefore all mention of eating herein
is made with this understanding.

We might also add the matter of exposure to sex. And here, as in the
matter of exposure to food, we have a behavior necessary to survival, a
behavior that can become over stimulated, function in excess and
sometimes in seriously troubled and dangerous ways (in sex crimes
for example). While procreation, mating, is essential (at least thus far
science has not entirely replaced this) to the survival and continuation
of the species, the programming to desire the pleasure of sex that we
carry within us can sometimes reach runaway dimensions. Excessive
sexual behavior, including excessive sex-seeking behavior, can (but
does not always) develop into serious and dangerous behavioral addiction. Many of the characteristics of patterns of addiction appear in sex
addiction scenarios, for example: continued engagement in the face of
potential or actual harm to self or others, withdrawal, and tolerance
where the highs get lower and the lows get lower.

CONTINUED USE AND ENGAGEMENT

Whatever the addiction, we know that *continued* engagement in an
activity in the face of *harm* to self or others can be a *problem addiction*.
It is the behavior, which goes beyond good judgment (and well functioning survival oriented instinct) to be driven to seek pleasure and
avoid discomfort and pain *at virtually all costs*, that renders an addiction
a problem addiction. After all, where an addiction does the opposite, is
ongoing in the face of contributing to the *well-being* of self or others or
in the face of making absolutely no difference to anyone, this addiction is likely *not* a problem addiction.

Here, we are concerned about the ongoing drive to engage in a
behavior, or to try to engage in a behavior, excessively, highly excessively, despite actual or potential harm. Still, excessive behavior is so
common within and around us, we might want to ask what can propel

us into excess itself. What is this excess that we are so attracted to? How does this thing called excess get the better of us, even override our own good judgment functions? (In the following chapter, Chapter 7, we first look at the psychological workings of judgment and then return to the matter of excess in Chapter 8. Later, in Chapters 11, 12 and 13, we consider the biochemical and neurological aspects of judgment and thinking in general.)

7
When Good Judgment Falls By the Wayside

Can good judgment function in the face of the pull of excess? Can good judgment function in the face of the pull of addiction? Clearly, understanding the universal nature of addiction teaches us a great deal about how the problem of problem addiction to patterns such as food, sex, gambling, and drug abuse can happen to "people just like us," and even to ourselves. People in trouble with drugs or food or sex or gambling, or something else, are people whose addictive tendencies have somehow fallen into one of the most dangerous of the problem addictions. It's easy to say, "But those addicted people are different from me. I could never do that. And no one in my family could either!" But don't kid yourself. That's what many addicted people and their family members once said, unaware of how readily one's—anyone's —good judgment can fall by the wayside.

As good judgment is in such great peril when the controlling hand of problem addiction grips us, let's step back here and consider in general the processes of both good judgment and of its falling by the wayside. In this chapter, I set forth some basic psychological and ethical aspects of good judgment relevant to every aspect of life as well as to addiction issues, as good judgment too frequently wavers and fails under the strain of the magnetic and domineering lure of problem addiction. Later, in Chapter 12, Degraded Decision-Making Functioning, I reconsider judgment as a biophysical function of the brain itself, one that can be detrimentally affected in the face of problem (and perhaps even some positive) addictions.

WHEN GOOD JUDGMENT IS NOT WORKING

What happens to "good" judgment? When under pressure from our patternings and their addictions, as well as from the overarching trends of chemicalization and mechanization (discussed in Chapter 3), and the powerful forces of addictive materialism and addictive inadequacy (discussed in Chapter 4), our judgment and decision-making functions may not be performing at their best. At this point, we want to ask, why is it, as we descend into troubled patterns, even become addicted to these negative patterns, we are not able to see ourselves doing so? And, where we can see ourselves doing so, why are we are not able to apply attentional, decision-making and thinking (including cognitive) skills to put a stop to this descent into cycles from which it may later be quite difficult to escape? Why is it that good judgment falls by the wayside as we descend? And why is it that the deeper we get into the programming to be problem addicted, the more difficult it is to exercise good judgment, to make a sound decision, and to implement a sound decision, a decision to leave that programming behind?

WISE AND RIGHT USE OF DECISION-MAKING ABILITY

Now, of course the wise and right use of decision-making ability does vary according to one's own world view, belief system, and other value systems. And this variation is a good thing, as it allows for diversity of world views. Still, there are some very basic and very universal aspects, core characteristics, of decision-making ability which rely on good judgment, the ability to make good judgments. This is a sort of *moral intelligence*—the ability to make good, even wise, decisions, and to know how to do so, when to do so, and what it looks like when others are doing so (or not doing so). This moral intelligence ability can be expressed in concert with one's own or one's family belief system, or it may reach beyond to broader, more universal themes. (Of course these may be one in the same.)

By moral intelligence I do not mean morality itself. Morality is a complex issue best reserved for another book. Much of what we call morality is actually what we have been taught that good is. Of course it is good that we learn about what good is, and what it means to do the right thing. And while social guidance (such as laws, religion, culture, family, and even tradition) can certainly help guide us in doing what is right and what is best and what is good, there is a fundamental difference between this *social guidance* and what I call *moral intelligence* itself. Although they do influence each other a great deal, social guidance comes from outside ourselves, and personal moral intelligence comes from within.

Our own personal moral intelligence is needed when we must decide something for ourselves—decide on an action or form an opinion on our own, sometimes in addition to, and sometimes independently of, law, religion, tradition, and teaching coming to us from outside ourselves. Even a young person needs a personal moral intelligence. Personal moral intelligence is necessary in many different situations. We see this need so often when young people are invited or pressured (by their peers or by television commercials, for example) to do things that are not necessarily the right or best or good things for them to do at their age or perhaps at any age.

Think of the common instance where a teen does not know what to do when pressured to play a game at a party, perhaps a simple one such as spin the bottle, a kissing game. Or think of another common instance when a young person is pressured to smoke a cigarette. There are many reasons why that young person may not be able to draw on teaching coming from outside her- or himself to respond to this pressure. In fact, even adults may find themselves in similar peer-pressure type situations from time to time. These situations do take place, for example:

- when we do not have a relevant teaching coming from outside ourselves to call upon; or,
- when we do not understand how the teaching coming from outside ourselves applies to a particular situation or issue; or,
- when we sense that perhaps the teaching coming from outside ourselves may not be being interpreted correctly or appropriately for a particular situation or issue; or,
- when events lead us to question the teaching coming from outside ourselves, leaving us only with what we have inside to guide us; or,
- when there is not teaching coming from outside ourselves, or we do not see that there is this teaching.

It is in these instances that we need our own internal compasses, our own personal moral intelligences to guide us, to guide our decision-making capacities. However, human development theories hold that morality itself does not fully develop until the age of 25 (and is said to actually begin developing at age 16). While I prefer to say that what I call moral intelligence actually begins developing in early childhood (by childrens' mimicking and following the modeling of parents and older children) and continues throughout life, the prime time for the development of certain abilities to identify and weigh moral issues is recognized as being in the 16–25 age range. (Moreover, the thinking now is that the prefrontal cortex does not fully develop until the age of 25, hence important executive functions of the brain await this development.)

So many experiences, whether or not traumatic, can hinder or even halt emotional and moral development. We have all heard comments such as these: "he may be 40 but emotionally he is 13" and "she is 50 but acts 11." Whether these comments are accurate or simply cruel, they do point to the sense that particular parts or components of the self do not mature at the same time. Emotional maturity, social maturity, intellectual maturity—all these aspects of the self (that should be working together) mature in their own time, and not necessarily concurrently. Some development can actually be arrested by internal or external events or traumas. Such traumas can take place in many forms, many of which are hidden to us. Even juvenile drug use can result in a developmental trauma. In fact, age at first use of various drugs is a good (although not 100 percent reliable) predictor of juvenile behavior and even of adulthood drug addiction. The latter is not necessarily because age at first use predicts a later addiction, but rather that early age of first use of a drug accompanies many later adult drug addictions to some drug or drugs. Whatever its cause, when there is the element of arrested development present, judgment even in adulthood may appear to be more like the judgment of one that is of a younger age, perhaps 15, or 13, or 11.

DECISION MAKING IS CENTRAL

So when we need to exercise good judgment or make good decisions about anything, we are calling upon brain functions that may not be fully formed, fully matured, or may be forever arrested. Where drug or other problem addictions are involved, we may be calling upon hindered, broken or virtually nonexistent judgment functions.

Decision making is central to the application of moral intelligence in daily life, especially in the face of the pull to enter or reenter a pattern addiction or addictive cycle. Decision making is something we all constantly engage in, whether or not we realize we are doing so. So many minor decisions are being made at all times, that we have to make some of these on the semi-conscious and even automatic level just to be able to go about our daily activities. For example, waving a fly away when we are in a hurry to write an urgent note, or turning on the windshield wipers when driving through a sudden rain shower, are decisions we may make almost automatically for good reason; however, these are still decisions we have made. And then there are the bigger decisions, such as what to do when someone says something cruel to you, or when you need to get a job done on time and put other important activities aside in order to do this. And then there are the sort of decisions made without much if any conscious thinking, on the spur of the moment, or on impulse, when these would have been better made after thinking through a conscious decision-making process.

Many decisions require placing importance—value—on a choice, and comparing the choices or options available so as to choose from among these. Should I go this way or that way? Should I spend my money on this or on that? Should I respond to this insult this way or that way? Should I say yes to this opportunity or that one? Should I say yes or *no*? Should I believe my parents, or the public service ads on television, when they say this drug or this activity is dangerous, even addicting, or should I not? Should I care whether this is dangerous or should I not? Will this be dangerous if I do it just this one time? How dangerous is this? And so on.... Clearly, decision making involves making choices, choices to or not to. Making a good choice is making a good decision, exercising good judgment. (The brain and the SELF itself need to have good judgment functions up and running at all times.)

MAKING A GOOD DECISION IS A PROCESS

What is a good decision? "Good" can mean different things to different people. The meaning of the word good varies. So let's focus on *decision* instead of on *good* here. What goes into a **good decision**? A good decision-making *process*! What is a good decision-making process? This is a series of steps that lead to a clear and logical and yes, morally intelligent, decision. So often we do not emphasize for ourselves, let alone for our children, what goes into a good decision-making process. Although making good decisions is a noble concept, and a fine goal, really making good decisions involves the process itself. Adults and children can learn to look for the process and the quality of the process of decision making, not just for the decision itself. By pulling the process itself into one's consciousness, the both quality and the moral intelligence of the process are consciously increased.

Too often, in our personal let alone work lives, we place all the emphasis on the decision and fail to look at how the decision was made. We can change this behavior by making the process of making the decision most important. We can learn a great deal about the importance of the process itself by watching political processes in democratic countries. For example, we do quite rightly care about the outcome of presidential elections, and yet, perhaps even more so, we care about the process by which we arrive at this outcome. In the United States, we emphasize the importance of the process of electing a president. We can learn to take the high value we place on this national process down to the personal level.

After all, a good decision is one that is arrived at through a good decision-making process. So we want to place value (for ourselves and for our children) on the process used to arrive at a decision. Returning to what I said earlier, so many decisions are made without thinking, and often it is after the fact that we wish we had thought before deciding. The old saying, "Think before you act," is great advice. We have all heard this many times. Now, let's take this to the next level, and let's *think about thinking* before we act. What does this thinking look like? Have we thought this decision through enough? What does this process of making a decision to (or not to) take an action look like? The process of thinking through a decision is the key here. When feeling the demanding pull of a problem pattern addiction, it is essential that one be highly conscious, so as to make any and all responses to this pull highly conscious (rather than impulsive). THIS ALLOWS THE SELF TO STAND UP TO THE LURE OF THE PROBLEM PATTERN ADDICTION—TO SEPARATE AND **DIS-IDENTIFY** FROM THIS TRECHEROUS AND INDISDIOUS PROBLEM PATTERN.

DECISION MAKING AND PROBLEM SOLVING: THE *HOW* MATTERS HERE

Decision making is a form of problem solving. The problem is: what is the best answer? The solving is: the process of getting the answer, the decision-making process of arriving at the right answer. The process requires us to stop, to slow down, to see ourselves think through the decision-making (or problem-solving) process. It is in this slowing down to hear ourselves think, to think about *how* we are thinking about the decision or problem, that we gain a great deal of control over our minds and behaviors. We can, and quite often must, pull ourselves out of the automatic behavior zone, take ourselves off of impulse.

When we take the time to consciously think through questions such as those listed in Figure 7.1, we are no longer making decisions without consciously thinking things through. Now we own our decision-making processes. We own the process of consciously asking ourselves and answering for ourselves key questions. The executive control functions of our mind-brains are working for us, not for our addictions.

WITH MATURITY CAN COME BETTER DECISION-MAKING PROCESSES, BUT WHEN IS MATURITY?

Young children tend to make most of their decisions based on how these will affect them and only them right now: Decisions in the now are only about them and only about the now. As they grow, young people (hopefully) make decisions based not only on how the outcome will affect them personally right now, but also on how these will affect themselves and others now and in the future. This growing concern for more than just now and for more than just oneself plays an ever-increasing role in decision making. Moral intelligence increases as the outcomes of decisions are understood to affect more than just oneself, and more than just the now.

Basically, good judgment is an ability that develops as young people grow up, an ability that never really stops developing, unless its development is arrested or damaged or otherwise blocked. We like to think that we make better and better decisions as we age. Whether or not this is true, what we should be emphasizing is that the process of making these decisions can become more and more conscious and intelligent. We learn to be purposefully morally intelligent—and then more and more morally intelligent.

THE GREATER GOOD

This highest value we can place on a decision-making process is the greater good value. We can ask ourselves, no matter how old we are:

How many people benefit from this decision and is this something I am thinking about as I decide? Here moral intelligence can filter into all we do and all we learn and all we think. Moral intelligence is an ability that can be learned, practiced, and developed. This is the human ability we are so much in need of as we become conscious of the conflicting pulls upon us, especially addictive and potentially addictive pulls. The question is, how can we empower good judgment to override automatic brain functions running awry and running into problem addiction? (See Chapters 11, 12, and 13 on brain functions that do run awry in problem addiction circumstances.)

Figure 7.1. General Decision-Making Questions

THE WHAT, WHEN, WHO QUESTIONS
> **What:** What is the decision I (or we) need to make?
> **When:** How much time do I (or we) have to make this decision?
> **Who:** Who is making this decision?
> **But who:** Who *should* be making this decision?

THE KNOW WHAT, KNOW MORE, KNOW WHERE QUESTIONS
> **Know What:** What do I know that will help me make this decision?
> **Know More:** Do I need to know more to make this decision?
> **Know Where:** Where can I find out more if I need to know more?

THE CONSEQUENCES QUESTIONS
> **Who Benefits:** Who benefits if I say yes, if I say no, if I say nothing right now?
> **Who Benefits When:** When do the benefits take place? Now? Later?
> **What Good:** What is the greatest good that can be done here?
> **What Outcomes:** What are the consequences?
> **What Harm:** Is anyone harmed? Who?
> **What Risk:** What are the dangers or risks?
> **What Value:** How do the benefits compare to the risks?

THE AM I READY QUESTIONS
> **Am I Ready:** Am I ready and able to make this decision right now?

(Chart by and courtesy of Angela Browne-Miller.)

8

Addiction and Excessive Consumption

Whether a drug or a nondrug behavioral process addiction, once the addiction is apparent, recognized, explicit—once this problem addiction surfaces—it is what I call troubled or problem *explicit addiction*. By the time the obvious, surface explicit addiction has made itself known, much has taken place on deeper, less obvious, less explicit and more implicit, levels. Moving up through the layers of the psyche into actual explicit behavior, we finally catch explicit addiction via its symptoms of EXCESS. Troubled explicit addiction is, in essence, a disturbance of our consumption and response to consumption functions. We consume an object or substance, or an activity, too much, in excess.

IN EXCESS

When we talk about substance addiction, we are talking about the actual consuming of particular drugs and alcohol, which may be legally or illegally acquired and used. Other problem addictions include consumption of other material things such as food (as in eating addiction) or consumer goods (as in shopping addiction). And other activities which may be engaged in *in excess* or addictively are also *consumptive*—consuming the object or activity or behavior of the addiction **in excess or to excess**: gambling addiction, sex addiction, pornography addiction, and other behaviors when they cross the line into excess such as excessive working and excessive television watching.

The phrase *in excess* generally refers to something done beyond what is considered normal, sufficient or healthy. Or, to further simplify, when something is done in excess, it is done too much, and with this "too much" being in the face of harm, or the potential of harm, to self or others. Of course, certain activities such as much of the drug use which is occurring throughout the world, are potentially too much from the first moment. For example, crack cocaine is said to be so immediately addictive that one "hit" is already too much. Hence, the door to, or threshold into, excess may be, in some cases, any use at all. Also note that some individuals are mentally or physiologically prone to become immediately addicted to certain substances or behaviors, which tells us that for these individuals, any use is similarly in excess for this reason.

SEVERAL TYPES OF EXCESS

I talk about two basic forms of excess here. One form of susceptibility to excess is based upon external factors, for example, where the drug the individual is being exposed to is, by its very nature, immediately and overwhelmingly addictive for virtually anyone exposed to it. I call this **externally-driven biological excess**. The other form of susceptibility to excess is based upon internal factors, e.g., where the particular individual who carries within a particular biochemical susceptibility is particularly prone to become addicted to a drug upon exposure to it. I call this **internally-driven biological excess**.

Adding to these forms of biological excess, there are other excesses, these being environmental or societal excesses. We live in a world where we are regularly, even constantly, pressured by advertising techniques to consume (yes, even to consume to excess) every time we turn on the television or radio, pick up a newspaper or magazine, walk past a store window, and many times when we answer the telephone or read our email. I call this **externally-driven societal excess aimed at the individual**. There are many other forms of excess occurring everywhere we turn—excesses of consumption we as a people are exhibiting, and for now, I will call all of this additional excess **broader overarching externally-driven societal excess**.

Here then we have four basic (although frequently overlapping) categories of excess, as listed below:

- **externally-driven biological excess;**

- **internally-driven biological excess;**
- **externally-driven societal excess aimed at the individual;**
- **broader overarching externally-driven societal excess.**

These forms of excess permeate all our behaviors, all our patterns of behavior, including all of our problem addictions. We are prey in the hands of these drives to excess—at least until we understand our programming, how it can run awry, and how to overcome and transcend it when we need to.

THE CONSUMPTION TRAP

Excesses in using a drug and excesses in engaging in a behavior (whether or not substances are involved) all involve consumption-type activity. While this is more readily understood in terms of substance addiction, and perhaps as per shopping and food addiction, as there is something quite tangible being consumed in these cases, consumption can also be applied to behaviors, activities. Interestingly, economists speak of the consumption of both goods and services, where consuming services tends to be consumption of an activity more than of an object, of a good. We can take this economic model a step further here and call consumption of activities—whether or not they are services—as consumptive in themselves. So here excess and consumption are linked and even inextricably linked with one leading to the other and vice versa as follows:

excess-driven → **consumption**
consumption-driven → **excess**

Once these conditions have hit runaway level, where the pattern of excess-driven consumption and vice versa is problem addiction, then we may have the sense that there is no way out of this situation or cycle, which feeds and fuels itself, as I have diagrammed in Figure 8.1. Of course the experience, once addicted to this cycle, is one of being *trapped in* the cycle, sensing a no way out sort of lose lose situation, a virtual trap or prison, a paradox, as diagrammed in Figure 8.2.

Sensing at a very deep level this trap, this no way out seeming sort of paradox, many individuals working to overcome problem addictions realize that any exposure to the drug or activity of choice is already crossing the threshold into excessive addictive use. For these persons,

Figure 8.1.   Consumption to Excess to Consumption to Excess Again Cycle

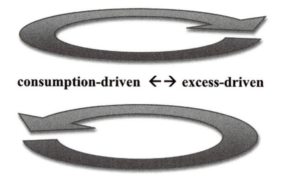

consumption-driven ←→ excess-driven

(Diagram by and courtesy of Angela Browne-Miller.)

any use is addictive and therefore is excessive. Recovery from problem addiction is fortified by and even hinges upon the full realization that one is a problem pattern addict, and that virtually any level of exposure to the object or activity of addiction is an invitation into excess, or back into the excess cycle—back to the **excess situation**—where already problem addicted.

Ultimately, we are slaves to our own internal brain-function programming to code patterns into ourselves—slaves until we can make our SELVES a key out of the trap, out of this biologically robotic tendency we have to indiscriminately give in to patterning whether it is good or bad patterning. And problem addicted persons well into their recoveries from excessive behavior patterns know this. They know that any crossing of the line back into any part of their problem addiction cycle is going too far. When presented with their drug or activities of addiction, they are able to say, in no uncertain terms, "No thanks, I am an addict and this will kill me," with increasing assuredness—and recovery continues. With the early stage of this attitude

Figure 8.2.   No Way Out Trap or Paradox

consumption → the no way out of the cycle paradox ← excess

(Diagram by and courtesy of Angela Browne-Miller.)

being perhaps tentative in early recovery, here is the time to practice making this statement and teaching the mind via repetition that this is the necessary response to all offers and cravings, the response to all invitations and lures back into excess (as pictured in the figure at the opening of Part Two of this book).

PART TWO

Recognizing Our Powerful Inner Coding to Be Pattern-Addicted

No Thanks, I'm an Addict and You Will Kill Me

(Illustration by and courtesy of Angela Browne-Miller.)

9
Our Rigid Yet Paradoxical Addictions to What We See As Reality

Our perceptions of our realities, our ways of being, all our behaviors, carry elements of the habitual. Our behavioral repertoires or spectrums are composed of *elements* of behaviors ranging from: use of genetic cross generational and through time memory; to within generation acquisition and application of acquired memory; to ad hoc association through learning; to individual attention-activating and attention-directing types of functions triggering, modulating, exacerbating (fanning the flames of) or even diminishing behavior. Many of these elements of our behaviors are part of our intrinsic programming, including our tendencies to respond to the cues or triggers leading us to reenter and repeat both healthy positive and unhealthy negative addictive cycles or patterns again and again—and then again and again and again.

WE CAN EVEN RESIST HEALING CHANGE

So deeply embedded within us are these tendencies that abandoning these tendencies can be immensely challenging. We are inherently programmed to resist many forms of change, to become addicted to something and to stay that way. And for good reason. This is how our biological machine (brain and its body) is designed to work. In fact, we as biochemical machines are not wired to find most change easy for us. Instead, we are wired to be addicted to the way things are, to what we have come to do repeatedly, and to what we have come to believe is our reality, even our identity in our reality.

We (both as individuals and as a population) tend to try to preserve the status quo. Living, even surviving, relies on our tendency toward life-protecting and life-sustaining pattern addiction. Yet, again I say that this valuable susceptibility to programming, an ability we have evolved over a long period of time, (according to the science of evolution), and passed from generation to generation via tradition and culture and even via genetic mechanisms, can and has run awry. **The very characteristic which helps us survive, even ensures our survival, can compromise, harm, endanger or even kill us.**

Let's call this our most basic, ever present and always underlying, susceptibility to the process of pattern-habituation and pattern-addiction. Surely this is an essential life-protecting function, yet it is one which now surely too frequently does run awry, morphing into a sort of self-induced or self-allowed brainwashing. I use the word *brainwashing* here as this is a handy label for the situation in which we succumb to drives almost unwittingly, as if being told from outside ourselves (or at least from outside our consciousnesses) to succumb to drives which can be dangerous, harmful, even fatal to self or others. Understanding the natural habituation and addiction functions we carry within us is essential to our clear understanding of the difficult time we have breaking habits and addictions, and in fact of the difficult time we have with many changes.

Let me emphasize again that we are addicted to what we think of as our reality. In this ever present, always underlying addiction to a reality, changing a behavior, any behavior, can feel somewhat like dying. Change can feel like losing the reality to which we are hugely attached and perhaps upon which we are entirely dependent—the only reality we feel we know, the only thing we feel we are. In essence, profound change calls for breaking an addiction to an entire reality.

OUR RIGID YET PARADOXICAL ADDICTION TO THE PATTERNED STATE ITSELF

We resist the change of pattern-breaking, even when the pattern we resist breaking is dangerous, life-threatening, counter-survival. **We allow the pattern we need to break to move into its own survival mode, to dominate our drive for overall survival for its own sake even when this pattern is a dangerous addiction.** There is a paradox in this resistance to the death of our problem patterns: stay addicted and the pattern addiction lives on, but stay addicted and you, your **self**, may die. The deep, genetically ordained drive within every genetically coded living organism to become addicted to patterns themselves—to even desire being patterned, dominates. Normalcy—no matter how troubled the normal pattern is—becomes the addicted state. A sense of normalcy (no matter how troubled that normalcy might be) is craved—and so is the **patterned state of mind** itself.

Living with the drive to be patterned, to always be patterning, we cannot avoid the deeply experienced conflict embedded within us, yes within all of us. On the one hand, this genetically ordained coding function is a survival-oriented tendency, reinforced by pathways we have inherited via our genes such as the pleasure pathway and the pleasure as pain relief pathway, virtually one in the same. The flight or fight function is a another good example of an essential program that can run haywire. Clearly, it is essential that we respond to life threatening situations automatically and rapidly, without taking the time to think, (such as when moving out of the way of a falling object or warding off a predator). However, many assaults and even murders are committed on impulse, in instances when this fight or flight reflex or related functions run awry.

Moreover, it is quite convenient that certain necessary behaviors are matters of genetic coding and therefore basic reflex, and that other necessary behaviors can become habitual via learning during life. How many people would stop their cars at red lights on time if they had to take the time to figure out from scratch every time what the red lights signify and how to stop the car? It is very good that we program ourselves to do some things automatically. On the other hand, however, we frequently fail to see that there is surely a downside to this automatic programming capability of ours.

THE TUG OF CHOICE

We feel the tug of choice, the yes-no tug actually embedded within us. We feel the pull of this two way tug as we have to choose which patterning to accept and continue and which patterning to resist and break where it is already in place, already instituted deep within us. This two way tug is a paradoxical condition we are born to experience, it comes with the package, the process of living with these bodies and brains. This tug is virtually a holding pattern, one that can actually render us ineffectual in making the very choice a healthy (non addicted) exit from this tug requires. This pull, this tug of choice paradox, works its way deep into our thinking and behaving processes, even into our physical conditions:

pull to accept patterning ← **(double bind trap)** → **pull to resist patterning**
pull to accept patterning → **(double bind trap)** ← **pull to resist patterning**

Here it is, the double-bind, the lose-lose, no way out sensation we all have experienced in some way. It may start early in life when even the best intending parent inadvertently (or advertently in some cases) gives the child a mixed message: Do this, no do that. Put on the red coat, no I said the blue coat. Be quiet, no speak up. Sit still, get up and get that. You are a good child, you are a bad child. Don't do that, it is bad, even though you see me doing that.

EXPLICIT AND IMPLICIT ADDICTIONS

Seeing how rampant and commanding these traps can be, we must take heed. We must also see how very obvious explicit problem addictions have become. And then we must admit to the less visible addictions driving them. We have to see the downside of implicit—deep level—patterning. In recent times, humans have become increasingly conscious of the problem of addiction to destructive and dangerous patterns, such as compulsive overeating, drug using, drinking, and so on, and this is a good advance in our awareness of what I call *explicit additions*—the more obvious, more visible addictions. This awareness can lead us to dig deeper and begin to see the more hidden patterns, what I call the *implicit addictions* driving the explicit addictions.

We have learned how explicit addictions tend to follow rather basic patterns, and appear almost cyclic, as is diagrammed in Figure 9.1, where we see the common **trigger-urge-response pattern**. (Note that Figure 9.1 also offers an escape route, a new response option, to which we will return later, in Part Three of this book.)

These explicit addiction—trigger-urge-addicted response—behaviors tend to be more readily recognized than do the other more hidden *implicit addictions*, such as the very obscure but very powerful addictions we have to our ways of life and realities. Yet explicit addictions are, basically, only symptoms of implicit addictions to deeper behavioral, emotional and energetic patterns. So the cycle, the addictive pattern in Figure 9.1, is merely the surface cycle pattern, the *surface or explicit addiction*.

Figure 9.1.   Basic Cycle of Addiction

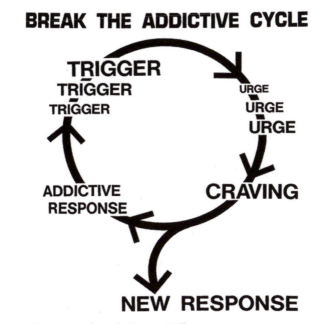

(Illustration by and courtesy of Angela Browne-Miller.)

HIDDEN IMPLICIT PATTERNING

Behind all surface, explicit, addiction is the less visible, less obvious, *implicit* pattern addiction. A warning: Implicit pattern addiction, even when life-threatening or quality of life degenerating, does not always signal its presence through explicit addictions. Implicit addictions are very difficult to detect let alone name. Still implicit patterning can make its presence known in a variety of ways we may or may not connect with it. We may find that hitherto unrecognized yet poor work habits, poor eating habits, poor emotional habits, poor posture habits, poor sleep habits, poor routing of internal energy habits, eventually catch up to us—whether or not we have first or ever realized these exist. The catch up can be a health alarm going off, or a family life deteriorating, or perhaps an explicit addiction emerging in the self or in the co-addicted persons or in the children (and teens as these are children of the family) as the result of underlying implicit patterning going off in all of these persons at once and more. A sad and quite common example of the surfacing of implicit pattern addiction can be found in the instance of two long term silently raging and seriously depressed parents raising a child. The child may eventually become the identified patient in the family, the one with the explicit addiction. Perhaps this child develops a severe eating disorder, or maybe a self cutting (self mutilation) pattern addiction, or perhaps this child becomes dually addicted to marijuana and methamphetamine. This child is the identified addict, as this child has formed an explicit addiction while the parents' pattern addictions are less obvious, more implicit.

UNDERLYING SOURCE PATTERNING TO BE ADDICTED TO A REALITY

And even deeper than the hidden energetic and subtle emotional patterns of implicit addictions is the **underlying source patterning program** which drives all other patterning, including that of implicit and explicit addictions whether these are positive or negative addictions, positive or negative—good or bad behavior patterns. The relationship of the underlying source patterning program to implicit and explicit addiction is diagrammed in Figure 9.2. It is here, at the deep level of the underlying source patterning program, that we again see the addict, and he or she is us.

We are all wired to form habits and addictions. The problem is, we are also all wired to form addictions to behaviors our brains tell us to be addicted to. The SELF falls prey to the underlying coding or wiring to be addicted to patterns and to be addicted to being addicted to patterns. Therefore, when we want to break an addiction, we have to rewire the SELF. We have to reach the SELF and assist the SELF in overriding its explicit and implicit problem pattern addictions, and in overriding or at least setting straight its underlying addiction to the addicted state itself.

Figure 9.2.   Full Patterning Addiction Hierarchy

EXPLICIT (SURFACE) PATTERN ADDICTION

↑

IMPLICIT (HIDDEN) PATTERNING/ADDICTION

↑

UNDERLYING SOURCE PATTERNING PROGRAM

(Diagram by and courtesy of Angela Browne-Miller.)

10

Underlying Source Patterning Driving All Addictions

We indeed have planted deep within us the coding to function as creatures of habits—of habit patterns—to inherit habits via our genes and via modeling from our parents and families and cultures, and also to develop habit patterns on our own while living our lives. As if this coding function was purposefully implanted within us, in our genes, to ensure our ability to live and learn, to ensure that we function as life forms, we are built to utilize this coding function every moment of our lives. It is this function which makes it possible for us to perceive (and even define for ourselves) a reality as a given, to tell ourselves we know where we are in time and space: It is this coding function that makes it possible for us to define our reality in every way in order to live "within" it—in order to live. And yes, part of living within a given reality successfully is buying into that reality entirely, or almost entirely.

SURVIVAL RELIES ON THIS PROGRAMMING

Although quite subtle, the tendency is to form an **addiction to reality** itself, (or to what is perceived as reality itself), to survive. In fact, organisms such as ourselves develop beneficial adaptations to the environment—to reality—that increase the likelihood of our survival. (We also change the environment where we can, sometimes increasing the likelihood of our survival, sometimes increasing the likelihood of our present-time survival but unfortunately failing to do the same for the long run. What a gamble changing our environment in the now with no regard for long term consequences is!) We have been doing this adaptation to the environment throughout our evolution. And we have been passing on the adaptations to our environments we have developed via our genes (as well as via our cultures and traditions).

So while the brain's reward system reinforces important behaviors today, in the now—eating, drinking, sleeping, mating—this survival oriented functioning itself has been passed on to us through time and we pass this on to future generations. However—and this is a big however here—all this is predicated on the *successful* passing on of an adherence to a reality in which these functions work and continue to be survival-oriented. While this is a rather lofty concept, it can be brought right down to Earth with the simple example of hunting prey for dinner. In the modern so-called "developed" world, we rarely have to directly hunt and kill prey for dinner. In fact, were we to engage in this activity in our neighborhoods and cities today, we might find ourselves mistakenly applying this drive to household pets and zoo animals. Health concerns, anger and havoc could emerge. Fortunately, we have adapted this drive to hunt and kill our prey for dinner to our modern environment and now control and even suppress this drive. By contrast, we have other drives which we need to continue today, such as the drives to sleep and to mate. Fortunately we still mate, although population and corresponding scientific pressures may be changing mating and related sexual behaviors. Let's take the behavior of sleep as a yet more general example. We need to sleep. Fortunately we are coded to need sleep, to feel the need for sleep, and to sleep when tired. Where there may be a point in the development of the species where sleep is not required, this new adaptation will require internal genetic coding (or external medical interventions) to ensure that whatever metabolic and behavioral changes are needed are made.

RISK AND STIMULATION AS TRIGGERS FOR GAMBLING AND GAMBLING WITH LIFE

Various readings of and responses to the sensation of risk have evolved over time and are in play in many problem addictions today. Gambling addiction provides a case in point. Brain scans have shown that when particular men are shown erotic pictures, they are more likely to make larger financial gambles than they are when they are shown frightening or disturbing pictures (such as pictures of dangerous animals). When they are shown something more neutral such as pictures of office equipment, they make gambles in the midrange. Brain scans reveal that when photos of snakes and spiders are shown to the men, the portion of the brain associated with pain, fear, and anger light up. Upon being shown these disturbing, even frightening pictures, the men are likely to keep their bets low, as the pain, fear and anger experienced causes the risk taking drive to minimize itself. By contrast, viewing erotic pictures results in other areas of the brain being lit up, and greater risk taking behavior (in gambling) follows.

There are numerous basic patterns we are coded to exhibit in both positive and negative ways. As is true for patterns of risk taking, many behaviors, deep virtually subconscious at their most active levels, are of value to us as we survive as a species. Yet the very coding which guides us as we live can drive us into, and hold us imprisoned in, a vicious cycle of a serious problem addiction. We take risks for both survival and counter survival reasons, but we do take risks. Risk taking is gambling, risking the outcome of action in the now regardless of the potential later cost of that action taken now. To make this gamble, we must either not know, or not want to know, the potential high cost of that action's outcome. Or we may know and deny what we know in order to whole heartedly take this risk. Denial rears its ugly head.

11

Slaves to Attentional Bias

We can run but we cannot hide. We cannot escape the reality that we are indeed creatures of, and **slaves** to, habit. We are actually creatures of the *mechanisms of habit and addiction*, the mental and biological workings that make habits and addictions possible. We do know, we understand on some deep level, that we are biologically coded to have working within our bodies these mechanisms of habits and addictions. We even count on this coding to take care of details and actions we may not be consciously thinking through. We actually **rely** on our own enslavement to our patterns.

Addiction is not as simple or straightforward as we may think. Take the very act of noticing, of paying attention to, something. When this something is a trigger for a problem addiction, **we can fall prey to that trigger simply by having noticed it**. If we dig deep enough, we have to admit that addictions to drugs, alcohol and various activities actually include **addictions to the specific triggers** for the particular drug use, alcohol drinking, or engagement in other activities that we are addicted to. Furthermore, on an even deeper level, we are not only addicted to addictions and their triggers, we are addicted to the very addiction-favoring attentional biases drawing us, again and again, to the triggers for the cycles of these addictions and their addiction responses. Hence, when we say someone is addicted to a particular drug or activity such as gambling, we are actually talking about a *complex set of addictions* to not only the drug or the activity itself, but also to the triggers for this addiction, and also to the attention-directing activities and associations the brain is undergoing to promote this addiction, to keep this addiction alive. Refer again to Figure 9.1 on page 69. Note the point on that cycle labeled "trigger trigger TRIGGER." We can conceivably map a new cycle of addiction to the addiction to each of the triggers and hidden triggers in this sequence. Suddenly we have addiction cycle upon addiction cycle all running at the same time, perhaps best described as a set of gears turning together, or perhaps more a web of moving and interacting sub-cycles spinning in all directions. Or the poor but brilliant brain who can make all this possible!

We have to see how these biological computers we call our brains become addicted to patterns, oft troubling patterns, and then allow the troubling patterns themselves to run the show, to even build in addictions to the triggers for these troubled patterns as insurance against the breaking of these addictions. Again, I want to suggest that the *domination of the brain by its problem addictions* takes center stage over most if not all—depending on how insidious the addiction is—activities of the brain. In this problem addiction dominated mind-brain, everything must serve the problem addiction itself. We are then having to rediscover and redefine the SELF to have it take its power back. The SELF must regain control of the brain that has been seized by the problem addiction pattern.

ATTENTIONAL BIAS PROGRAMMING

Among the many mental functions we are coded to engage in (albeit relatively subconsciously) is the addiction to triggers—and the addiction to the addiction to triggers. Here is the powerful attentional bias toward those things that habitually remind us of, call our attention to, bring on cravings for, our habits and addictions, favoring items and situations that will kick off the entire addictive cycle again. We have to take a moment to think of cows out to pasture. When the dinner bell rings, the cows proceed, as if having been ordered, like four legged automatons, in line over hills, even along dangerously narrow and steep pathways, to dinner. (The cows are programmed to respond to the dinner bell, the food has reinforced this program or pattern. More than this, the cows are pattern addicted to the trigger, the dinner bell itself.) How readily programmed living organisms can be, even have to be. We all have wired into ourselves our own dinner bells.

Numerous behavioral studies point to an abnormality in the allocating of attention to what are called drug cues (reminders or triggers of various forms) in drug addicted persons. Basically, more attention is paid to details related to the addiction than to other details. Attention is more rapidly, more firmly, and with more holding power, captured by items associated with an addicted person's substance or activity of choice. Studies show that, when an addicted person is presented with two visual stimuli or "cues" (also called "targets"), one on each side of a screen, one a drug related stimulus, the other a nondrug (or neutral) stimulus, the person who is addicted to the drug will stay focused on the addiction related images. Addicted persons will respond more quickly to the first type of target or cue, the one related to the drug addiction. And then in later showings of pictures, this time neutral pictures on both sides of the screen, these same persons will then respond to whatever is now in the location of the side which had pictured the first drug addiction-related item. Findings are telling us that in drug addicted persons, attention is captured and then held by drug-related stimuli over other nondrug related stimuli, and by memory of drug related stimuli over nondrug related stimuli. Attention is automatically drawn back to—attention automatically seeks and favors—the source or location of the drug related stimulus. The brain—or its problem pattern addiction, that is—has programmed the brain to seek and place priority on triggers for its addiction, frequently to the exclusion of other cues or information.

Another type of experiment looking at attention in general finds drug-related bias again, this time in a modified version of what is known as a Stroop Task. The original Stroop Task presents words (including color names) displayed in different ink (or screen) colors. Subjects are tested for their speed in naming the color of the letterings. When a word is printed in green ink, the correct response will be green. Now, when a word is the word for a specific color, such as red, but is printed in the color of another color ink, such as green, subjects tend to be slower in naming the ink color. Clearly, for color words that do not match the ink that they are naming, the brain requires more time to know the color of the ink the word is written in; while, for neutral, noncolor words, the color of the ink is correctly named more quickly. And again for color words written in a congruent font color, the color of the ink is correctly and rapidly named most of the time. This is what is known as the Stroop Effect, which occurs where attention devoted to reading the word interferes with attention devoted to naming the word's ink color. When this task is modified to test for the possibility of drug-related attentional bias, similar results are acquired. Here, drug-related words are presented to drug addicted persons in varying ink colors, and neutral words are also presented in varying ink colors, with the results indicating that drug-related words demand more attentional resources than do neutral words. In other words, the ink color of more neutral words is named more rapidly than the ink color of drug related words because the drug-addicted brain places *more attention* on drug-related words themselves rather than on their color.

Other tests of attentional bias reveal much the same, that greater attention to, attentional bias toward, drug related stimuli is common among persons addicted to the drug that a particular stimulus addresses or suggests in some way. Other sets of tests for attentional bias include what are called change blindness tasks, in which participants detect slight changes between two rapidly alternating pictures or visual scenes. Drug addicted persons more readily detect drug-addiction-related changes in a pictured scene than do those who are not drug addicted. And yet another test for attentional bias is the attentional blink test, which is used to study responses to stimuli and also addiction-related attentional abnormalities. A stream of visual stimuli is rapidly presented, with instructions to detect two specified stimuli within the stream. The first and second targets or cues are separated by a certain amount of time, such as a separation of between 200–400 milliseconds. Subjects are generally more likely to miss the second target because attentional resources are already allocated to processing the first. And this is the "attentional blink." When the first stimulus is an addiction-related stimulus, addicted persons demonstrate a longer and more extended attentional blink. However, when the second stimulus is an addiction-related stimulus, an addict's first attentional blink is reduced.

In drug-addicted persons, we see that words and images associated with drug use have a heightened capacity to capture and hold attention, and that such stimuli interfere with attention to other things in their environment. This heightened attention toward drug-related stimuli occurs in a wide variety of addictions including addictions to: cannabis, cocaine, opiates, tobacco, alcohol, caffeine, food, gambling, sex, relationships, love, violence, and even shopping-spending. We are slaves to our programming to be attentionally biased.

CONSCIOUS ATTENTION TO TRIGGERS

Some studies show that in some addictions, the attentional bias toward drug-related stimuli over nondrug related stimuli will be far more powerful when the stimuli are perceived consciously. For example, data suggest that attentional bias toward tobacco cues more often require the stimuli to be consciously perceived; when the smoking cues are presented too quickly or are masked by another stimulus, they do not affect attentional allocation. By contrast, some studies of alcohol attentional bias find that heavy social drinkers (but not light drinkers) show even subconscious attentional bias toward alcohol cues, suggesting that such subconscious bias may serve as an early warning sign of alcohol addiction. These findings also bring up another possible explanation for the bias: stimulus familiarity. Furthermore, evidence suggests that the magnitude of this attentional bias is directly proportional to relapse risk. Many studies report that the magnitude of the attentional bias is directly proportional to the level of craving during drug abstinence and withdrawal.

Repeated use of the drug of addiction and or repeated engagement in the activity of the addiction (even where the activity is a nondrug addiction related activity), may and most likely always does produce at least some, if not major, changes in the brain. Again, these changes cause the brain to attribute excessive significance or salience to people, places, and things—to cues, triggers—associated with the addiction. Recognizing that we can become—even be programmed to become —so very hypersensitive to the things that call us back into our habit patterns, that can actually pull us back into crash and burn mode, is critical to our overcoming troubled addiction patterns.

BAD LEARNINGS

Some attention favoring is even associated with our brain's learning function. While learning is highly desirable and while, quite rightly, a great deal of society's budgetary resources are directed to means of enhancing learning processes in children and in adults, we must stop for a moment and understand that *not all learning is constructive or positive*. Again, a highly desirable and even essential to survival function of the brain can and does run awry: **The brain can learn, can teach itself, to pay greater attention to triggers for reentry into a negative habit pattern.** The pattern addiction can take central stage and *teach, even program, the brain* to maintain the pattern itself, to do what ever it takes, to learn what ever it needs to learn, to hold that pattern in place, no matter how dangerous and destructive that pattern is or can be.

We have to see that addiction to stimuli are powerful **learned associations** between the drug or activity high and the reminders of this high. So powerful are these learned associations that the brain's *ability to inhibit* the problem addiction's behavior can be overridden by the learned associations between the addiction's highs and its triggers. Inhibiting response to triggers can fall by the wayside, be overpowered by the associative pull of the triggers right into the highs. Based on the deep association between the triggers or cues and the highs, the triggers that become associated with drug use (or other addiction behavior) can themselves produce intense cravings for and reminders of the high itself, leading directly down a nonstop road to relapse.

TRIGGERS THEMSELVES MAY INDUCE HIGHS

What is perhaps of ultimate significance here is the fact that the cues or triggers for addicted persons' drug use or other addictions can themselves produce intense cravings, therefore even relapses. At the same time, these cues or triggers can kick off near and sometimes actual entry into the very altered state of consciousness (the ASC referred to in Chapter 2) the drugs would induce were they to be used, even before they are used, enhancing the cravings all the more. Attentional bias favoring—even demanding, even making automatic—the entry or reentry into the altered state associated with one's addiction: How remarkable the brain is that it can wire us for such an experience, yet how dominated it is by its own remarkability. Once addicted we are slaves to our patterning. In fact, our troubled patterns can take precedence and assume (or just grab) directive position over all control of all functions. Every conscious and subconscious effort then becomes organized around the problem pattern addiction.

12

Degraded Decision-Making Functioning

At the heart of most of our behaviors is the moment of deciding: the go/no-go, do/do-not-do, yes/no, proceed/stop. This most primary, and at the same time ultimate, moment in our behaviors is THE MOMENT—the decision-making moment. This THE MOMENT is actually a chain of moments, as any one decision is actually a chain of decisions, many of which are so subtle we are not conscious of them. Most behaviors, when broken into small steps, increments, actually involve long chains of conscious, subconscious and unconscious decision-making processes.

GO AND NO-GO

One analysis of the process of selecting responses is called the go/no-go model. In go/no-go testing, different types of cues that indicate to the subject whether to respond or to refrain from responding to the cue are presented. Many drug addicted individuals have difficulty avoiding responses to pictures or stimuli related to their addictions. In laboratory go/no-go studies, addicted persons demonstrate greater inability to refrain from responding—greater inhibitory impairment —when presented with drug-related cues.

A decision-making task commonly used to study addicted person's thinking is the so-called delay discounting task. This type of task requires subjects to decide between a reward (such as a sum of money) being available sooner and a larger reward (such as a larger sum of money) being available at a later time. Addicted persons tend to choose the smaller, more immediate addiction-related rewards more often, despite their relatively small size and thereby diminished reward amount: **The delay which is part of the delayed but larger reward diminishes the perceived value of the delayed but larger reward in the now**. This is called delay discounting and it has been reported for a variety of addictive disorders, including addiction to nicotine, alcohol, amphetamines, cocaine, opiates, gambling, and shopping. While this tendency for problem pattern addicts to more steeply or more frequently discount delayed monetary rewards is quite consistent, it also appears that delayed rewards consisting of the drug of choice are discounted even more severely by drug addicts. For example, heroin-addicted persons who are participating in risky needle-sharing behaviors show greater delay discounting of both heroin and monetary rewards. The drug of choice with a cleaner needle *later* does not register as as valuable as the drug of choice *now* with no insurance of clean needle. And, it is also seen that money later is not as valuable as money, albeit less money, now to buy the drug now.

Whether or not addicted to heroin, or any substance, it is becoming increasingly clear that we all carry within us *mechanisms for overvaluing immediate rewards* (what may only seem to be rewards) over delayed perceived or actual rewards. This very mechanism primes us to continue problem addicted behavior in the now in the face of its negative consequences later. (We tend to think of this tendency as belonging to an adolescent state of mind, that the young are so very focused on today that planning for tomorrow can be too low a priority. Refer again to Chapter 7 on why good judgment falls by the wayside.) Hence when we say that addiction is the continued use or behavior in the face of adverse consequences, we are frequently saying that addiction NOW is the continued use or behavior NOW in the face of CONCEIVABLE adverse consequences LATER, whether that LATER be a moment, an hour, a day, a week, a month, a year, or several years later. The reality of later recedes as the problem pattern dominates one's reality.

ACTION SELECTING AND INHIBITING

The brain plays a major role, in fact virtually the only role, in both selecting and inhibiting our actions. The brain makes our decisions about our actions for us. Our biocomputer brain is always working, always serving either us—or our positive and negative pattern addictions. In that our brain is responsible for the programming that addicts us, (for example that addicts us to drugs and to nondrug activities), we have to wonder **at what point the brain becomes invested in our selecting addiction-fueling behavior over addiction-inhibiting behavior**. (In my years of working with problem addicted persons, I have come to recognize the matter of *investment* in addiction as central.)

A great deal of evidence regarding the role of the brain's frontal areas in action selection and in complex decision making comes to us from neuroimaging data. Among the findings is the understanding that the brain's right hemisphere's frontal lobe is involved in our efforts to prevent or deter what of our behaviors we may want (or may think we want) to prevent or deter. Another area of the brain, the fronto-median cortex, plays a role in voluntary response inhibition. Other studies point to the importance of dopamine in regulating discounting behavior. How amazing it is that the brain employs biological, biochemical mechanisms to make the right (and wrong) decisions about problem addiction in the face of present and future adverse consequences. We have to wonder, how much is the failure of our *response inhibition function* actually voluntary and conscious, and how much of this is subconscious and out of our conscious control? What can we do to convince our mental main frames, our brains, to bring these decisions back into conscious control? Who is in charge here, our troubled patterns or our SELVES?

Who *should* be in charge here, the pattern addiction or the SELF? The answer may be obvious—the SELF—unless you speak for the problem pattern which has taken control of the SELF.

13

Compromised Thinking and Situation Responsivity

It is all about SITUATIONS. It turns out that we think quite differently in different SITUATIONS. How surprising. After all, it is the same brain doing the thinking for you this morning as it is thinking for you last night. It is the same brain running you when you talk to Dan or Sandy as it is when you talk to John or Mary. Yet you express such different parts of yourself and such different messages to these people. Thank goodness, you may say, there is no way you want Dan or Sandy to hear what you said to John or Mary, and vice versa.

But why are we doing such different thinking in different situations? It turns out that we have mental functions which actually think about our thinking for us, and actually select the thinking we will do in particular situations—tell us what sort of thinking to do when. This function is a cognitive control function, an executive sort of command center function of the brain-mind.

SITUATIONS, SITUATIONS, SITUATIONS

What is emerging as central here is that we are slaves to not only our coding to form, preserve and feed pattern addictions, but to our brain's decisions regarding what to do in various situations. Cognitive control (our brain's own executive and overall organizing behavior) involves processes essential to our survival, including our ability to act and react in a **situation-specific** manner. Situation-specific reactions are reactions not general to all situations, but rather to specific situations. A large shark behind glass at the aquarium may evoke interest, yet the same large shark swimming near you at the beach may evoke alarm, fear, desire to get away quickly, perhaps the desire to hide. This indicates great flexibility in our cognitive control. We have great cognitive flexibility which allows us to make key decisions in complex and changing contexts or situations. This same cognitive flexibility allows us to direct our attention to what we find important, and to remember what we learned about what we found important. Cognitive control allows us to respond to specific situations rather than oversimplify and over-generalize, and also to recall how we have responded so that we know, when a new situation arises, how much of the situation is similar and how much is different.

EXECUTIVE CONTROL

We can experience disruptions in our cognitive control functions: when this disruption occurs it is described as **dys** executive behavior. In fact, this dysexecutive behavior is a key element of an addictive disorder. Persons who are problem addicted are frequently unable to engage in **situation-appropriate responses** to stimuli or events. (I have discussed two of our major cognitive control functions, attentional bias or attentional control, and decision making, and how these can run awry, in the two previous chapters.) Cognitive control malfunctions inhibit our general functioning as well as our functioning with the goal of survival in mind, always in mind. (I have realized that, in working with persons who are addicted to problem patterns, I am seeing a vying for control of the SELF, a struggle for control in which the problem pattern seeks to fool the SELF into thinking the problem pattern *is* the self. Keep in mind here that we are talking about survival of the SELF rather than of the problem pattern that fools the SELF into calling this problem pattern the SELF.)

As noted in the previous two chapters, clinical evidence indicates that both attentional abnormalities and decision-making deficiences are present among people who exhibit substance use disorders. Note again that generally speaking, persons who are addicted do show a greater immediate reward bias; that is, they are more likely than non-addicted persons to choose a smaller immediate reward over a larger reward for which they would need to wait. This tendency holds true for various types of rewards, including for the addict's drug of choice and for monetary rewards. Laboratory-controlled gambling tasks have also linked abnormal decision making with addictive disorders. All related cognitive processes (decision making, attentional control, and various forms of enforcement- and association-driven learning) are processes that fall under the general umbrella of executive function and are associated with frontal circuits within the brain.

ACTION SELECTION DECISIONS RESPOND TO SITUATIONS

Decisions can be made regarding minor and major mental and behavioral choices. In that any decision involves some action, even if only a minor or a biochemical action, virtually every decision is an action selection. It follows that **every decision is an action selecting event**, even when there is nothing done, as a decision to do nothing, to take no action, is a form of decision. Decisions to respond to particular situations may require us to work or to call upon behaviors we have not already recorded. Numerous findings suggest that the brains of substance abusers are generally working harder to recruit the usual brain areas needed to perform tasks, that there may be some degree of neural inefficiency interfering with action (and thus also non-action) selection. Where the selection is nonaction, or not to engage in the problem addiction's behavior (such as to take another drink), the nonaction is inhibition. In that there appears to be a neural inefficiency in problem addicted persons, there may be a problem with inhibiting behavior in certain situations, especially where addiction to even the triggers for reentry into the addictive cycle is so powerful.

In the case of more complex decision making, beyond the already so complex TO DO OR NOT TO DO decision, it is becoming clear that some persons' neural frameworks have greater abilities to make decisions based on future outcomes than do others'. We detect an **actual inability to consider future outcomes** when choosing whether to continue drug use (or other addictive activity) despite continued negative consequences. Given the lowered resistance to triggers, and derailed decision-making functions, when inhibition functions are weak, problem addiction is a rather natural problem. **Addicted persons tend to be more unable to make situation-appropriate decisions-responses to stimuli, events, SITUATIONS. As is the premise of this book, we are all addicted persons. Therefore we are all faced with the potential of sharing, at some time in some way, the inability to make situation-**

appropriate decisions-responses to SITUATIONS. How many times have we made situation-*in*appropriate decisions? Why?

So very critical is our ability to cope with situations in **situation appropriate** ways, that I have seen the importance of working with the perception of the situation itself in helping persons who are problem addicted overcome their problem patterns. This is what has inspired me to design the Situational Transcendence conceptualization and program I discuss in Part Two of this book.

PART THREE

The Importance of Promoting Situational Transcendence

The Journey Starts Here

... though I walk
through the valley
of the shadow of death,
I will fear no evil ...
Psalm 23

(Illustration by and courtesy of Angela Browne-Miller.)

14
The Case for
Situational Transcendence

Many of our problems with troubled addictive patterns bear hidden gems of wisdom, insight, realization. Perhaps we even feed some of our addictions, somehow aware that we are providing ourselves with the opportunity to transcend them. We are not entirely trapped, entirely prisoners of the programs we burn into ourselves. As human beings we do have a choice. We can either become so overwhelmed by our problems that we miss out on the value of challenging opportunity, or we can realize that addiction is a *potential-laden* SITUATION. And here again is that word, SITUATION. Those of us (which is all of us) who are addicted to a problem drug or nondrug pattern, or to a more implicit emotional or energetic pattern, maybe an overt co-addiction or something yet more subtle, have a wonderful opportunity to experience a special form of learning and change or transcendence —specifically this awareness and experience of change I call herein, **Situational Transcendence**.

Situational Transcendence works on all levels of the self to bring about within the self a lasting new way of perceiving and responding to a situation (including any triggers in that situation). When Situational Transcendence is engineered, the brain is washed with a sort of firing on all levels—a sweeping and immediate realization that reaches across its various regions, and in so doing the mind-brain and the behavioral patterns it executes can leap into a profound change. New learning has taken place, new avenues of behavior and response to situations are opened, and their entry or aha sustained. In essence, the problem pattern addiction situation is overridden, transcended by a wave of new more powerful more global signals.

SITUATION DEPENDENCE AND SITUATION RESTRICTION

The previous chapter discusses aspects of *situation-dependent behavior*, in which it becomes clear that we behave differently in different situations—when the situations call for us to, or trigger us to, behave in **situation-specific** ways. Adding to that discussion of *situation-specificity*, we can say that each situation contains or does not contain within it, specific characteristics, cues and triggers for entry and or reentry into a problem addiction cycle. So the situation itself is not just a place, it is a time, person, place or thing, including nutritional situations, emotional situations, financial situations, and so on, each of which is loaded with its own situational conditions and triggers.

We can say that any given situation may be so very loaded with triggers for entry and/or reentry into a particular cycle of problem addiction that there appears to be no exit—that any behavioral pathway out is blocked by behavioral pulls in to, and to stay in, the situation and its cycle of addiction. Let's call this no way out situation, **situation restriction**. A great deal of energy is trapped, stuck, in this situation. Consider Figure 8.2 on page 60 and its diagramming of this situational and quite rigid restriction, trap or no-exit paradox. The problem pattern offers no obvious and easy way out of itself. Why would it? The problem pattern is driven to survive in tact as the problem pattern that it is. The problem pattern is driven to commandeer all available resources, whatever biochemical and emotional resources it needs to feed itself. The problem addicted pattern is one that locks energy into its pattern, and even seeks to engage other surrounding energies to support its cause.

We now can build on this diagram the release of addicted-pattern-maintaining energy when such a trap is exited, as is diagrammed in Figure 14.1. What is taking place in Figure 14.1 is the release from the trap, the release from the situation from which there appeared to be no escape, no exit from the pattern of addiction. Here the diagram shows the release of trapped energy, energy which had been devoted to holding the person, the person's brain, and the SELF, trapped in this problem addiction pattern. Energy freed is energy available! Energy available is energy available to a NEW PATTERN! (Also, in Figure 14.1 note the fork just above the escape from the paradox of addiction. At this fork in the road, we can fall back into the trap, or stay out of the trap.)

Figure 14.1.   Release from the Paradox of No Exit Addiction Situation

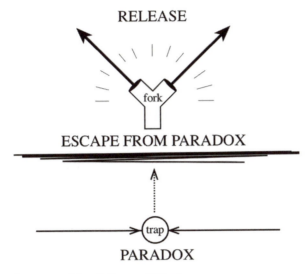

(Diagram by and courtesy of Angela Browne-Miller.)

ADDICTION-SPECIFIC SITUATIONS

There are great and healing opportunities to harvest energy that has been locked into maintaining problem patterns. An understanding of the structure of addictions is required. First, problem addicted individuals can learn to recognize how the addiction-specific situation feeds the addiction-specific response to this situation which in turn feeds the addiction situation:

addiction-situation-specific response to addiction situation →
continuation of addiction situation →
continuation of addiction-situation-specific response to addiction situation →
more continuation of addiction situation →
more continuation of addiction-situation-specific response to addiction situation →
and so on.

Ultimately, exit from this situational trap of problem pattern addiction involves: identifying this as a trap; recognizing the store of energy locked into this trap; seeking the intentional, conscious, and careful release of energy from this trap; harvesting this energy to promote, to fuel, a leap in the mind-brain's ability to overcome, transcend, this problem pattern, this problem situation. This is, in essence, a rewiring of the self, a taking back of the self from the problem pattern addiction.

Prior to the Situational Transcendence, the self as it was wired was wired to remain in this problem addicted situation. Situational Transcendence requires of, and brings about in, the mind-brain a new outlook on the situation, and a new situation-specific response to each and every trigger—and trigger to be triggered and so on. No matter how bleak and painful a situation may appear, it can be changed by being seen differently, by being *re-perceived, and therefore by being experienced differently. A new pattern can be formed. An old pattern can be escaped.*

Of course, before any changes can occur, we must be convinced that we **can turn things around**! We must believe in the possibility of Situational Transcendence. We must also understand the process, which must be studied and practiced continually. No matter what level of understanding we reach, there is always more to be learned. This and the following three chapters are a basic introduction to the process of Situational Transcendence used in my work with clients. What is being addressed here is the means of empowering the SELF to overcome its problem addicted programming to take back control of itself. First, let's look at problem patterns which can be broken by Situational Transcendence. To override our problem addicted responses to our problem situations, we must first recognize our problem addicted patterns. Then we must speak to the brain by teaching it new understandings and patterns.

15

Patterns of Progression into Problem Addiction Situations

We all know how easy it is to slip or progress into increasingly predictable ever more rigid patterns of behavior. It is what we do, how we live, how we learn. And sometimes this slipping into patterns is not what we would choose to do. The old "bet you can't eat just one" commercial says it all. It is quite difficult to engage in something which has some form of seemingly positive reward—such as a sense of relief, or a high, or an escape perhaps—without wanting to do it again. This desire to repeat the receiving of a reward is quite natural and even healthy. Do not fault yourself for this, as this is part of our programming, our coding. Even addiction is part of our coding, as addiction itself, addiction to positive patterns of behavior, is a useful program. Hence the underlying source patterning program (described in Chapter 9 and Figure 9.2 on page 71) is as much as part of who we are as is our body and personality, perhaps even more so.

It is where the brain runs awry, where this underlying ability to code a positive program (of responding or behaving or learning) works in a detrimental way, that we find potentially and actually detrimental addictions arising. We see troubled patterns arise not only as drug and alcohol addictions (such as those diagrammed in Figures 15.1, 15.2, 15.3, 15.4, and 15.5), but also as every form of problem addiction we know, plus several forms of addiction not so readily recognized as explicit addiction. We can even look into more subtle patterns such as relationship patterns, to see models of *problem patterns of relating*, to find potentially detrimental relationship addiction patterns arising within the pleasure and relief from discomfort pleasure pathways. For example, see Figures 15.6. through 15.13. (All figures appear at the end of the chapter.) Note that this "relating" can be to a person or to a drug or activity of addiction, and the patterns of relating, once into a problem addiction cycle, are quite parallel across addictions. Also of note is the illusion suffered by many persons experiencing problem addictions, whether to lovers, or to drugs or food or gambling and the like: LOVE! A sense of being in love with whatever the object or experience of the addiction may be permeates all too many problem addiction patterns and makes these pattern addictions all the more difficult to leave. We can also look at other patterns, they are every where around and within us, to see how common the patterns, even the troubled patterns, are to all our behaviors.

CASUAL TO REGULAR

We slip so easily into troubled patterns. Typical movement into addiction is one of stepping from impulsivity to compulsivity, and moving only in one direction, rather than ever turning back from compulsive behavior to impulsive behavior. (Attentional bias distortion, degraded decision-making functioning, compromised thinking, all make turning back increasingly difficult.) This can be then, a one way street for the person with a troubled addiction, with the danger of returning to impulsivity being a full return to compulsivity:

impulsivity → compulsivity → compulsivity → ongoing compulsivity

We can dissect this progression from impulsive to compulsive to look deeper into the stages of this progression. The first step in this behavior can be described as a movement from no use to casual use, where its opposite, ongoing non use or non behavior (as we are talking about substance use as well as behavioral nondrug addictions here) can be an alternative and more positive ongoing pattern:

Non Use or Non Behavior → Non Use or Non Behavior →
Non Use or Non Behavior

However, once there is experimentation or casual use or casual behavior, then the step from no behavior in this area to casual behavior has been taken:

No Behavior in this Area → Some Casual Behavior

Frequently, the next step into addiction can be a casual, even an intermittent behavior, even a somewhat repetitive behavior, moving to a regular behavior. We can diagram such a progression this way:

Casual Behavior → Regular Behavior

And it is along this simple pathway that a pattern can be born. Always as this movement from casual to regular behavior progresses, there is a deeper patterning at work, a source patterning, an underlying yet quite simple tendency, even drive, to create a pattern out of a behavior, as seen here below where the above continuum is added to the basic structure as was seen in Figure 9.2:

Casual Behavior → Regular Behavior
EXPLICIT (SURFACE) PATTERN

↑

IMPLICIT (HIDDEN) PATTERN ADDICTION

↑

UNDERLYING SOURCE PATTERNING PROGRAM

Certainly we have all witnessed this tendency in others or perhaps even experienced this process ourselves. For example, while some persons can drink alcohol casually and never find themselves developing a pattern of regular use, others cannot. A once in a while drinking pattern can shift to a pattern of every weekend or every night. (Let us be clear here. This does not necessarily mean the increasingly regular use of alcohol is the development of a problem pattern, as more is involved.) Always as this movement from casual behavior to regular behavior is taking place, there is a deeper source pattern fueling the process.

REGULAR TO TROUBLED

At some point, some regular behaviors become a bit too regular, too repeated. The easy ability to stop the behavior reduces. Decision making regarding this behavior is not working well. Good judgment recedes. Attentional biases favoring this behavior increase. Learning of the pattern of behavior instills ever deeper into the brain. The regular behavior may thus become a troubled behavior, again always fueled by the implicit pattern as well as by the underlying source patterning program where the deeper biological and biochemical workings of surface patterns are always at work.

$$\frac{\text{Regular Behavior} \rightarrow \text{Troubled Behavior}}{\text{EXPLICIT (SURFACE) PATTERN}}$$

$\uparrow$

IMPLICIT (HIDDEN) PATTERN ADDICTION

$\uparrow$

UNDERLYING SOURCE PATTERNNING PROGRAM

People who are exhibiting troubled behavior continue a behavior even in the face of its adverse effects to themselves (their health, their mind, their work), their families, their businesses, their neighborhoods, or their societies. It is easy to slip from regular behavior to troubled behavior because the early signs of troubled behavior are subtle and often go undetected. And, of course, where the signs are detected or noticed in some way, they are all too frequently blocked out or denied if perceived at all.

TROUBLED TO ADDICTED

People who are caught in troubled patterns tend to not even be aware of how easily they can slip from troubled behavior patterning into full blown patterns of addicted behavior:

$$\frac{\text{Casual} \rightarrow \text{Regular} \rightarrow \text{Troubled} \rightarrow \text{Addicted Behaviors}}{\text{EXPLICIT (SURFACE) PATTERN}}$$

$\uparrow$

IMPLICIT (HIDDEN) PATTERN ADDICTION

$\uparrow$

UNDERLYING SOURCE PATTERNING PROGRAM

Fortunately, not every one who tries alcohol or other drugs, or overeating, gambling, or compulsive theft, travels this tragic path. Some of these persons, these casual behav**ORS** try a behavior once and then consider the experiment completed. But all too commonly, casual behav**ORS** unwittingly slip into regular behavior. They confidently tell themselves, "It can't happen to me. I'm too much in control of my life to develop an addiction to anything. I'm just having a little fun."

DESCENT INTO DETRIMENTAL PATTERN ADDICTION

We may say, "well that can't happen to me." Yet, in reality, we are all too often deluding ourselves. Case history after case history demonstrates that casual problem behaviors, without training regarding how to avoid programming oneself, dramatically increases the probability of developing a fully addictive behavior. *And any behavior conducted regularly increases the chances of its pattern being programmed into the person conducting that behavior.*

This is an explanation of the descent into detrimental pattern-addiction. Any behavior can be expressed once or twice. Yet, somehow we can too often be blind to the crossing of the boundaries between casual and regular, regular and troubled, troubled and addicted. Why? Because we are programmed to slip, unaware, into pattern addiction, almost blindly, whether it be a negative or positive addiction—unless we are highly watchful. Remember, the same underlying template of coding that allows positive patterns to self reinforce and program into us allows detrimental negative patterns to self reinforce and program into us as well.

THE FREEING AND RIGHT USE OF OUR ENERGY

Is this genetic tendency to acquire programming mere happenstance? Is it the misfiring of the survival-oriented function (developed to have us respond automatically to falling boulders, red lights and other safety signals)? Or, are we prisoners of a source mechanism buried deep within our coding—a mechanism rendering us readily programmed creatures of habit, almost eager to succumb to automatic behavior?

Are we prisoners of coding which tells us to live pattern addicted and then to die? Compulsive addiction to drug consumption, food consumption, sex consumption, and other consumptive and repetitive behavioral patterns—while we may be unaware of the effects—can actually make us emotionally and even physically ill. Such pattern addiction can be life threatening. Some people physically die of detrimental addictions without first breaking these addictions. We must *go conscious* to be able to catch ourselves slipping blindly into negative patterns of thought and of behavior. Going fully conscious will allow us to take ourselves off of automatic, to have the self fully recognize and transcend addictive situations. The first step in going conscious is to become hyper-conscious of the patterns we fall into. The patterns illustrated in the following figures are examples of what addicted persons can do to begin to see, to actually visualize, their pathways into addiction to their patterns.

Note again that while Figures 15.6. through 15.13 model troubled addicted relationship patterns, these also suggest patterns of relationships we develop with the objects and activities of our addictions (as in falling in love with the drug or the game or the gamble). Having problem addicted persons visualize and then diagram their surface, most explicit patterns of addiction is the first step in calling subconscious mental workings and pathways to the surface. Following these patterns (in Figures 15.1 through 15.13), where we see what sorts of troubled surface patterns we form in our lives, we turn to what is involved in breaking free of these explicit addiction patterns, and what patterns we can take on to override undesirable patterns. (We will return to these patterns in Chapter 21.)

Figure 15.1.   Cocaine Addicted Person's Trigger Chart: All Triggers Leading to One Point

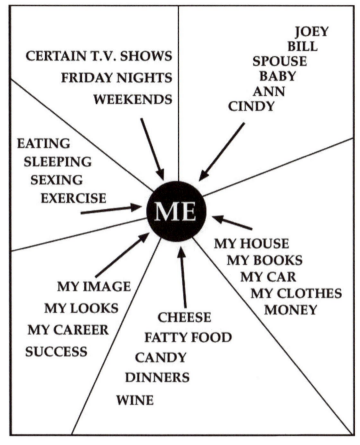

(Illustration by Anonymous, courtesy of Angela Browne-Miller.)

Figure 15.2.   Trigger Chart of Individual Who Has Chronic Head-aches and Painkiller Addiction: All Triggers Leading to One Sensation

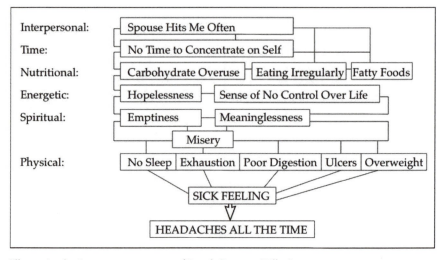

(Illustration by Anonymous, courtesy of Angela Browne-Miller.)

Figure 15.3. Alcohol, Tobacco, and Stimulant Dependent Individual's Triggers: All Triggers Feeding Addiction

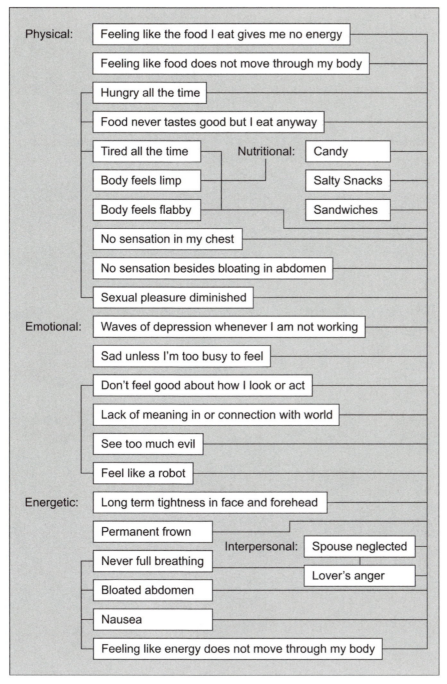

(Illustration by Anonymous, courtesy of Angela Browne-Miller.)

Figure 15.4.   Alcohol Addicted Person's Trigger Chart: All Roads Leading to the Same Place

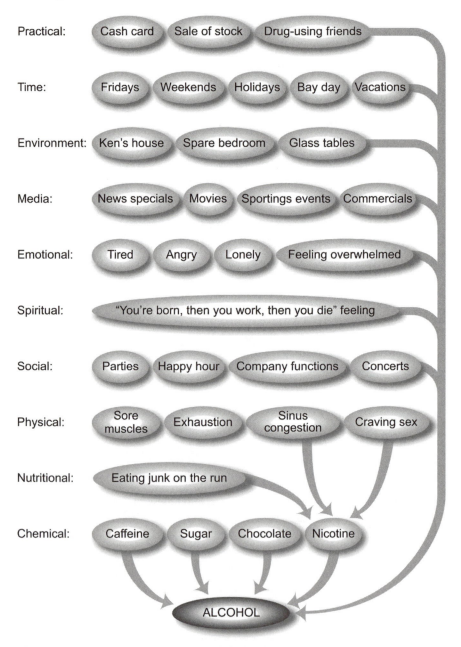

Practical: Cash card   Sale of stock   Drug-using friends

Time: Fridays   Weekends   Holidays   Bay day   Vacations

Environment: Ken's house   Spare bedroom   Glass tables

Media: News specials   Movies   Sportings events   Commercials

Emotional: Tired   Angry   Lonely   Feeling overwhelmed

Spiritual: "You're born, then you work, then you die" feeling

Social: Parties   Happy hour   Company functions   Concerts

Physical: Sore muscles   Exhaustion   Sinus congestion   Craving sex

Nutritional: Eating junk on the run

Chemical: Caffeine   Sugar   Chocolate   Nicotine

ALCOHOL

(Illustration by Anonymous, courtesy of Angela Browne-Miller.)

Figure 15.5.   Alcohol and Pain Killer Addicted Person's Trigger Chart: The Compounded Trigger Trap

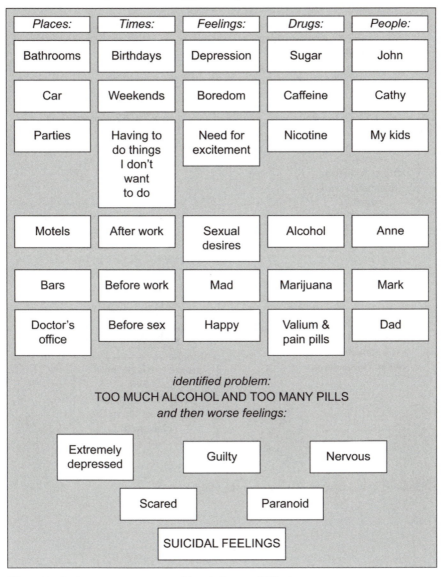

(Illustration by Anonymous, courtesy of Angela Browne-Miller.)

Figure 15.6.   Troubled Relationship (to Person or Drug or Activity) Pattern #1: Common Addictive Discomfort-Comfort Cycle or Pattern

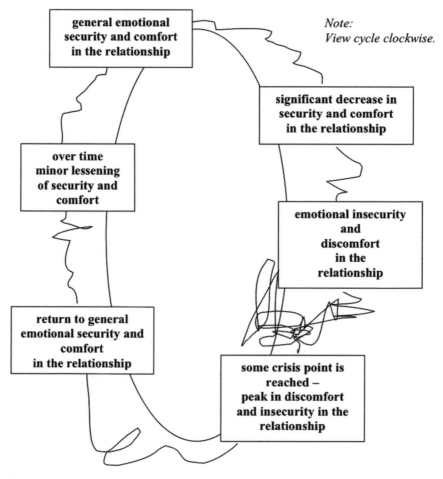

(Illustration by and courtesy of Angela Browne-Miller.)

Figure 15.7.   Troubled Relationship (to Person or Drug or Activity) Pattern #2: Common Addictive Longing for Contact Cycle or Pattern

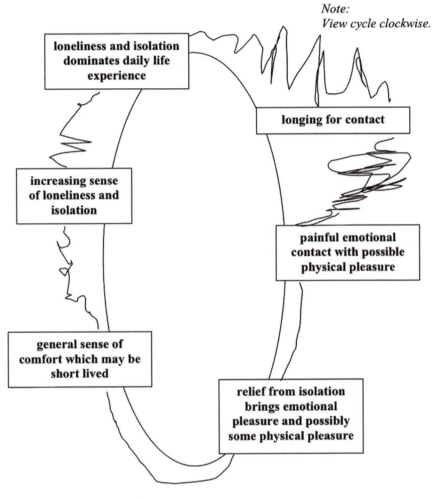

Note:
View cycle clockwise.

loneliness and isolation dominates daily life experience

longing for contact

increasing sense of loneliness and isolation

painful emotional contact with possible physical pleasure

general sense of comfort which may be short lived

relief from isolation brings emotional pleasure and possibly some physical pleasure

(Illustration by and courtesy of Angela Browne-Miller.)

Figure 15.8.   Sample Positive Relationship (to Person or Drug or Activity) Progression Pattern: Common Anatomy of a Positive Bond Progression

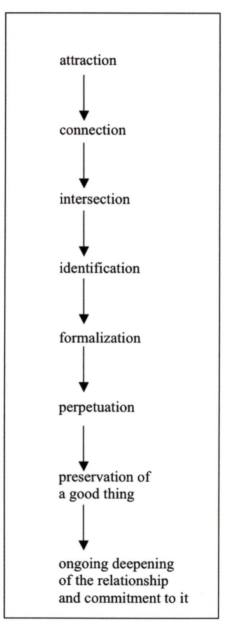

(Illustration by and courtesy of Angela Browne-Miller.)

Figure 15.9.   Sample Troubled Relationship (to Person or Drug or Activity) Progression Pattern: Common Anatomy of a Negative Bond Progression

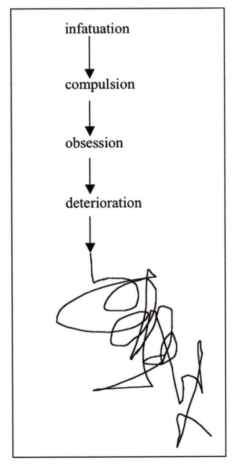

(Illustration by and courtesy of Angela Browne-Miller.)

Figure 15.10.   Sample Mixed Positive and Negative Bond (to Person or Drug or Activity) Progression: Pattern with Reversals

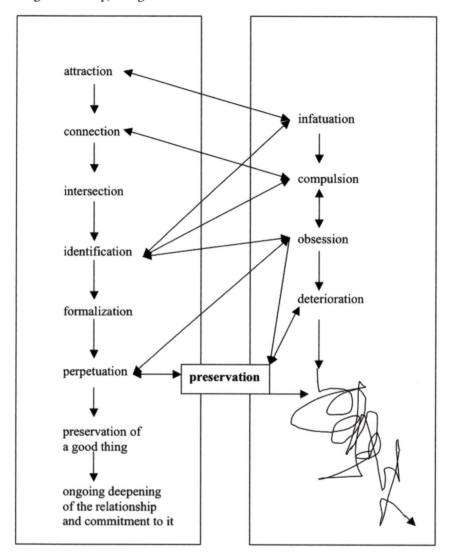

(Illustration by and courtesy of Angela Browne-Miller.)

Figure 15.11.   Sample Patterns of Cyclic Emotional and Sexual Relationship (to Person or Drug or Activity) Behaviors: With Pleasure and Pain Driving the Cycles or Patterns

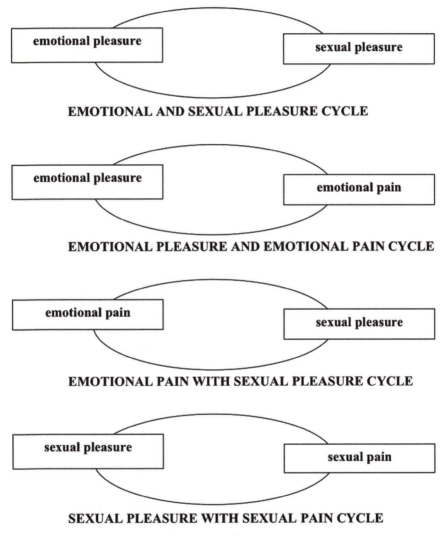

EMOTIONAL AND SEXUAL PLEASURE CYCLE

EMOTIONAL PLEASURE AND EMOTIONAL PAIN CYCLE

EMOTIONAL PAIN WITH SEXUAL PLEASURE CYCLE

SEXUAL PLEASURE WITH SEXUAL PAIN CYCLE

(Illustration by and courtesy of Angela Browne-Miller.)

Figure 15.12.   Emotional and Sexual Pleasure-Pain Cycles or Patterns: Patterns Can Interlink and Compound

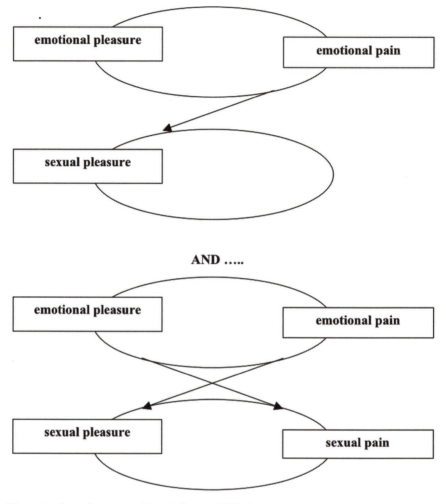

(Illustration by and courtesy of Angela Browne-Miller.)

Figure 15.13.   Sample Pain-Pleasure Confusion Mini-Cycles or Sub-loops: Pleasure, Pain and the Illusion of Escape from the Patterns

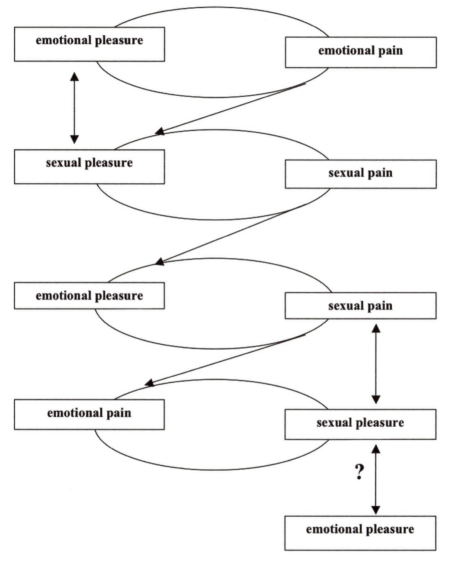

(Illustration by and courtesy of Angela Browne-Miller.)

16

Achieving Situational Transcendence

It is said that there is no such thing as a free lunch. Overcoming problem patterns is frequently described as very hard work. Surely in the anguish and life draining and damaging wreckage a troubled addiction can leave in its path, relief may come neither readily nor cheaply.

Finally and fully seeing, recognizing, and mapping the problem patterns that must be changed (such as those in Figures 15.1 through 15.13) is indeed hard work, as what has gone into generating and sustaining these patterns is hard work. You know this on all levels. While slipping into a problem addiction pattern may feel quite easy, and may have seemed to just take you over unbeknownst to you, your brain and body have been working hard all along. Part of you has been fighting the take over of the problem addiction pattern, and part of you—well perhaps not you, but part of your patterning—has taken you over.

Mapping these patterns is calling them to conscious attention. Where denial of the existence of the addiction pattern, and domination of the SELF by the addiction pattern, is taking place, even drawing a detailed map of the pattern onto paper can be demanding. The denial that must be stopped from blocking full conscious attention to the pattern has to be set aside. And, the domination of the SELF by the pattern addiction has to be overturned—at least enough to see the full pattern and to express its existence, even by a simple act such as mapping it onto paper.

Mapping the process of entry into, passage through, and exit from or elevation out of, the problem addiction pattern is a helpful process which can even prove revolutionary as the SELF takes its domination of the SELF back from the problem addiction pattern, first by mapping it, seeing it for what it is: I KNOW YOU ARE HERE, I SEE YOU, AND NOW I CAN DRAW BOUNDARIES AROUND YOU AND DIMINISH YOUR POWER OVER MY SELF.

This mapping can be designed to raise understanding of and then generate direction toward the very Situational Transcendence I have been referring to in previous chapters. Setting the stage for this transcendence requires creating a state of the SELF in which such a transcendence can be cultivated and then harvested. Four basic conditions or psychological states can be cultivated in the SELF by the SELF, to fuel full participation in the process of this Situational Transcendence: *commitment, attention, fortitude,* and *faith* in the process. These are interactive states of mind and can be generated as detailed below.

A word here before proceeding. This material on generating Situational Transcendence to overcome problem patterns is not only non-denominational but also is readily used by anyone whether of a particular religious or spiritual orientation or of no spiritual orientation. (Also note that this material is compatible with Twelve Step as well as non Twelve Step approaches.) The aim of the material contained in this part of this book is to: (a) provide psychological means of profound change; (b) provide a guide to mental states involved in change; (c) see how to map the process of change and to find oneself in this map; (d) use this understanding to map desired change, to transcend deeply embedded programming; and (e) to thereby actually shift attentional bias, and decision making, regarding our responses to problem situations themselves.

CONDITION ONE: COMMITMENT

The most basic condition for transcendence is the decision to make a commitment to the process. Calling for a commitment to the process suggests that this Situational Transcendence does not just "happen." Situations for conscious transcendence are not just something that one stumbles into. If it were, many more addicted people would be experiencing Situational Transcendence "by chance" every day. The Situational Transcendence process I describe here requires a strong *commitment*, a sense of tenacity and determination. It means telling the self to put everything on the line for change.

But just how does one develop commitment? It is surely easy to shout, "This is it! I'm going to change my life! Hooray!" However, momentary excitement and ongoing commitment are not the same thing. Excitement can be a temporary high. Commitment is a process of working to sustain that temporary enthusiasm, to morph it into ongoing sensation rather than a flash in the pan. Commitment makes it possible for us to have ourselves select a different behavior and then decide to practice it every day, for a long, long period of time. Where the brain has deficient internal (subconscious) inhibition processes as is seen in many addicted persons (recall Chapters 12 and 13 on this), we must commit to doing what it takes to consciously inhibit addictive responses to triggers for the addiction. The following exercises suggest to the mind a commitment-generating focus.

Decide to Be Committed

First of all, being committed does require making a conscious decision to be committed. It sounds simple, but many people find this initial decision difficult to make and hang on to. Making and keeping decisions takes practice.

Begin to experience the process of commitment by doing this exercise: Set aside six consecutive days of the week, perhaps Monday through Saturday, to work on transcendence. Then take Sunday (or the seventh day) off as a little vacation for yourself. If you like, take another day of the week off. Just make sure you choose the same day every week. Consistency will help you be firm about your decisions.

On the morning of the first day, make a conscious decision to be committed. Wake up and make the decision, and then really feel that decision for a day. Then, the next day, wake up and make a decision to not be committed. Feel that lack of commitment for the entire day. On the third day, repeat the first day. And on the fourth day, repeat the second day. Continue this on-off, committed-uncommitted exercise for two more days. This will total six days. You are alternating between deciding to be committed and not deciding to be committed. You will learn about commitment by experiencing the contrast between it and the absence of it. This exercise trains you to tell the difference. As you learn to do so, you will find that your commitment gains clarity and strength. After this six-day exercise, take your vacation day.

When you are able to clearly make a decision to commit yourself to Situational Transcendence you will have overcome a major stumbling block. Many people who approach transcendence are interested in the profound personal, spiritual, emotional, and intellectual change that it entails, but are still somewhat afraid of that change. Because of this fear, they hesitate to truly commit to the process. Making this decision is the first step on the road.

Feel Committed

Commitment requires more than just a decision. A feeling must accompany that decision. Too often, people who want to change their lives have difficulty understanding what "commitment" means. This is because commitment must be felt, not simply talked about.

There is a difference between deciding to be committed and feeling committed. Decision making rationally commands the intellect, the logical faculties of the mind, to carry out a specific set of actions or intentions. This is the necessary first step. The second step is feeling this commitment, which is more than employing one's logical faculties. We are talking about employing one's *psychological* faculties—getting one's feelings and emotions involved in the process.

Try this next exercise. Again, experiment by alternating days of commitment with days of non-commitment for six days. On the days that you are feeling committed, try to increase the level of feeling over the previous days. Play act if you have to. Exaggerate your feelings, get "psyched up" about your commitment. Just make sure you get a good idea of what it might feel like to be really committed. If you continue this day-on, day-off process for six days, you will begin to get the sense that there is a difference between feeling committed and not feeling committed. By working on it, you can increase the degree of feeling in your commitment. The seventh day is, again, your day of rest.

Feel Committed on All Levels

Once you understand the difference between feeling committed and not feeling committed, it is important to look at commitment on various levels of your being. In this third step, you will add depth to the second step. Instead of simply feeling committed, you will learn to feel committed to specific areas of growth leading to transcendence.

There are many levels of being to which we must be committed if we are to experience Situational Transcendence. Among these are the intellectual level, the psychological and or emotional level, the spiritual level, the physical level, and the economic or financial level. To be committed to transcendence is to be committed on all of these levels. To bring about purposeful transcendence, we must be committed so thoroughly, with so much feeling and on so many levels, that everything we think or do reflects that commitment. In other words, the whole person becomes committed. Every moment spent is spent while feeling that commitment. Partial involvement in the process of commitment to transcendence is almost no involvement at all. The rules here apply to the whole mind, the whole self, and the whole heart. If you are to fully succeed in rewiring your self, there can be no other, no higher, no competing allegiance. You must be loyal to your commitment to transcendence, to overcome your problem pattern.

Practice feeling committed on an increasing number of levels for six days. On the first day of this six-day period, feel committed on one level, say the economic level. Any money you spend must be spent with your commitment in mind. On the second day, feel committed on the economic level and another level, say the physical. Everything you do with your body, you must do with your commitment in mind. And on each of the next four days add a new level of commitment and feel committed on all the levels you have selected up to that day. By the sixth day, you will have six levels upon which you are actualizing your commitment, that is, the economic, physical, nutritional, social, emotional, and time-management areas. Here are some examples of how to actualize your commitment on these various levels:

Economic—On this day, draw up a budget for the month; include no expenditures on or in any way related to the object or activity of your addiction. Apply the money you save toward some other cause—bill paying, therapy, health care, donations, etc. Be highly conscious of your use of, and thoughts about, money on this day. Money represents economic energy. Learn about what money means to you.

Physical—On this day, carve out more time than you usually would to care for your body. Exercise, stretch, and bathe it well. Your body is the temple of your soul.

Nutritional—On this day, stop and pause before each bite of food that you take. Ask yourself if the food you are about to eat will nourish you.

Social—On this day, make each social contact reflect your commitment to transcendence. Say something in some way about this exercise each time you speak to someone, even strangers. Be brave. Be open. Be honest.

Emotional—On this day, concentrate on each emotion that ripples through your soul. How much do you know about what you feel? How sensitive are you to what you feel? Find a way to connect each emotion to your sense of commitment.

Time Management—On this day, plan your time for the next month. During the first day of your new schedule, plan short breaks (even thirty seconds, if that's all you have time for) every hour to be certain you can feel your commitment. Time is a river. You are a passenger on this ride, an explorer traveling on or in time. Chart the territory.

CONDITION TWO: ATTENTION

Commitment is essential to transcendence. Attention is equally important as a condition of the process of transcendence. There is no free lunch here either. To achieve transcendence, one must *pay* attention. All too often, commitments are made and strongly felt, but a clear and continuing attention to the commitment is not maintained. Our minds wander at the slightest invitation. In order to learn Situational Transcendence, the student must pay tuition—in the form of attention. This is an exercise that will help you to begin to pay close attention.

Go Conscious

Open your eyes. Strive to see all there is to see. Go conscious as a way of staying out of your automatic habit mode. We are so much less conscious of the world around us than we can be. There is always room for greater observation. Most of us have never experienced truly natural higher states of perception. Some people, however, have turned to drugs in order to achieve what they think of as heightened states of perception. Drugs are viewed by some users as being a shortcut to these heightened states. The truth, however, is that drugs only produce an illusion of a fully heightened state. You can learn to achieve natural heightened states of perception without drugs. You can actually learn to "go conscious." This means turning on your eyes, ears, sense of taste, of smell, of touch, even turning on your own sixth sense—your intuition. Practice looking carefully at everything around you.

> *Spend one day deciding to see as much as possible. On the following day, decide not to see as much as possible. Spend the day after that seeing as much as possible again —you know the routine. Do it for six days. Learn that there is a difference. On the days when you are perceiving as much as possible, really go for it. Listen for sounds that you have never heard or never paid attention to before. Try to smell and taste things that go otherwise unnoticed. As you continue to alternate days, you will notice that you can continue to increase your level of sensory perception simply by deciding to do so.*

By concentrating on increasing your awareness, you become conscious of the process.

Focus

Learning to focus is difficult. Most of us have not been taught to focus, that is, to truly concentrate. Yet, we can choose to focus.

Do this exercise. Think of yourself using a precision camera, the lens of which you must focus manually. Use your hand to turn the ring on the lens until the image you are looking at through the camera comes into sharp focus. If it looks only somewhat sharp, you haven't gone far enough. Do not stop until the image is perfectly sharp. Only at this point are you in focus. Now take this experience and apply it to the way you perceive the world—to the way you see, hear, taste, smell, and feel. Your eyes are precision lenses. Your ears are ultrasensitive microphones. Your tongue is a sophisticated tasting machine. Your nose is a fine instrument for smelling the world. And your skin is a "lens" on all things you touch and feel. Focus your "lenses." Continually sharpen your focus. Spend the next set of six days working on your focus. Focus a different sense each day, that is, day one: sight; day two: hearing; day three: taste; day four: smell; day five; touch; day six: intuition. Rest on the seventh day.

Call Details into Consciousness

After doing these exercises, you will find that you notice details more often and more clearly than ever before. You will find that you see shadows, reflections, nuances of color. You will begin to feel the texture of the foods you eat, the richness and variety of smells in the world, the feel of the wind on your skin.

As you notice more details, recognize that you are becoming more perceptive and strive to increase the quantity and clarity of the details that you experience. Whenever you find yourself with a free moment, sharpen your focus and look for details. Look hard for these details. Call them into your consciousness. They will not merely sit there, readily available for your examination. You will have to work hard to bring them there; you will have to say, "Come to me now, details."

When Your Mind Wanders, Refocus It

Your mind will wander. There will be times when you will not notice that it has wandered until an hour, half a day, a day, a week, a month, perhaps even a year has gone by. Don't let this discourage you.

As soon as you notice that your mind has wandered, refocus it. Go back to thinking of yourself as a camera lens. Turn that lens ring; focus your mind.

Seek Intentional Awareness

Awareness of your surroundings does not happen by accident. You must choose to be aware. Awareness must be intentional, and this requires that you pay attention to what you are perceiving. Without intentional awareness, there can be no Situational Transcendence. So *pay attention*.

CONDITION THREE: FORTITUDE

The greatest threat to continuing commitment and attention to transcendence is a lack of fortitude. Fortitude is more than commitment and attention. When a person has fortitude, he or she can endure hardship, pain, and adversity with courage. Imagine the fortitude of the mountain climber who climbs through blizzards and below-freezing temperatures, who continues on the journey in the face of extreme hardship. With fortitude, the student of transcendence is unwavering, even in the face of problems and distractions. There may be countless obstacles to progress: family fights, divorce, job loss, illness, discrimination, loneliness, insecurity, fear. These hardships call upon you to develop fortitude.

Learn to Recognize Your Fortitude

Decide again, as we have done with earlier exercises, to work at this on alternate days.

> On the first day you will decide to feel fortitude. On the second day you will decide not to feel fortitude. Continue in the normal alternating pattern. As you continue to alternate days, you will begin to notice the difference between feeling fortitude and not feeling it. Try to increase the feeling each day you decide to feel it.

You will learn, as you have in other exercises, to detect two different types of experience. One is that you can feel your fortitude—you will be able to discern between the presence and absence of it. The other is that you can increase the *intensity* of the fortitude that you feel.

When a Problem Arises, Generate Fortitude

As you are working on the exercises described in this chapter, both unforeseen and predictable problems will confront you. They will interfere with your work toward situational transcendence. You can however, use any obstacle or problem to generate strength and fortitude, as an opportunity to grow. You can turn the way you see the problem around. Any time a problem comes along, whether it is a ringing phone while you are trying to concentrate, news that your bank account is seriously over drawn, or a sudden craving for drugs or food or gambling, use it as an opportunity to practice feeling fortitude, and as an opportunity to increase the intensity of that fortitude with each new obstacle. Remember: use problems to strengthen fortitude.

CONDITION FOUR: FAITH

Faith is the ultimate condition for Situational Transcendence. Without it, there will be doubt in the process of transcendence and in oneself. Doubt can be hidden or obvious, subconscious or conscious. Whatever form it takes, it undermines the flow of energy into the transcendence process. The feeling of faith is subtle and may be difficult to experience in the beginning: but with practice and patience, faith grows stronger. Faith is a belief in the process of a Situational Transcendence. Faith is an optimism of the spirit, a hanging on to the positive view, no matter what argues against it. (Note that herein, the faith being discussed is not associated with any religion or a particular spirituality. Rather, this faith is a state of mind, as in having faith in something, e.g., faith in the process of Situational Transcendence, and can be experienced by persons of any religious or non-religious persuasion.)

Experience Faith

Survivors of shipwrecks and storms and other struggles often claim that they never lost faith in a positive outcome. You too can learn not to lose faith by developing your ability to have faith. (Again, faith here is not associated with a religious orientation.)

As you have done with other exercises, learn to experience faith by alternating days. On the morning of the first day, wake up and decide to experience faith all day. Overdramatize your faith. "Fake it till you make it" applies here. On the second day, decide to not experience faith. As you continue to alternate days, you will notice that you are learning about the difference between experiencing faith and not experiencing faith. Through the difference you will begin to learn what it means to have faith.

Strengthen Faith

The development of faith is probably one of the most important components in the entire process of learning transcendence.

On each day that you decide to experience faith, decide to experience more of it than you did the previous day. You will learn, as you have with the other exercises, that once you are able to recognize a feeling, you can learn to develop and strengthen that feeling.

The stronger your faith, the more power and energy you will be able to direct into the process of transcendence. Your faith will grow from a trickle into a rushing river of energy, flowing from you to you, from the world around you to you, and from you into the world around you. Commit yourself to strengthening your faith. You will feel the abundant rewards.

Sustain Faith

Once you have learned to recognize faith and your ability to strengthen it, you must work to sustain it.

When you feel faith, say to yourself, "Oh, this is what faith feels like, and this is what it feels like to decide to have it and then to actually follow through on strengthening my faith." Learning to sustain faith is like learning to ride a bicycle. At first it will be difficult to keep your balance. You will be able to sustain your faith for a little while and then you may begin to waver and lose your balance. But if you keep trying, you will eventually find that you can strengthen your faith and hang on to it. And once you have truly learned to sustain your faith, you will not unlearn it. Try sustaining your faith for six consecutive days.

CONDITIONS FOR SITUATIONAL TRANSCENDENCE

These conditions—commitment, attention, fortitude and faith— are state of mind, states of mind that must be continuously developed. There is always room to grow. Fix these conditions in your mind. Continuously repeat the above exercises and address the above considerations until you develop your own exercises for strengthening your commitment, attention, fortitude, and faith in the Situational

Figure 16.1.   Four Basic States of Mind, Mental Conditions, for Transcendence

Commitment
  Decide to be committed.

  Feel committed.

  Feel committed on all levels.

Attention
  Go Conscious.

  Focus.

  Call details into consciousness.

  When your mind wanders, refocus it.

  Seek intentional awareness.

Fortitude
  Learn to recognize your fortitude.

  When a problem arises, generate fortitude.

Faith
  Experience faith.

  Strengthen faith.

  Sustain faith.

(List by and courtesy of Angela Browne-Miller.)

Transcendence process. Life will present you with tests of your progress. The conditions for transcending problem addiction are as summarized in Figure 16.1.

Have a wall calendar you can write on, and write in what items listed in Figure 16.1 you plan to do on each day (in advance of actually conducting the steps in Figure 16.1). This will help you accomplish this in a conscious and planned manner. This will also help you begin to take conscious control of the functions of your mind that may be running your problem addiction. Take your time back, take your mind back, take your SELF back.

17
Phases of Situational Transcendence

Release from the paradoxical trap of a problem addiction pattern fuels Situational Transcendence. This release can be generated by maximizing recognition of the stages of this transcendence, promoting movement from one stage to another, and by promoting the energy release involved in these. Situational Transcendence is a continuous process through which an individual achieves elevation to a higher level of awareness, understanding and functioning—ideally again and again. For purposes of this discussion, I say transcendence is composed of four profound phases, each of which is necessary for the process, and each of which is enhanced by the conditions described in the previous chapter. The phases of or life passages in Situational Transcendence are:

> **Phase 1—Struggle**
> **Phase 2—Paradox**
> **Phase 3—Insight**
> **Phase 4—Elevation**

PHASE CHARACTERISTICS

Each phase has its own special characteristics. I have included diagrams of these phases. As you examine each diagram, try to think of the movement, the highs and lows, and calm or even flat times, of your life in terms of the phase. How many times have you found yourself in such a life passage or phase? Make the diagrams part of your own mental imagery. Thinking in pictures often helps to learn on a deeper level. Thinking in new and conscious pictures, pictures we consciously impose upon ourselves rather than have come upon us, also allows us to reach deeply into thought processes we have linked to words. Thinking in pictures also allows us to even get behind images we are used to seeing or visualizing and responding to. I would suggest new pictures that are creating new mental pathways, alternatives to what has been attracting our attentional biases . . . .

PHASE 1: STRUGGLE

Many days, if not every day, we have at least minor highs and lows, minor or perhaps some other degree of struggle to cope with. Struggles take various forms, and can be struggles with other people, with family relationships, with work relationships, with ourselves, with morality, and maybe also with our cravings for simple human contact. Or the struggles can be around cravings for food or drugs, or maybe with balancing our checkbooks, with heavy traffic, with our health, with our tempers, with our moods, with living up to what we think we or others would like to see us live up to. You name it —it fits the struggle scenario. We often struggle without recognizing or seeing beyond the struggle, and often acclimate to the state of struggle itself as natural, as a given. We may acclimate to such a great degree that we do not see ourselves struggle. Or we may see the state of struggle we are living in as terrible and perhaps ongoing, even a never ending condition. We can become so deeply caught up in struggle, subconsciously or consciously, that it becomes impossible to step back and say, "Oh, look, I am struggling. This is important to know. This can be the first phase of Situational Transcendence." But it is just this observation that can set us on the path to amazing transcendence experience. When we are struggling, we must take the time to tell ourselves that we *are indeed struggling*— and that seeing this can be good, because this is the first phase of transcendence.

Consider Figure 17.1. This pattern illustrates ups and downs, pushes and pulls, and highs and lows so typical of the struggling phase. During a true struggle, there must be low points in order for there to be high points. Both extremes are integral to struggle.

Figure 17.1.   Phase 1: Struggle Pattern

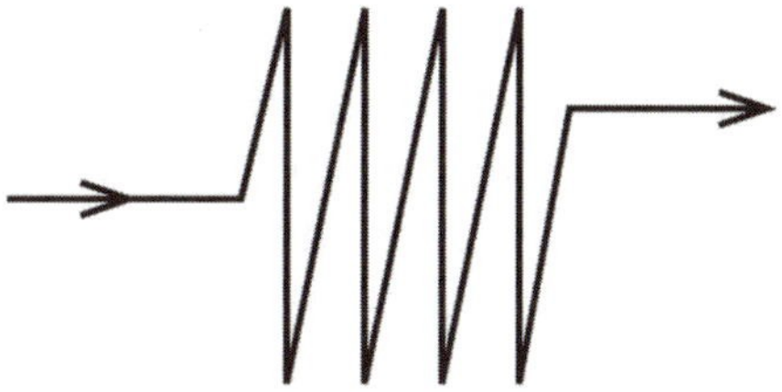

STRUGGLE

(Illustration by and courtesy of Angela Browne-Miller.)

PHASE 2: PARADOX

And then there is paradox. Paradox is a fantastic experience. Paradox can be confusing. It can be painful. It can be frightening. Whether a personal paradox is minor or major, it can produce in some a zombielike effect, in others agitation. Paradox is the experience of being in a situation from which there seems to be no escape, no resolution: NO WAY OUT. The person in paradox feels trapped.

As noted earlier, sometimes parents quite unwittingly put their children into paradoxes in the form of a double bind, something like this: "Which coat do you like?" a parent may ask a child. "The red coat or the blue one?" If the child says, "The red coat," the parent says, "That's not a good choice, you should like the blue one." And when the child says, "OK, blue one," the parent says, "Oh that is too bad, because the red one is much better." When this happens, the child is experiencing a double bind. In this case, there is nothing the child can do that would be the right thing to elicit a positive response from the parent. The child is bound by an unpleasant consequence no matter which choice he or she makes. There seems to be no escape. The situation holds, or so it would seem, no real choice. In living life, both children and adults create double bind situations for themselves with or without the help of other people.

One double bind many people find themselves in these days is the massive amount of TRUE NOT TRUE and YES THIS IS A PROBLEM NO IT IS NOT denial everywhere around as well as within us. This double bind is apparent in our denial of the massive chemical dependences of our times (see again Chapters 2 and 3). This is more than but includes a personal drug and alcohol addiction. This is the entire species becoming ever more chemically dependent. Where the species does not confirm its chemical dependence, the species confirms that individual members of the species suffer from problem addictions. (It is easier to point the finger at others then at oneself.)

The individual takes a drug to escape a painful, stressful, or boring situation but the situation from which the person is trying to escape becomes even more painful, stressful, or boring when the person returns to it, as is inevitable upon coming down from the trip. While no escape is no escape, the seeming drug or problem addiction escape is also no escape.

Paradoxes like this are extremely stressful and often painful. But faith in the Situational Transcendence process shows us that paradox serves a purpose. Without the tension, the feeling of being trapped in an unwinnable no way out situation, there may be no energetic impetus for moving on. This is to say that the tension created by your paradoxes, when used well, can generate enough energy for you to break out of them. Without the tension of the paradox, we may not be able to work up to—to fuel—the release—the jump or shift in perception—that is produced by breaking out of the paradox, the energetic double bind.

Paradox is illustrated in Figure 17.2. Study this diagram for a few minutes. This is the stand off or holding pattern in which people who need to grow and experience transcendence can get caught or trap themselves. The only way out of this holding pattern is to grow past it, break out of it and move on, increase your perception so that you can see beyond the limits of the double bind that holds you there. The two arrows ending up against each other and going nowhere represent the forces that hold an addicted person in his or her trap. One force is the powerful tendency to stay stuck or addicted, to use the problem situation or drug to avoid the *perceived* stress and pain of breaking out from paradox. The other force is the stressful and painful effect of being in the problem situation itself, that situation that seeks

Figure 17.2.   Phase 2: Paradox Pattern

(Illustration by and courtesy of Angela Browne-Miller.)

to avoid the stress and pain of being without the problem behavior, or even of getting out of the problem behavior.

This is a deadlock, an energetic deadlock. This can hold you in its grip indefinitely. Or, if you choose the way of transcendence, it can provide a take-off point into another level of being. When the paradox of addiction explodes, energy is released and this energy can bring insight. Whatever your addiction, you can harness the energy in its paradox and then move into transcendence. To do so, you must become highly alert to the tensions you feel and to your implicit pattern addictions which generate them.

PHASE 3: INSIGHT

Insight is a profound experience. This is the aha phenomenon, the startlingly sudden glimpse of something more than what has been obvious before that moment. But insight is frequently followed by lack of further insight, or even a return to the situation just prior to that insight. Much insight comes in small packages. Sometimes we experience insight without even realizing it. You may be driving along and suddenly "get" or "grok" or grasp viscerally something about a problem that has been bothering you. Perhaps you even pull over a moment. Or you may be working—perhaps on a relationship issue, or perhaps on reorganizing a room, or perhaps on a scientific issue—and suddenly figure out an unexpected solution. All at once a new idea comes into your mind. You suddenly discover a new way of looking at a problem. This is an insight. Yet, only if you maintain this insight, hang on to it, is this insight a real elevation in awareness and understanding, as explained in the subsection below regarding Elevation.

Insight is illustrated graphically in Figure 17.3. Compare this to the diagram of paradox illustrated in Figure 17.2. See that insight is a brief leap out of the paradox. Consider Figure 17.3 further; see what this symbolizes to you. Upon viewing this figure for a while, you may find that it suggests the glimpse, or perception, of another way of seeing the world and of being in the world. The highest point in this diagram is this **flash of realization**. It represents a peek (and a peak) into a higher level of understanding. Notice that the line falls back, or almost back, to its original level. This is because the insight I am talking about here is a temporary jump in understanding or awareness. The insight itself does not automatically bring a real change, there is no

Figure 17.3.   Phase 3: Insight Pattern

INSIGHT

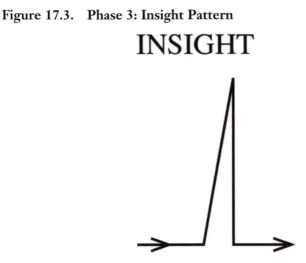

(Illustration by and courtesy of Angela Browne-Miller.)

real growth. In order to grow, insight must be recognized and sustained. When it is, a sort of spiritual elevation of the self, or perhaps better stated—of the spirit, is possible. By use of the word spirit or spiritual in this and the following discussion, I do not mean something belonging to a particular religion or religious experience, but rather a sense that one's self, espirit of self, has grown, expanded to see more and cope with more, and to change as a result.

PHASE 4: ELEVATION

Elevation is illustrated in Figure 17.4. Here, the leap of insight is sustained. The term, spiritual (elevation), is used in this figure to emphasize the sense that the spirit, the self, has been uplifted, has risen to a new level of awareness and understanding. (Note that the use of the term spiritual here does not refer to a particular religion or spirituality. While spiritual elevation may be for some a religious experience, religion is not required here. This elevation of awareness and perception may register differently for different people.) Consider this diagram in Figure 17.4. What does this diagram symbolize? There is an elevation from one level to another. What might this look like in your own life or in your own state of mind? How might you feel if your

Figure 17.4.   Phase 4: Elevation, a Situational and Spiritual Pattern for Transcendence

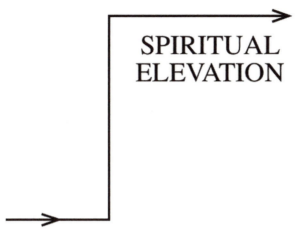

SPIRITUAL
ELEVATION

(Illustration by and courtesy of Angela Browne-Miller.)

understanding of what was going on in your life shifted to a new, a higher, level of awareness?

In this diagram, there is an elevation from one level of understanding or awareness to another. This diagram signifies a jump in perception. This jump, as diagrammed, is actually an insight that is being sustained this time. The awareness of self, the spirit of oneself, rises to a new level of being and maintains this level. This "holding on" to this new level is the experience of sustained insight, or what I call here, elevation. Without this holding on to the new level of understanding, the insight is usually brief, and the people experiencing the insight return to or close to their original ways of seeing themselves, their situations, and the world, as was seen in Figure 17.3.

Elevation differs from insight in that there is no just falling back to one's previous perceptions as if the experience of sustained insight was never achieved. Elevation is the elevating of one's self or spirit in a profound Situational Transcendence.

From the new level of awareness achieved by elevation, each of the phases of transcendence may have to be repeated in order to reach new and greater levels or elevations of understanding. One can always discover new struggles, paradoxes, and insights to generate further elevations.

Figure 17.5.   Four Basic Phases of Situational Transcendence: Model Pattern

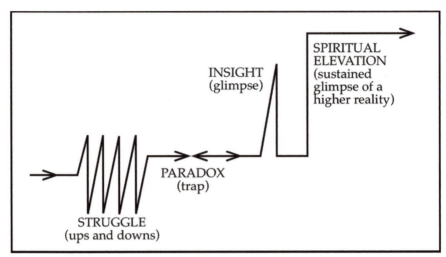

(Illustration by and courtesy of Angela Browne-Miller.)

LIFE PHASES AND PATTERNS

This exciting and adventurous process of Situational Transcendence is suggested in Figure 17.5. It shows the four primary, building block phases of Situational Transcendence linked together. The cycle of phases is repeatable, as in the passages of Figure 17.6. Contemplate these diagrams for a while. Can you map the passages of your life in this manner?

Be certain that you understand that each phase may take barely a few seconds or last for years. Some people experience a state of struggle all their lives. Others live in a perpetual stage of paradox, of being trapped. Some rotate between struggle and paradox, as Figure 17.7 demonstrates. Some people have insights but do not recognize or sustain them, and thus continuously return to the same paradox that produced these insights, or to similar paradoxes.

Each of us follows his or her own life pattern. We each live out our own version of Figure 17.6. (Some of us experience patterns that are variations of the ones diagrammed in Figures 17.6 and 17.7.)

Figure 17.6. Life Map: Ongoing Process of Situational Transcendence: Ideal Pattern of Progression

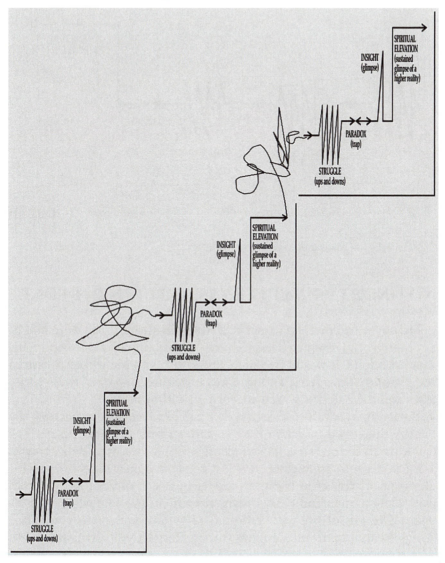

(Illustration by and courtesy of Angela Browne-Miller.)

Figure 17.7.   Variation on Life Map: Ongoing Struggle to Paradox to Struggle: Common Pattern

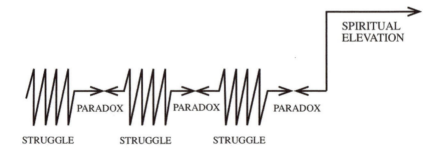

(Illustration by and courtesy of Angela Browne-Miller.)

NO ONE'S LIFE PATTERN IS WRITTEN IN STONE

However, no one's pattern is written in stone. If we were taught as children to recognize these phases of Situational Transcendence, then, as adults, it would be much easier for us to see where we are in the process of our lives, and to take conscious control of these processes and the patterns which are formed within these.

But no matter how old we are, we can always learn to harness the energy produced in each phase to move on to the next phase. We can learn to see our struggles as fertile ground for astounding growth. We can learn to appreciate paradox, recognize insight, and strive for elevation. If you keep trying to see this pattern of your life you will eventually understand that you are already on the path of transcendence. The gift of life will then make itself very clear to you. Your struggles are important stepping stones. Respect your struggles.

18

Foundations of Situational Transcendence of Addiction

The last two chapters have analyzed the concept of Situational Tran-scendence—what this is, and what it takes to achieve this shift in awareness of one's situation. The concept can be applied to virtually any behavior and certainly to any obstacles or difficulties we may feel we encounter, whether these be emotional, financial, physical, or other types of problems. Remember, any ongoing behavior has a pattern-addiction component. Addiction to a problem pattern, any problem pattern, is the specific problem being addressed in this book, but the Situational Transcendence I offer herein is infinitely transfer-able from one situation to the next, and then the next, then the next, and so on. Problem pattern addiction, whether it be to a problem behavior, to an addictive drug, or to a troubled relationship, or to something else, offers everyone lessons in transcendence. This chapter considers seven basic ideas about Situational Transcendence as it relates to problem addiction.

IDEA ONE

Problem addiction to a seriously burned in pattern is a powerful bondage that can only be broken by something more powerful. One must accept this as a fact and appreciate the size and seriousness of the task of overcoming a problem pattern addiction.

IDEA TWO

Pattern addiction can be very subtle and difficult to recognize. Therefore some individuals either present themselves, or are presented, with the challenge of an explicit pattern addiction so that they may recognize how addicted to patterning we all are. They then undergo the struggle to break out of their most explicit addictive patterns and, in the process of that struggle, experience growth. Some people have found the recognition of explicit addiction to be their primary opportunity for growth. Drug, alcohol, food, sex, relationship, spending, and gambling addictions are some of the easiest patterns to spot and thus offer some of the most accessible opportunities to practice situation transcendence and to grow. Yet we are all are pattern addicts.

IDEA THREE

The ultimate form of learning can be said to be the situation transcendence I am describing here, a process composed of the four phases described in the previous chapter: struggle, paradox, insight, and spiritual elevation. This pattern is a repetitive, never-ending process. Your entire experience of living is transformed the moment you identify the phase of the process you are currently experiencing and locate this phase on a map of your life as you know it to be thus far. (See Figures 17.6 and 17.7.)

IDEA FOUR

One way to promote insight, spiritual elevation, and thus transcendence is through the pain, struggle, and paradox of pattern addiction. There are many ways to encourage transcendence; addicted individuals have *selected* the vehicle of addiction to reach their goal of transcendence and discovery.

IDEA FIVE

Remember that the transcendence we are describing is a process that gains power as it progresses. Progressive transcendence can overcome addiction and then move beyond. *There is no end point to this process.* (See Figure 17.6.)

IDEA SIX

One must *work* to maintain the insights and spiritual elevations gained in the process of transcendence.

IDEA SEVEN

With every full cycle of transcendence comes an entirely new way of seeing the self and the world. Be ready and open to total change and new life. Only total change and an ongoing commitment to transcendence will fully heal the wounds to the SELF that are caused by problem addiction.

It is essential that every one of us commit to development of the self. Both personal and planetary pressures are calling us into action. Lifestyle change, when incorporated with the steps to the situation-specific change of Situational Transcendence presented in the previous chapter, is exciting and challenging. This type of change is no small event in a person's life. It changes whole situations, whole lives.

PART FOUR

Conducting Lifestyle Surgery

Time to Overcome Addictions

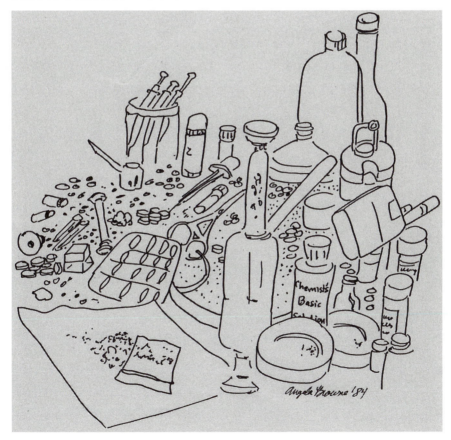

(Illustration by and courtesy of Angela Browne-Miller.)

19
Lifestyle Surgery: Breaking Addiction

In overcoming detrimental habits and addictions, the counterpart of the elevation of self or spirit is the effective management of daily life. While development, fortification and elevation of the self deals with the more immaterial, abstract part of the human process, life management deals with the material, practical, down-to-earth aspects of living. To conquer addiction, Situational Transcendence and life management must work hand in hand. The qualitative juxtaposition of these two areas in the process of overcoming a deeply ingrained problem addiction generates a growth-nourishing and growth-producing balance.

The reason that life management skills are so very important is that many problem addicted and otherwise troubled individuals have a difficult time with the job of just being a person. Their personal lifestyles are often disorganized, disrupted, and out of synch or harmony. While this degree of disorganization can itself fuel or invite detrimental patterns of addiction, especially the more explicit addictions, the reverse is likely more prevalent: detrimental addiction patterns can wreak havoc on the lives of the persons so addicted.

Let's not be fooled by the absence of visible disorganization. Some problem addicted persons may appear tidy, neat, and organized, however what is not seen is the internal distress, the disorganization and even chaos in what may have once been healthy patterns of life management. Sometimes disorganization is taking place on emotional and relationship, or maybe financial and work life, or other still less visible levels. The erosion of healthy life patterns may be taking place while this disruption is moving from the inside out.

One of the key paradoxes in detrimental addiction is the reality that while the life of the addicted individual is eroding under the force of negative addictive patterning, the addictive patterning itself is organizing itself to SURVIVE, sucking on everything and everyone around it, and all healthy patterns around it, to hold its ever growing dominance over other patterns, to force other patterns into eroding. There is a profound relationship between problem patterns and surrounding disorganizing factors. Again, the organization of the destructive addictive pattern not only fuels the disorganization of the surrounding healthy life patterns, but it promotes this disorganization. These disorganizing factors feed the problem patterns.

Poor life management skills make an addicted person much more vulnerable to problem addiction. When life is disorganized, it is much easier for people to fall prey to the whims of the powerful addictive programming they have stored in their bodies. And where there is no preexisting poor life management skill or pattern, the detrimental addiction pattern will sway the balance of organization far in its favor. This is why healthy life management patterns can help to organize a life as prevention and or healing of addiction.

THE REACHING HAND

Consider the legal concept, "The dead hand reaches out." This is the described ability of someone who writes a will to influence the distribution of his or her estate long after he or she has died. This "dead hand" reaches out into the realm of the living—from the past into the present. Addiction acts in a similar way. Let's look at how the dead hand of addiction reaches out. Addicted people have repeated their addictive behaviors, including countless actual physical motions and gestures, so many times that eventually they simply "go through the motions" of their addictions automatically. Many people who try to break even simple habits, such as fingernail biting, find that they perform their habits without thinking about them. Whether a relatively simple habit like nail biting, or a more intense habit, such as addiction to drugs, the behavior has been repeated so often that it has worn a memory pathway through the brain and nervous system.

This memory pathway can be thought of as a deep ravine into which spill connected sensations, memories, and gestures. These spill like water rushing over land and falling into gulleys and grooves worn into the ground. For example, a man who has spent ten years biting his fingernails while watching television may find that, each time he sits down to watch television, his hand automatically ends up at his mouth. If he does not **pay very close attention** to what he is doing, he will unconsciously begin biting his nails. Likewise, a man who has been drinking or using drugs at social gatherings for fifteen years may find that, every time he is in the company of three or more people, he craves his old drink or drug. In this situation, it is likely that, if he breaks down and "has just one," he will slip easily into having another and another, without paying any attention to what he is doing. The memory pathway is alive and well, just trigger it.

Memories of addicted individuals are like the will writer's dead hand—they reach out into the land of the living. They reach into the present from the past. They can reach out long after the addiction has been, or seems to have been, put to rest. The only way for a person who as been addicted to gain control over the powerful programming he has stored in memory—burned into brain cells—is *to manage his life very carefully.* Only by paying careful attention to every aspect of his life—by being highly conscious—can he control the automatic behavior that will seek to control him. To win out over the insidious, intrusive, and seemingly omnipotent dead hand that addiction creates, concentration on life's details and life's management skills is essential.

When an addicted person gains an understanding of just how effective a job he has done, of how well he has programmed addictive behaviors into his mental circuitries, he can feel quite discouraged, frightened, and overwhelmed. If you are addicted to something, you may be feeling this way right now. You may be saying, "I'll never change. This pattern is in me too deeply. It controls me. I can't control it." These fears will continue to pop up until you learn self-confidence and self-control through life management, until you see that you need life management tools for change, to conquer your impulses. With these tools, profound change can become a reality in your life.

Most of us have not really experienced how good a healthy approach to organization feels. We either compulsively over-organize or we weakly under-organize. Either extreme fails to address basic management issues and fails to integrate all of the levels of life management into a stable, healthy, and energetic package.

Once some experience and skill in life management has been gained, a person who is trying to overcome a behavioral hurdle will increase confidence. And increased self-confidence brings *hope*, and it brings a sense of self competence which makes personal change believable, even possible, no matter how large the obstacles to change seem to be. In developing management skills, addicted individuals learn that they actually can override their deeply entrenched programming.

OVERCOMING PROGRAMMING

A man who has taken twenty swallows of wine (maybe two glasses, depending on the size of the swallows) a day for five years—36,500 swallows—has lifted a glass to his mouth and swallowed alcohol at least 36,500 times. The physical gesture of bringing the glass to one's mouth, the act of drinking and swallowing, and the psycho-biological experience of tasting and absorbing alcohol into the system, are remembered along with the places, times, people, physical feelings, and emotions that have been repeatedly associated with those gestures. By sipping alcohol over and over again, this person has programmed himself to connect the gestures of drinking and swallowing with the experience of absorbing alcohol into his system and with all those related events, places, people, and feelings. Any part of this memory configuration, a particular gesture or feeling or place or person, may call back the entire memory and reactivate the programming. That "little addict person" who lives in his nervous system and brain cells wakes up again. Because so many levels of existence are tied into the addicted person's memory configuration, an experience or action on any level of existence can trigger addictive behavior on any other level. This is why an individual seeking to change his or her programming must pay careful attention to all levels of his or her existence.

Addictive behavior is automatic and subconscious. To override an automatic, subconscious behavior, one must become highly *conscious* of that behavior. The breaking of an addictive behavior cannot be left to chance. *Pay attention*, a lot of attention.

DOING SOMETHING NEW

To do something new, to break out of a problem addiction pattern, one must first recognize, really see for what it is, this pattern and its details. Patterns of problem addiction do vary, as addictive behavior takes many forms. Every person who is problem addicted has at least one, if not many, very personal problem addiction patterns. Nevertheless, it is possible to generalize these patterns and to construct the simple three-point addiction cycle discussed earlier (see again Figure 9.1 on page 69) as underlying most problem pattern addiction, in fact as underlying most addiction whether problematic or positive. This is the trigger-urge-addicted-response pattern.

ELEMENTS OF ADDICTIVE PATTERNING CYCLE

The cycle usually begins when a deeply ingrained *trigger response mechanism* causes the addicted person to feel the *urge* or craving to use the substance or to perform the action part of the pattern to which he or she is addicted. If the cycle continues, as it usually does, the addicted person actually responds to the urge with his or her *addictive response*. (Again, you will find these cycle points in Figure 9.1.)

Breaking addiction requires breaking the cycle at one or more of these points. At cycle point one, basic and complex, obvious and more hidden, triggers can be identified. Once they are identified, triggers can be eliminated, altered: perceptions of them can be changed. When this has been successfully done, the cycle can be broken. Now when the addicted person experiences one of the triggers, that trigger may no longer set off further movement through the cycle.

The cycle can also be broken at point two. Here urges (or cravings) can be identified, controlled, and lived through, provided that close attention is paid to the nature and course of one's urges. A break in the cycle at this point means that the urges will cease to lead to addictive responses. Finally, at cycle point three, addictive responses can be replaced with other, new responses. When the old addictive cycle is broken, something new happens.

OVERCOMING RESISTANCE TO CHANGE

One of the greatest obstacles in overcoming addiction to any pattern is *overcoming the resistance to change*. All too often the addicted individual is reluctant to change because change necessitates moving into the unknown, in other words, *doing something new*. This is why the process of breaking the addiction cycle must incorporate some highly methodical elements. There is no secret or magic recipe for overcoming addiction. As we know, this takes a great deal of commitment and hard work. But this commitment must be backed up by a willingness to undergo radical change. We must be willing to perform *lifestyle surgery* on ourselves, to make whatever changes are necessary to break the addictive cycle. Let's call this lifestyle surgery. At the end of Chapter 22, you will find an outline for effective lifestyle surgery, a life management plan. Lifestyle surgery is not a magic process requiring little or no effort. Breaking addiction takes a difficult, and sometimes very mundane, daily injection of discipline.

20

Dictionary of Triggers

One of the most important steps in breaking an addictive pattern is to identify the *triggers* that have been deeply embedded in that pattern. By recognizing these triggers, pattern-addicted people can take concrete steps to either change their triggers or change their responses to those triggers.

Remember that a trigger is anything that the addicted individual thinks of as being, or responds to as, a trigger. You already know this on some deep level if you are addicted: triggers are all in your mind. Sure there are real things in the world that affect you, but your *reaction to anything and everything is generated by you!* A trigger can be any object, experience, event, relationship, person, predicament, idea, or impulse that sets off or magnifies a chain of events. As a pattern-addicted individual, you are continually surrounded by, and experiencing, a variety of emotional, practical, social, psychological, physical, and chemical triggers. You must identify—become conscious of —as many of your triggers as you can in order to control their influence on you. Bring important data about yourself out of your subconscious and into your consciousness. This will help you pay better attention to yourself.

This chapter provides examples of over thirty triggers and categorizes them into ten problem areas. This will help you make your own list of your own triggers. The triggers listed here are, in the main, triggers of explicit addictive behaviors such as cyclical drug use, spending, and eating. As you read through this chapter, go ahead and write down your own list of triggers. Copy the triggers listed here if you feel that they pertain to you. Add anything else that comes to your mind—that the lists trigger in your mind—even ideas that may represent more implicit triggers. Write down *everything* that comes to mind, even if you do not have a category for it, even if you cannot explain it. You are brainstorming now.

PROBLEM AREA ONE: PRACTICAL TRIGGERS

Practical triggers are those which make it easy, that is, "practical," to obtain and to use the objects, or to do the behavior, of your addiction. Among those practical triggers most commonly listed by addicted individuals are:

Availability of Money With Which to Purchase the Objects of One's Addiction: such as cash on hand, too much money, too much credit, a bank card that makes it possible to get cash when the bank is closed.

Affordability: the object of one's addiction is affordable—often in large quantities—to the addicted individual.

Paybacks and Favors: gifts or returns of favors (i.e., in the form of alcohol or drugs given to the drug-addicted person).

Invisibility: energy pattern problems are frequently invisible to untrained observers, and, therefore, the mere invisibility of problem energy patterns makes it practical to continue to have them.

PROBLEM AREA TWO: TEMPORAL TRIGGERS

Temporal triggers are all those time-related factors that influence, or are connected with, addictive behavior. Time periods of activity or inactivity and particular times of the day, week, month or year may have meaning to an addicted person. Common temporal triggers are:

Free Time: having enough time to reinforce and respond to one's programming often brings that programming out. (This is one of the most common triggers.)

Lack of Time: time-shortage conditions can also bring out one's automatic behaviors, because when there is no time to think about what one is doing, one just does whatever is programmed in—one runs on automatic.

Particular Times of the Day: certain times such as family times, meal times, the "happy hour," the time right before or right after a workday begins or ends.

Particular Times of the Month: for example, many women report anticipated and actual premenstrual stress as a trigger, and some men also report monthly behavioral cycles; the full moon is listed by some as a trigger time. Hormonal and perhaps even gravitational changes are cyclical, and neurological patterning can be built around them.

Particular Times of the Year: these include winter months, the first hot spell, etc. Seasonal changes can, over the years, bring out automatic emotional and behavioral shifts.

All the Time: even the passage of time triggers some addictive behavior, and just getting time to pass is the goal of a great deal of addictive behavior.

PROBLEM AREA THREE: ENVIRONMENTAL TRIGGERS

Addicted persons are reminded of their previous addictive behaviors, and of other triggers, by their environments. Environmental triggers clearly bring out explicit addictive behaviors, but they also trigger implicit pattern cycles. While this list focuses on triggers of explicit addictive cycles, the transfer to the implicit is easily made. Typical environmental triggers include:

Particular Cities
Specific Street Corners
Bars and Restaurants
Particular Houses
A Room in a House: the bathroom, the kitchen, the room with a bar, and any room associated with the habitual behavior.
Furniture and Appliances: mirrors, refrigerators, dresser drawers where "stashes" (i.e., secret stores of alcohol or drugs or food or money) are kept; often furniture and appliances can be triggers.
Outdoor Environments: beaches, forests, sports stadiums.
Vehicles: i.e., cars, trains, and planes on short or long trips.
Particular Objects: the paraphernalia associated with the preparation for using an addictive substance, and any other objects identified with other triggers. (OBJECT TRIGGERS can easily become a separate trigger category.)

PROBLEM AREA FOUR: MEDIA TRIGGERS

The media are loaded with triggers for the pattern-addicted individual. Again, familiarity and association with images and memories that are somehow tied into a habit cycle can trigger that cycle. Among the media triggers are:

Television Commercials
Television Programs
Movies
Magazine Covers

PROBLEM AREA FIVE: EMOTIONAL TRIGGERS

This is the largest category of triggers cited by addicted individuals. The power of emotional triggers is compounded by the fact that most of the particular emotions (or emotional patterns they represent) listed as triggers below can, in themselves, be addictive. Many of these triggers are also associated with triggers in other categories:

Boredom
Depression
Anxiety and Stress
Feeling Overcommitted
Mental Exhaustion
Humiliation
Fear of Failure
Failure to Meet Obligations
Agony of Defeat
Low Self-Esteem
Bitterness
Rejection
Envy
Jealousy
Resentment
Anger and Arguments
Risk Taking
Feeling Challenged
Excitement
Fear of Success
Success
Thrill of Victory
Happiness

Desire to Reward Oneself
Need to Consume and to Hoard
Need to Experiment
Gambling With Oneself
Desire for New Identity
Search for Inner Peace
Confusion
Not Knowing What To Do
Feeling No Feelings (*No feeling is a feeling.*)

PROBLEM AREA SIX: SPIRITUAL TRIGGERS

Many individuals suffering from detrimental addictive behaviors report a sense of spiritual malaise. Spiritual triggers, while addressing abstract and elusive feelings, can be important in mapping addiction. Among these are:

Having No Values
Feeling a Void
Feeling of No Meaning in Life
Searching for Meaning
No Inner Peace
No Sense of Center
A Desire for Ritual
Replacing a Structured Religious Activity of Childhood with an Adult Addiction

PROBLEM AREA SEVEN: SOCIAL TRIGGERS

Social triggers are numerous and interact with emotional, environmental, chemical, practical, and other triggers to strongly affect the addicted person. Social triggers involve other people, or the anticipation of other people. These include:

Social and Peer Pressure
Parties and Events: both actual and the planning of any and all get-togethers.
Spectator Sporting Events
Business Lunches: you know the two martini lunch?

Workplace Interactions: fellow employees may share their alcohol and drugs with each other, or there may be peer pressure to use drugs or drink among co-workers. Co-workers may push other habits such as spending, eating, and sex pattern addictions.

Discussing One's Habit With Fellow Addicts: whether it be "war stories" or other forms of discussion, just talking about the addictive behavior can trigger it.

Association With Dealers: drug addicts may have within their social circles their "dealers" or "suppliers"—people from whom they buy or get their drugs. Overeaters may find their local restaurant, bakery, or deli owners playing the role of dealers.

Implicit addictions also respond to social triggers. Any social contact or experience which has been built into a holding or other energy pattern will serve as a kickoff point or trigger for that pattern. Be very aware of the silent social pressures and triggers you may feel.

PROBLEM AREA EIGHT: PHYSICAL TRIGGERS

Temporary and permanent conditions are frequently unavoidable and often trigger addictive behavior. (Not all are unavoidable however.) For example, among physical triggers are:

Pain: headaches, body aches, injuries.

Hunger: this can trigger all sorts of mood swings, and physical sensations.

Overeating: feeling full and fat.

Trouble Waking Up in The Morning: for a range of reasons.

Fatigue: tiredness, drowsiness, physical exhaustion.

Physical Depletion: that run-down feeling.

Lack of Exercise: this can lead to fatigue, trouble waking up, physical depletion, and a general malaise, and more.

Sexual Activity: anticipation, arousal, activity, postactivity (or lack of, for some people, not all).

Sensory Stimuli: such as the smell of object of one's addiction, other odors, sounds, and sights. (SENSORY TRIGGERS can easily become a separate category.)

PROBLEM AREA NINE: NUTRITIONAL TRIGGERS

Eating habits are a source of both obvious and hidden triggers. Eating fuels the body, and eating patterns fuel the body's energy patterns.

The power of these nutritional triggers is compounded by the fact that eating itself can be addictive. These nutritional triggers include:

Irregular Eating
Overeating
Undereating
Not Eating
Empty Calorie, Junk Food Eating
Binge Eating
Nutritionally Imbalanced Eating

PROBLEM AREA TEN: CHEMICAL TRIGGERS

Chemicals taken into the body may trigger a psychobiological chain of events leading an addicted individual to turn to the object or activity of his or her addiction. When the addiction is to an emotional, behavioral, or energy pattern, mind- and body-altering chemicals such as those listed below can tie right into a cyclical habit pattern. When the object of addiction is a natural or artificial chemical (marijuana, alcohol, codeine, etc.), taken into the body in some way (via injection, eating, sniffing or smoking, for example), the primary or explicit drug addiction is often triggered. Chemical triggers can include:

Sugar
Nicotine
Caffeine
Alcohol
Marijuana
Cocaine
Other Illegal Drugs
Legal Drugs (Prescription and Nonprescription)
Poor Nutritional Foods or Food Combinations
Toxic Chemicals in the Workplace or Home
Environmental Irritants

Your list of triggers is actually never ending. In making a list such as the one above, you are brainstorming—searching your mind for as much information about yourself as you can possibly uncover. Be certain to write your list down on paper. Create more problem areas if that helps you list more triggers. Vigilantly search yourself and your environment for both explicit (obvious) and implicit (hidden) triggers. The more triggers you write down, the more previously unrecognized triggers will float to the surface of your mind.

21

Trigger Charting: Seeing the Addiction Process

The pattern-addicted individuals who have identified their *general* problems (usually explicit addictions or health conditions), often feel overwhelmed by the task of identifying *specific* addictive patterns. The variables seem to be too numerous to identify. The addicted persons' behavioral idiosyncrasies may be entirely invisible to them at first, obscured by the perceived immensity of the problem. Once at least some of an addicted individual's triggers have been identified, the basic habit cycle or cycles can be dissected, diagrammed, and mapped, in order to better understand how they work.

MAPPING ADDICTION

To break a pattern addiction of any form, you must be able to clearly see how that addiction works. You must be able to call this awareness of the process into consciousness at any time. What I like to call pattern mapping is one way to "see" this process. Mapping increases the level of awareness that you have of your pattern.

Mapping can be simple or complex, depending on the level of detail. All addictive behavior is multivariate; that is, a number of interrelated factors determine the behavior of the addicted individual. Usually the causes of an addictive behavior are so numerous and so inextricably linked that the roots of a particular addiction are difficult to pinpoint. The trigger chart I propose in this chapter is a powerful tool that helps "map out" addictive behavior. It is a personal behavioral inventory. The trigger chart allows you to draw a profile of your trigger/response network.

Addiction is a confusing and uncertain territory. That is why, in the beginning, the trigger chart must be simple and clear. Triggers are elusive. When you first begin to identify yours, you may only spot one or two: "a fight with my spouse," or "social pressure to drink," for example. With proper guidance however, you will be able to map a much larger network of triggers.

The trigger chart is created by first defining problem areas in your life and then listing triggers (i.e., objects or events that bring out addictive behaviors) by their relevant category (see Chapter 20).

Mapping addictive behavior in this way enables you to "see" or define your condition. Gradually you will recognize, and add more triggers to, your chart. A trigger can be any experience, event, predicament, or impulse that sets off a chain of events leading to the manifesting of an addictive behavior. Anything can be a trigger, and every addicted individual has a unique set of triggers. These must be identified if you are to be able to work with the habitual response patterns that you have developed.

Once the process of trigger identification is started, many addicts report that it is never ending. Connected to every trigger are other triggers. Behind and connected to every obvious, explicit trigger is a web of less obvious, implicit triggers. For example, a refrigerator full of delicious desserts may trigger an overeater into an eating binge. Behind this explicit trigger, the refrigerator, is a network of other triggers which are either entirely unacknowledged or are lingering on the edge of the overeating addict's awareness. An argument with a spouse may trigger a bout of chronic back pain. The argument is the explicit trigger, but a web of tensions, energy blocks, physical injuries, and emotional memories compose a set of interlinked, networked, implicit triggers. Countless other implicit triggers can exist.

Whatever your addictions may be, the process of mapping your pattern addictions becomes an investigation into your entire lifestyle. Once the unwieldy problem of addictive dependence is diagrammed and dissected, it *can* be understood. It can slowly be unearthed and brought to your awareness. One must *see* the cycle of detrimental patterning in order to break it. As was pointed out before, a *trigger* stimulates your *urge* to manifest your addictive behavior. When you give in to your urge, you are experiencing the addictive *response* to that urge.

Prior to the detailed identification of your triggers, you experience such urges without insight into the intricate web of causality leading to them. But once you understand the pattern or cycle, you can break that cycle at any of its three points: at the trigger point, the urge point, or the response point. Understanding your addiction cycle begins with identifying your triggers. This is how you create a trigger chart:

Step One: Begin to List Your Triggers

This is a brainstorming process. Uncovering memories and ideas will take the lock off the door to your mind. For every trigger identified, there will be at least one, if not several, other triggers that come to mind. Over time, other triggers will surface into your consciousness, as if lifting the obvious triggers by listing them allows implicit triggers to float to the surface of your consciousness. List everything that comes to mind in all or most of the following categories:

PRACTICAL TRIGGERS
TEMPORAL TRIGGERS
ENVIRONMENTAL TRIGGERS
MEDIA TRIGGERS
EMOTIONAL TRIGGERS
SPIRITUAL TRIGGERS
SOCIAL TRIGGERS
PHYSICAL TRIGGERS
NUTRITIONAL TRIGGERS
CHEMICAL TRIGGERS
OTHER CATEGORIES OF TRIGGERS

Refer to Chapter 20 for examples of triggers within many of these categories. Recognize that these categories overlap. They are listed separately to stimulate your brainstorming. Work with a large piece of paper, perhaps an 18" by 24" sheet of paper. Try to use a different colored felt-tip pen for each category. List as many triggers as you can think of in each of these categories. Some triggers will fit into more than one or into no category. Write these categories and triggers down on your paper anywhere you like. This is *your* map.

Step Two: Add Triggers to Your List

Add at least five triggers in each category. If this is difficult, think in terms of primary (explicit and obvious), secondary (less explicit and less obvious), and tertiary (very implicit and very hidden) triggers. For example, cocaine addicts will find that a pile of cocaine is a primary trigger. A secondary trigger for them might be an empty plastic bag of the sort they have used to store their cocaine. A tertiary or incidental trigger might be something that reminds them of either the primary trigger, say a pile of sugar, or the secondary trigger, perhaps a clear piece of plastic. Another and more implicit tertiary trigger might be a drop in energy caused by a shift in blood sugar level, or a mood swing related to some family problem. That drop in energy and mood swing into depression may stimulate a craving for the cocaine, which is a stimulant

However you go about your brainstorming, be sure to write down *anything* that comes to mind, no matter how trivial. Any association at all is ripe material for the trigger chart. Do not try to make sense out of everything just let it all come into your awareness and write it all down. Write as quickly as you can without trying to be neat. You can clean up your list and organize it later.

Once you have listed everything that you can think of, draw a box or a circle around each individual trigger.

Step Three: Connect Your Triggers to Form Patterns

Now examine all of your triggers. Do you feel that any of these are connected? Draw a line between these triggers. Some connections will seem logical, others will seem to make no sense at all. For example, at five o'clock Friday (a time trigger) Bill, a person addicted to the drug alcohol, may go to a particular bar (an environment trigger) where he may see Mark and Sally (social triggers), feel like partying (a psychological trigger), and eat a large amount of salty nuts and potato chips instead of a real dinner because he is hungry but too lazy to eat right (a nutritional trigger). And after all that salt he may be so thirsty that he finally "breaks down" (probably a state of mind, a psychological trigger driven by a physical or psychological trigger) and has a beer (a chemical trigger), which leads to several more drinks (more chemical triggers), each of which invites the next drink.

This is a fairly obvious pattern. Other patterns will be less clear, but any patterns that come to mind should be recorded. People who are addicted to drugs (including alcohol, nicotine, and caffeine) often experience triggers that seem inexplicable at first glance. For example, the smell of flowers may remind you of the incense you once used to cover the smell of marijuana, which, in turn, reminds you of other drugs. However, you may, at first, just see that the smell of the flowers leads to a craving for drugs. Or a favorite song may make you want to have a glass of wine. Or the smell of a cigarette burning may lead you to want to smell marijuana smoke. Or the sound that a knife makes on a cutting board as you chop vegetables may remind you of chopping a line of cocaine with a razor blade.

If you are working on a chart of a more subtle, implicit pattern, you will have to be even more open to the seemingly random associations your mind makes. For example, if you have a habit of pulling out your hair strand by strand or lash by lash, you assume you do this automatically and have no triggers. However, upon study, you may find that having nothing, or nothing of interest, to do with your hands is a trigger. You may also discover that you only do this when you are alone. If you have digestive problems such as an ulcer or a pre-ulcerous condition, you may think that this problem arises when you eat spicy food and when you are under stress. Yet you can dissect these two explicit triggers into the many triggers that they really are: many foods and multiple stressors. You may also eventually discover that you rarely breathe deeply and that you hold your abdominal area tense without realizing that you are doing so. Holding this area tense results in pressure on, and reduced blood flow to, the digestive organs.

Whatever your pattern addictions may be, continue to map out relationships among the various triggers you have listed. Observe the patterns that emerge. The charts at the end of this chapter (Figures 21.1 and 21.2) are actually simple maps of several different addicted individuals' "habit territories." Notice the similarities and differences in these charts.

ONGOING CHARTING

Your addiction chart should be reconstructed regularly. Add to your first chart daily for a week. Make a new chart each week for ten weeks, incorporating everything from your old chart and pushing yourself to add new details. For the next ten months, make a new chart once a month. Then shift to two or three times a year. This will provide you with an amazing journey into your behavior and a new level of awareness about yourself.

In the beginning, you may focus on one habit at a time, such as a drug habit or an overeating habit. Later, when you feel comfortable with the basic trigger mapping, you may want to draw two or more charts on a giant piece of paper and look for connections among your addictions. You may want to begin with the most obvious, explicit addictions that you feel you have and then move to your more implicit addictions as you find them.

Whenever you find connections among triggers, draw lines to demonstrate those connections. Long after some of your more explicit patterns have diminished (and they will if you so desire), this mapping process will reveal significant information about your emotional, behavioral, and energetic patterns.

I have included sample trigger charts here as well as earlier in this book (in Chapter 15). Figures 21.1 and 15.1 were done by people explicitly addicted to drugs who were just learning to chart. Figures 15.2 and 15.6 through 15.13 are addressing both explicit and somewhat more implicit patterns via trigger charts and other pattern maps. Figure 15.3 is a more detailed chart done, with my help, by a multiple drug user who had been studying charting for some time. Although many of these charts and pattern maps are presented in a top-to-bottom or vertical fashion, many people I have worked with have chosen to draw their charts in circular form, as I do quite frequently. As you repeat the charting process for your own pattern addictions, your own chart will gain details and levels. Its format (linear or circular) may change. Eventually, you will draw something more complex than any of these charts.

Figure 21.1.   Sample Trigger Chart #1: Seeing the Internal Map or Pattern for Change

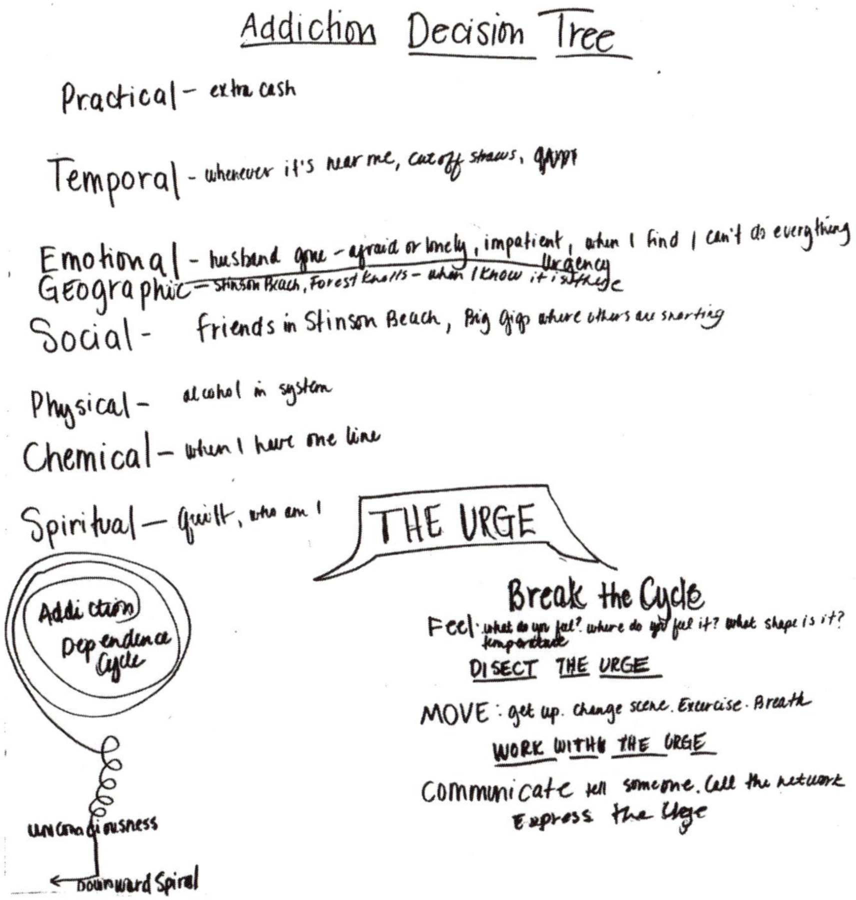

(Illustration by Anonymous and courtesy of Angela Browne-Miller.)

Figure 21.2.   Sample Trigger Chart #2: Mapping the Problem Addiction Pattern

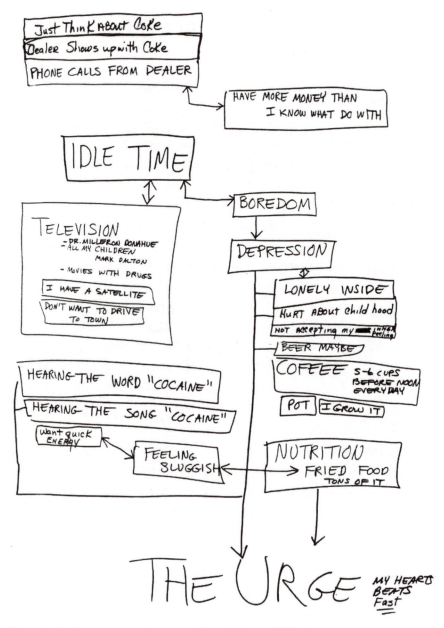

(Illustration by Anonymous and courtesy of Angela Browne-Miller.)

22

Life Management Planning

Once your triggers have been clearly identified, they can be changed, responded to differently, or avoided. This takes a lot of work and a lot of commitment. Mostly this takes solid *life management planning*.

Fix the following principle in your mind:

**TRANSCENDING
PATTERN ADDICTION**
is a
WILLINGNESS TO DO SOMETHING NEW
to make a
COMMITMENT
to
HARD WORK
on many levels, including the:
**PRACTICAL
PHYSICAL
NUTRITIONAL
CHEMICAL
ENVIRONMENTAL
SOCIAL
PSYCHOLOGICAL
ENERGETIC**
and
**PSYCHO-SPIRITUAL
LEVELS OF BEING.**

This is what I call *lifestyle surgery*. Hard work on only one level results in change on only one level; and, change on one level is not enough to overpower the force of any pattern addiction. Holistic change is necessary. This takes a combination of close scrutiny of every level of your life and a marked effort to change on all of these levels. The following multilevel *Life Management Plan* is a practical fleshing-out of the program for lifestyle surgery. It is a sound, methodological program for change. You may want to begin the plan, one segment at a time, adding a new level to your life management each week. Write yourself a schedule sheet to keep track of your progress. Schedule in advance the dates on which you will add a new level to your plan. A careful following of this plan will enable you to change or avoid your triggers and break the cycle of detrimental pattern addiction. Whether you are working on an explicit or an implicit addiction, the matter of life management is critical.

A LIFE MANAGEMENT PLAN

Set up one or more three-ring binders with as many dividers as you need to organize the ongoing notes you will make in each of the following categories.

The Practical Level

Time Management

Time and *time* again, poor *time* management leads people back into the storm of addiction. Commit yourself to developing time management skills by continuously tracking, and then improving through careful planning, the use of your time.

ORGANIZE YOUR LIFE MANAGEMENT PLAN by writing a long term schedule or calendar which designates days and times for beginning and continuing each segment of this plan.

KEEP A SLEEP DIARY of every time you sleep, whether it be a nap or your night's rest, during each week. Evaluate and amend these times to implement the following goals:

- *Regularity:* Go to sleep and wake up at approximately the same time every day. Also, if you nap, try to nap at about the same time every day.

- *Adequacy:* Get enough sleep. Enough is variable. If you already know what constitutes a good level of sleep for you, aim for that level.

While not everyone sleeps seven or eight hours a night, this is a healthy average to aim for if you are uncertain about your own needs.

- *Satisfaction:* If you feel sleepy too often, you either need more sleep, more exercise, better nutrition, or perhaps have some other physical or psychological need. Aim for a deep sense of satisfaction with your sleep habits. Other elements of this life management plan may also help to reduce your fatigue.

KEEP A DAILY RECORD OF YOUR SCHEDULE FOR A MONTH. Record everything that you do and note how long you do each activity. Once you have an accurate picture of your schedule, evaluate and amend it to incorporate the following goals:

- *Regularity:* Live a life with a regular and predictable pace to do it.

- *Variety within the free time periods:* Although you want to achieve a regular and predictable pace to your life, build in regular free time periods that include a variety of recreational activities.

- *Adequacy in terms of health-promotion:* Examine your schedule for its intensity. Find a reasonable midpoint between days with a sluggish pace and days that are *over* booked.

- *Utility in your addiction-affliction recovery process:* Be certain your schedule leaves room for and includes specific therapy sessions and other prescribed activities that are essential to overcoming your addictions and other health problems.

- *Satisfaction:* Develop a sense of satisfaction with each day of your life. Continue for one or more years to consciously revise your daily schedule to achieve this. One way to track your level of satisfaction is to review each day for five minutes each night before falling asleep. This review also helps you become more conscious of the time of your life and how you are spending it on a day-to-day basis.

KEEP A RECORD OF HOW YOU SPEND YOUR FREE TIME. Write down how long you do which free-time activities each day, the initials of the person with whom you do these things, and any items of particular interest for each day. Then evaluate and amend these times for:

- *Effects upon your recovery:* Be careful not to use your free time in ways that will trigger further urges to manifest your explicit addictions such as overeating or drug or alcohol using. Examine your free time for friends, places and experiences that may trigger your addictive behavior. (*Remember, these people do not actually trigger your behaviors, but you may react to them as if they do.*)

- *Pleasure derived:* Are you enjoying your free time? Your free time is valuable and should be used effectively. Look around. Find pleasurable and healthy free-time activities.

- *Satisfaction:* Aim to feel satisfaction with the use of your free time.

- *Learning:* Learn as much as you can about what *free time* means to you.

REMEMBER TO ALWAYS:

- *Plan ahead:* Do not leave yourself open to automatic addictive behavior by leaving unplanned hours and days.

- *Have back up plans:* Be certain that you have other options in case a date is cancelled or plans fall through. Not having a back up plan can trigger addictive behavior.

- *Do not change your schedule on the spur of the moment:* This means just what it says: Do *not* change your schedule on the spur of the moment. You can easily succumb to addictive patterns this way.

- *Build useful activities into your lifestyle on all levels:* Be sure to plan to sleep, eat, exercise, work, take time for yourself, call or see friends who know that you are working to transcend your addiction, and do whatever else your doctor, therapist, counselor, or other advisor (if you have one) has prescribed for you. Write these and other activities into your weekly schedule.

Money Management

The ability to organize one's money—using spending, budgeting, and saving skills, can bring about confidence in the material world. This is not about the size of one's income; this is about he sense of self-awareness that comes through monitoring one's economic participation.

KEEP A MONEY DIARY of daily spending and savings for one week. Leave *no* loan or purchase out of the diary. Then evaluate your spending and savings habits by the following criteria.

- *Sense of Control:* If you find that you have trouble handling "cash on hand" (in your hands, pockets, wallet drawers, etc.), arrange ways to not have cash or get hold of it easily. Gain a sense of control over your use of money by doing what it takes to make it difficult to spend money on your habit or in response to emotional or other triggers. Pinpoint all the areas in which you have money management difficulties: paydays, credit cards, automated teller machine cards, cash on hand, compulsive spending. Be certain to come up with a plan for, or seek counseling regarding, each difficulty. Bookkeepers, accountants, and financial counselors can be helpful.

- *Useful spending:* Decide what expenditures are essential (such as rent, food, and taxes). Then decide what expenditures are necessary in your fight to transcend your addictive behavior. Not your many unessential expenditures. Prioritize your spending categories.

BUDGET. Write a budget for each month before the month begins. Stick to your budget for that month. Do not make changes during the month. If you think that you've budgeted too much for a particular item, do not change mid-month. Unless you have a life-threatening emergency, wait and amend next month's budget. Notice when, and under what emotional conditions, you have trouble sticking to your budget. This is especially important for spending, credit card use, shopping, and gambling addicted persons.

The Physical Level

Exercise Management

If you do not manage your body, it will manage you. Take control. A healthy body has fewer cravings for the consumption of unnecessary and unhealthy food and drugs and for doing other self-destructive activities. And, awareness of physical health reflects itself in awareness of psychological well-being.

SEE YOUR DOCTOR for advice regarding the appropriate exercises for your age and physical condition. Do this immediately.

KEEP A LIST OF ALL EXERCISE that you perform each week: the types of exercise, the times of day, and their durations.

EVALUATE AND AMEND THIS LIST for:

- *Regularity:* Regular exercise (as approved by your doctor if you are or should be under medical supervision) is a must.

- *Adequacy:* Be certain to select exercises that suit your level of physical health. Be certain to get enough exercise, without overexercising. If you have never exercised before, begin with a leisurely 20 minute walk each day. Even a very brisk 30–60 minute walk 4 times a week can be excellent exercise. If you have a heart condition, or if you experience shortness of breath or dizziness when you walk or jog, see a physician. Whatever your level of athletic ability, avoid sports injuries; these can lead to or trigger a recycling back into full expression of your pattern addiction.

- *Satisfaction:* Strive for satisfaction with your physical exercises. Try different exercises until you find those that fit your temperament and tastes.

Hygiene Management

Stay clean. This may seem an extraneous activity, but the upkeep of your personal hygiene is a vital key to the upkeep of your self-respect and self-image.

TAKE A LOOK AT YOURSELF. Note any areas of your body that you feel could use some attention, i.e., your fingernails, your gums, your hair, your skin. Learn to improve and take care of these trouble spots.

BUILD HYGIENE INTO YOUR SCHEDULE. Write personal hygiene into your weekly plan, even if you feel that you are already a hygienic person.

The Nutritional Level

Nutritional Management

Caring about yourself means caring about what you put into yourself. Manage what you eat and you will learn to manage a lot of other areas of your life. Nutritional imbalances can affect your energy, your emotions, your addictive behaviors, your health, and your attention functions.

EAT REGULARLY.

EAT BALANCED.

EAT ENOUGH.

EAT NOTHING IN EXCESS.

EAT CALORIES WITH NUTRITIONAL VALUE.

KNOW WHAT YOU EAT. Ask yourself and write down the answers to these questions:

- *What did I eat and drink yesterday?*
- *What did I eat and drink each day of last week?*
  for breakfast?

for a morning snack?
for lunch?
during the afternoon?
for dinner?
for dessert?
for a midnight snack?

KEEP A RECORD OF WHAT YOU EAT by listing *every* thing you eat and the time of day you eat it. The best way to see your eating behavior is to do this for at least one full month. Some people choose to do it for at least a year, or for one month every few months for many years, in order to maintain a high level of awareness about what they put into their bodies. When you do keep the list, leave no day and no food off the list. Include all snacks and any empty calorie foods as well as all nutritious items. Use the back of the page or extra list pages if you need more room to be thorough. Also note your mood, location, and other information about what is going on when you eat the food.

IMPROVE YOUR EATING by evaluating your eating habits for:

- *Regularity:* Try to eat and snack at approximately the same times each day.

- *Balance:* Begin by eliminating your overeating in one or two of the food groups. First cut down on the salt, for example, then on empty calorie, non-nutritious junk foods. Survey your eating habits for undereating and irregular eating as well as for overeating. Be aware of your eating patterns and pinpoint changes that you want to make in them.

- *Food Groups:* Eat food from each of the following five food groups every day: nuts and grains, vegetables, fruits, dairy products, and fish/poultry/meat. If you are a vegetarian, leave out the fish, poultry and meat food group, but be sure to achieve a balanced protein intake. Work with a nutritionist if you are uninformed in the area of dietary health.

- *Water:* Be certain you drink at least eight 8 ounce glasses of water each day. This is a lot of water, but it really helps your body to function more smoothly. Drinking water helps to control weight, water retention, and the pile-up of wastes.

- *Empty Calorie Eating:* Examine your food intake for the presence of drugs and additives, fast foods, junk foods and foods that have a high salt or sugar content. Stop eating foods whose calories carry little nutritional value.

- *Satisfaction:* Seek to feel satisfied and happy with what you eat. Search for healthy meals that you can enjoy.

The Chemical Level

Chemical and Craving Management

This book has used drug addiction as its primary example of explicit addiction. Drug and food addictions can also be implicit addictions when they are not recognized as explicit addictions. Far too many of us live with little and big drug and food addictions and fail to realize this. Whether or not you think you are addicted to drugs (including alcohol, caffeine, nicotine, prescription drugs, and over-the-counter drugs), or food:

> NOTE ALL CRAVINGS that you experience for alcohol, caffeine, nicotine, other drugs, or foods. Every time you experience a craving, even a mild craving, note down the:
> - *Day.*
> - *Time.*
> - *Duration.*
> - *Object of craving.*
> - *How you respond to the craving.*
> - *How you could respond differently to this craving.*

> PLAN NEW RESPONSES. When you discover a hitherto unrecognized craving, study it. Whether they be new or old cravings or urges, think of ways you could respond differently to them, such as calling a friend, taking a walk, beating a pillow, eating a healthy meal. Incorporate these new responses into your weekly schedule—build them into your life by writing them into the schedule in anticipation of future cravings. Plan these responses ahead of time to break the habit cycle and get out of automatic mode.

The Environmental Level

Living Environment Management

A clean, organized, and attractive living environment is a manageable living environment. Your physical world is, or can be, a representation of your emotional world.

> EVALUATE YOUR ENVIRONMENT for its:
> - *Cleanliness.*

- *Organization.*
- *Attractiveness.*
- *Comfort.*

IMPROVE YOUR ENVIRONMENT ON A REGULAR BASIS in each of the above categories. Expensive, radical changes are not always necessary. Simply make a continual effort to make small improvements.

Environmental Triggers Management

Many physical objects, large and small, serve to trigger the addicted individual's addictive behavior.

IDENTIFY THE PHYSICAL TRIGGERS IN YOUR ENVIRON-MENT. Analyze the affects that particular objects and places have on you.
WHEN NECESSARY, REMOVE THESE TRIGGERS from your environment.

Family Life Management

Family life changes when one or more members of the family decide to break their addictions. Because all family members are affected by your decision to transcend addiction, you should include all your family members in your:

TIME MANAGEMENT.
MONEY MANAGEMENT.
NUTRITIONAL MANAGEMENT PLANNING.
OTHER MANAGEMENT AREAS RELEVANT TO THE FAMILY.

Work Life Management

Work life is a central element of many addictive patterns. Evaluate and amend your work life to:

CONTROL WORK-RELATED TRIGGERS.
SUSTAIN WORK LIFE WITHOUT BEING OVERCOME BY IT.
FIND SATISFACTION IN YOUR WORK.

General Social Life Management

Certain friends and social activities are likely to pull an addicted individual back into the snare of his or her addictive behavior. Manage your social life to:

AVOID OR RISE ABOVE SOCIAL OR PEER PRESSURE (pressure to resume your addictive behavior).
GENERATE POSITIVE SOCIAL CONTACT.
FIND SOCIAL SUPPORT.
ENJOY HEALTHY SOCIAL TIME.

The Psychological Level

Feel and fully express the pain and confusion of addiction, and the joy and fulfillment of rising above addiction. Do not shut these emotions out. Do not ignore them. Do not feel that, if your addiction is implicit, you have nothing to express. Give full voice to any feelings you have in this process. Tell friends, write in a diary, talk to a tape recorder, have someone make a video tape of you, or talk to a psychotherapist or other counselor.

Commitment Management

Fully decide to transcend your addiction. Experience the many setbacks and successes that are a part of this process. You must always strive to *believe in yourself.* As discussed in Chapter 4 and in this chapter under "The Spiritual Level," develop the ability to:

DECIDE TO BE COMMITTED.
FEEL COMMITTED.
FEEL COMMITTED ON ALL LEVELS.

Stress Management

Stress is the result of an unresolved problem or an incomplete development. The lack of resolution and completion creates tension. Sometimes this tension is healthy and growth promoting, but sometimes stress can make you nervous, ill at ease, sick, and perhaps even kill you.

KNOW STRESS. There is no way around stress. Every profound life change is stressful. This means that even change for the better, such as stopping a destructive pattern addiction, generates stress. You may have adapted to the stress of your addiction so thoroughly that you may not even recognize it as stress. But when new stresses—typical of healthy change and the growing pains of transcendence—appear, you feel their impact because they are new. You may even feel afraid of this newly recognized stress. However, this stress can be used well by turning this tension into valuable, productive energy. *Good stress management is essential.*

RECOGNIZE STRESS AS AN OPPORTUNITY. Stress is always taking place in our lives. Our response to that stress determines whether we will become ill or turn it into a chance to master the challenges of life. Addiction offers this opportunity to those who recognize it. To begin healing your addiction, manage your stress.

- *Remember that life can be stressful:* Addiction is stressful. And recovery from addiction is stressful.

- *Identify stressful events in your individual and family history:* Be certain to discuss stresses with a counselor or therapist. Comb your emotional make-up and the storehouse of your heart to identify, and then express and work through, any unresolved stresses you find.

- *Stay current with your feelings:* Check yourself out at the end of each day. Ask yourself, "are there many unexpressed feelings that I am carrying?" If there are, make a note about them, and then cry, yell, laugh —express them. If you are angry at someone, find a healthy way to express your anger to that person, or to a photograph of that person.

- *Identify stress as it appears:* Pay close attention to your physical reactions to stress. Are you grinding your teeth, perspiring, salivating, aching, twitching? Is your heart pounding? Are you breathing rapidly or gasping for air? Sometimes your body will recognize that you are feeling stress before your mind does. Sometimes your mind will not recognize the body recognizing stress until you teach it how to. Ask your mind to pay attention in detail to your body.

- *When you identify a stressor or a symptom of stress, take measures:* Focus on the physical symptoms whether they be vague or profound; concentrate on your breathing; do some physical exercise or stretching, if you can; call a friend.

- *Always remember that life can be stressful at every turning point:* There is no way to avoid stress, but honest communication and a good social support system, combined with exercise, good nutrition, and paying attention to emotions, do a lot to reduce stress.

- *Remember the opportunities that stress provides:* Stress gives us all a chance to master the challenge of life. It is not a challenge we can macho, bulldoze through, or overpower. We must learn to feel and listen and share. When we master and then overcome negative responses to stress, we gain the strength, power, and understanding that will propel us forward on our journey of transcendence. Stress can be used as jet power fuel for personal growth.

The Energetic Level

Pattern Recognition Management

Write a new trigger chart (see Chapters 15 and 21) for yourself each week, trying not to consult your old one and trying to dig deeper, adding more explicit and implicit triggers each time.

Pattern Repair Management

Identify patterns by regularly drawing trigger charts and pattern maps (as in Chapters 15 and 21). Find small identifiable changes in behavior that can change one part of the pattern at a time. Do this on an ongoing basis.

The Spiritual Level

Condition Management

Practice the exercises provided in Chapter 16. Use the schedule suggested in that chapter for at least three months to continuously practice:

COMMITMENT.
ATTENTION.
FORTITUDE.
FAITH.

Phase Management

Learn to recognize which phases of Situational Transcendence you have been through and which phases you are presently in, as explained in Chapter 17. Remember, these are:

PHASE 1: STRUGGLE.
PHASE 2: PARADOX.
PHASE 3: INSIGHT.
PHASE 4: SPIRITUAL ELEVATION.

Here at the close of this chapter is a summary of the preceding Life Management Plan. Sit down once a week and review the plan to see if you are addressing life management on *all* of its levels. Commit at least one hour a week to planning activities. Manage your life as if you were a chief executive. After all, your life *is* your business. And keep the journal or diary mentioned at the beginning of this plan. Write it in every day. Use binders with dividers—at least one divider for each level. Add your own levels and activities if you desire:

A LIFE MANAGEMENT PLAN

THE PRACTICAL LEVEL
Time Management
ORGANIZE YOUR LIFE MANAGEMENT PLAN.
KEEP A SLEEP DIARY.
KEEP A DAILY RECORD OF YOUR SCHEDULE FOR A MONTH.
KEEP A RECORD OF HOW YOU SPEND YOUR FREE TIME.
REMEMBER TO ALWAYS:
- *Plan ahead.*
- *Do not change your schedule on the spur of the moment.*
- *Build useful activities into your lifestyle on all levels.*

Money Management
KEEP A MONEY BUDGET.

THE PHYSICAL LEVEL
Exercise Management
SEE YOUR DOCTOR.
KEEP A LIST OF ALL EXERCISE YOU DO.

EVALUATE AND AMEND THIS LIST.
Hygiene Management
TAKE A LOOK AT YOURSELF.
BUILD HYGIENE INTO YOUR SCHEDULE.

THE NUTRITIONAL LEVEL
Nutritional Management
EAT REGULARLY.
EAT BALANCED.
EAT ENOUGH.
EAT NOTHING IN EXCESS.
EAT CALORIES WITH NUTRITIONAL VALUE.
KNOW WHAT YOU EAT.
KEEP A RECORD OF WHAT YOU EAT.
IMPROVE YOUR EATING.

THE CHEMICAL LEVEL
Chemical and Craving Management
NOTE ALL CRAVINGS.
PLAN NEW RESPONSES.

THE ENVIRONMENTAL LEVEL
Living Environment Management
EVALUATE YOUR ENVIRONMENT.
IMPROVE YOUR ENVIRONMENT ON A REGULAR
BASIS.
Environmental Triggers Management
IDENTIFY THE PHYSICAL TRIGGERS IN YOUR
ENVIRONMENT.
WHEN NECESSARY, REMOVE THESE TRIGGERS.
Family Life Management
TIME MANAGEMENT.
MONEY MANAGEMENT.
NUTRITIONAL MANAGEMENT PLANNING.
OTHER MANAGEMENT AREAS RELEVANT TO
THE FAMILY.
Work Life Management
CONTROL WORK-RELATED TRIGGERS.
SUSTAIN WORK LIFE WITHOUT BEING OVER-
COME BY IT.
FIND SATISFACTION IN YOUR WORK.

General Social Life Management
AVOID OR RISE ABOVE SOCIAL OR PEER
PRESSURE.
GENERATE POSITIVE SOCIAL CONTACT.
FIND SOCIAL SUPPORT.
ENJOY HEALTHY SOCIAL TIME.

THE PSYCHOLOGICAL LEVEL
Feel and Fully Express the Pain of Problem Addiction
Commitment Management
DECIDE TO BE COMMITTED.
FEEL COMMITTED.
FEEL COMMITTED ON ALL LEVELS.
Stress Management
KNOW STRESS.
RECOGNIZE STRESS AS AN OPPORTUNITY.

THE ENERGETIC LEVEL
Pattern Recognition Management
Pattern Repair Management

THE SPIRITUAL LEVEL
Condition Management
COMMITMENT.
ATTENTION.
FORTITUDE.
FAITH.
Phase Management
PHASE 1: STRUGGLE.
PHASE 2: PARADOX.
PHASE 3: INSIGHT.
PHASE 4: SPIRITUAL ELEVATION.

PART FIVE

Knowing Addiction

Addiction Troubles on the Mind

(Illustration by Anonymous, courtesy of Angela Browne-Miller.)

23

Addiction As a Family and Social System Affair

Whether it is an explicit drug addiction, or an explicit nondrug addiction, or a much more subtle energy pattern of implicit addiction, the problem addicted individual is actually part of a *problem addicted system*. Many of the most subtle, implicit problem patterns begin developing, or are at least initiated, set in motion, at home, amid family life, and in the community, amid social life. Because an examination of drug (including alcohol) addictions within families aptly demonstrates this relationship between personal patterns and surrounding patterns, I focus this chapter largely on this model, using the relationship between families and drug addiction as the primary example. However, clearly we are talking about the workings of all kinds of drug and nondrug addictions and coaddictions (which themselves are also addictions) here. Sections below that discuss communication, lies, grudges, and hurts, most definitely apply to drug as well as nondrug addictions, as well as more hidden, implicit pattern addictions.

Think about the way children are programmed by their parents as they experience the same emotional and behavioral (and even energetic) scripts again and again. Family communication and energy expression patterns are woven deeply into the young and developing human biocomputer and are difficult to reprogram later on. Similarly, what is patterned into the social system—which is composed of individuals who have come from, and many of whom are still in, families —is patterned in the mind of the individual and vice versa. The family—of one's childhood and even of one's adulthood—can be the point of transfer back and forth between individual and societal patterning. While patterns of addiction are entirely biochemical within the brain's functioning, they are surrounded by external to the individual patterns as well. Given that there is the additional level of genetic, inherited coding to acquire patterns, even problem patterns, the combination of the pressures to pattern, even to pattern problem addictively, is profound.

CHEMICAL DEPENDENCE

Chemical dependence is one of the most blatant and pervasive addictions on the planet. People of all ages everywhere can get into trouble with drugs and alcohol. Children *in utero* are exposed to highs and lows of caffeine, nicotine, alcohol, cocaine, meth, and other drugs when their pregnant mothers take or absorb these chemicals into their biological systems. While drugged with a stimulant such as sugar, caffeine, or cocaine, the fetus may increase its activity or become disturbed. When the stimulant is a vasoconstrictor such as caffeine, nicotine or cocaine, the veins and arteries in the pregnant mother's body constrict and sharply reduce the flow of oxygen into the womb. When alcohol is consumed by the mother, fetal alcohol effects may result. (Also note that infants absorb compounds and drugs from within their environments, beyond the womb. Children in meth lab homes, for example, can absorb the material from their home environments.)

Childhood is a time when foods with sugar and caffeine are tasted and frequently consumed in large quantities. These *psychoactive* compounds are provided by adults who either cannot say no or do not understand that children can develop sugar and caffeine dependencies. In some cases, parents actually use these dietary drugs—the psychoactive compounds found in food and beverages—to control their children: "if you are good, I'll buy you a candy bar," or "if you eat all your dinner, you can have cake for dessert." When parents complain that "My children just won't calm down enough to go to bed without their ice cream," they are revealing that their children have become dependent on the effects of sugar on their young bodies in order to calm down. Sugar causes a brief increase in energy, which is then followed by the calming release of serotonin in the brain, accompanied by a depressive drop in blood sugar levels.

As children grow older, they see their parents eating poorly, smoking, drinking, and using various other drugs. Then they see and hear countless advertisements showing happy and attractive people eating sugar-filled foods and drinking alcohol. Given that children have been born and raised in a chemical society, it is not surprising that they face the risk of becoming chemically dependent as adolescents and, later on, as adults. It is also difficult to sort out patterns of chemical use from other more implicit pattern addictions, because almost all of us have been influenced toward a high use of drugs (dietary and nondietary, legal and illegal) in our systems.

Adolescents and even adults feel social or peer pressure to "do what everyone else is doing," to "fit in" and, at an increasingly younger age in this materialistic society, to "keep up." Especially among preteens and teenagers, the desire not to stand out as odd or different may be a prime motivation to experiment with, and even regularly use, alcohol and other drugs. The sense of social pressure begins at a tragically early age. Unfortunately, the younger people are when they first experiment with both legal and illegal drugs, the greater the likelihood that they will have trouble with drugs later on.

Parents struggle with their children's and teenager's desire to experiment and to respond to media and peer pressure. Yet parents often undermine their struggles by simultaneously creating the poor nutritional standards and types of dietary intake that render young people susceptible to biological cravings for drugs. After all, a childhood of high refined white sugar consumption programs a young person's body to accept chemically induced highs and lows. To use drugs such as alcohol and cocaine to achieve highs and lows later on in life is simply to switch drugs or to add another drug to the list of those already being taken through the diet. The chemicals may be different, but the process is virtually the same.

HAVEN IN A HEARTLESS WORLD?

The ideal family has been described as a "haven in a heartless world." Yet for many, family life is no haven. On the contrary, family life can be cold, heartless and hypocritical. How can parents protect their children from being lured into troubled pattern addictions, when they, the parents, are already enslaved to these themselves? How many parents who smoke or drink or use other drugs attempt to tell their own children not to? How many parents criticize drug use and then unwittingly provide their children with magazines and take them to movies that glorify the use of alcohol and drugs? How many parents have time to notice the confused messages regarding problem drug use patterns and any other problem patterns, and the heavy patterning pressure around these, that they are sending their children? Given that we are faced with the chemicalization of our world (see again Chapter 3), we must see that emotional and spiritual connection is needed to preserve individuals in the face of this chemical onslaught. But, many parents do not have the know how or time or energy to create a healthy problem pattern free home, let alone a *heart-full* family environment. And of those parents who have the time or who make the time, how many really know how to bring about a sense of family as a haven of humanity in their homes? Parents are confronted by the demands of modern adulthood: being breadwinners, home managers, child bearers, child raisers, and, at the same time, being fulfilled people. When a morning has been tiring, a coffee break may *seem* to replenish one's energy. When a day has been difficult, a drink at the end of the day may *seem* to make an hour happy.

The only answer that seems obvious is that no individual gets into trouble all by her or himself. Whether or not people live with their families, whether they are children, teenagers, or adults—their conditions are always a family (and a social system) affair. This means that transcendence of this situation, problem addiction patterning, is a family and a social system affair. The systems that have locked the problem patterns in place must release its individual members to transcend these problem patterns, to grow, change and transcend undesirable situations.

THE SYMPTOMS AND EFFECTS OF FAMILY DRUG PROBLEMS

A family feels the effect of one of its member's drug problem patterning whether or not it officially, that is, explicitly, knows about the problem. Hidden drug problems may make themselves evident via lies and communication breakdowns, and in the development of grudges, hurts, and co-addictions. Even when the family knows about the problem, when the problem is not hidden, when one of its members' use is visible, these and other symptoms can still surface. Let's examine some of the behaviors characteristic of the *problem pattern addicted family.*

LIES

Lies take many forms. Some are more visible than others; these are the *obvious* lies. Others are more difficult to detect. They are *hidden*. Sometimes a person lies so often that lying becomes a way of life. These are *continuous* lies.

Obvious Lies

Obvious lies are easy to spot. If Johnny says, "I was with Mark at his house until midnight last night," when Mark was at your house with you waiting for Johnny until midnight, it is obvious Johnny is not telling the truth. But watch out! Just because this lie is obvious does not mean that it is easy to understand or respond to. Many families need a great deal of practice in the confrontation of obvious lies. Fortunately, though, although obvious lies can be extremely frustrating, they are relatively innocuous. They are, however, a large part of problem addiction and co-addiction patterns.

Hidden Lies

Hidden lies are insidious. They do their damage without revealing their presence. One of the most dangerous aspects of the hidden lie is that family members often "allow" a lie to remain hidden by choosing not to acknowledge its presence. Sometimes obvious lies are simply ignored. In other circumstances, when a family knows that something is "not quite right" but is not clear what lie is being told, the family may choose to "look the other way." Certainly, some hidden lies are very deeply hidden. These lies are part of a pattern of lies supporting a problem pattern of addiction. These lies may not come out—become obvious—until a crisis forces them to the surface. Perhaps Dad only goes on a drinking binge when he is away on fishing trips. By the time he gets home, he has dried out and recovered from his hangover. He may not have caught any fish, but it is a standard family joke, "what a terrible fisherman Dad is." Finally, Dad has a serious boating accident as a result of his drinking. The hidden lie about his alcohol problem may then, in this time of crisis, be revealed. The pattern addiction has become explicit to the family now.

Continuous Lies

In a family with a drug or alcohol addiction, or other behavioral addiction, an array of obvious and hidden lies can easily develop into a stream of continuous lies. Over time a terrible confusion arises from the continuous lying. Lies are told to cover lies, and more lies are built over those lies. New lies cover old ones, weaving a web of deceit and denial. It becomes very difficult to figure out what is the truth. It also becomes difficult to stop lying. Family members may reach a point where they know nothing about each other. They lose touch with each other, lose awareness of each other's feelings, fears, and aspirations. They lose the ability to confront each other with the truth. When one or more family members gets into trouble with drugs, or with other problem addicted behaviors, the entire family may become enmeshed in continuous lies, in doing whatever it takes to fuel the pattern of problem addiction because this IS the **family's** pattern. The family acts like a family of ostriches who, when threatened, put their heads into the sand so they won't have to face reality. They would rather be blinded by the lies than know the uncomfortable truth. This desire to avoid the truth is apparent in two more common types of lies: *excuses* and *denial*.

Excuses As Lies

A family with a drug problem will often find that one member of the family is constantly making excuses for himself, or for some other member of the family. These excuses are part of a problem pattern that helps to direct the attention away from the real problem. They are lies.

Denial As Lies

Creeping denial invades the family that does not want to see the drug problem of one or more of its members. "Our children do *not* use drugs. Do you Dick and Jane?" "Of course we don't, Mom and Dad. And neither do you." Although denial can be a very obvious hidden lie, it is often the most difficult to expose because of the pattern of implicit cooperation that every member of the family is lending to the lie.

COMMUNICATION BREAKDOWNS

Every single lie, whatever type it may be, results in non-communication. Whether caused by lies or other difficulties of expression, families with drug and other addiction problems suffer from many forms and patterns of broken communication.

Lack of Communication

"Hello. No time to talk. Goodbye. I'm late, I'm late, I'm late." This is a typical scenario in far too many families. Family members rush around like mad hatters—rushing to work, rushing to school, rushing through family meals, and generally rushing away from each other. Little or no effort is made to communicate and share feelings. In many cases even simple communication, such as "I'll pick you up at four o'clock" or "Dinner is at six o'clock" or "I'll be home at eight," is never made. Lack of communication has become so very common that most people have adjusted to it and no longer find it at all unusual. This lack of communication is in itself a problem pattern.

Inadequate Communication

Even when communication does occur in a drug problem family, it can be inadequate. "I told you to be home by six," says the mother. "I didn't hear you," replies her son. "That's your problem. No dinner for you now." "Who cares? I had two milkshakes while I waited for you to pick me up. You never came." "You didn't tell me you needed a ride." "Yes I did." "Next time, tell me when I'm within earshot." This kind of conversation is inadequate in that it does not express the fact that one person was wondering where the other person was and was concerned for his welfare, while that person was hurt that no one came to pick him up. Inadequate communication is when feelings and facts are buried under accusations and counteraccusations. Inadequate communication is another problem pattern.

Confused Communication

Reality is further distorted when communication becomes confused. Family members who deal with other family members when they are craving a drink or drugs, are high on alcohol or drugs, or are experiencing hangover or withdrawal symptoms, may and typically do find their communication confused. The family member with a drug or other addiction patterning problem may change his or her mind or mood or entire personality several times a day, week, or month. This can be frightening, as users cannot be trusted to be consistent in their reactions. One minute they will be loving and kind to the members of their families, and the next day they can be threatening and cruel. A pattern of confused communication can lead others to become confused communicators in order to fit in. It can also plant, and then cultivate and reinforce, the seeds of deep emotional disturbance in children and adolescents—seeds that may emerge later in adult life as deep neuroses, or other troubled patternings.

GRUDGE DEVELOPMENTS

Lies and broken communication lead to unexpressed, partially expressed, or indirectly expressed pain and anxiety. When this hurt is not fully expressed, the person who has been hurt is likely to develop a grudge.

Private Grudges

A private grudge is a strange thing, a stuffed away, unexpressed emotion that is always un-stuffing itself and breaking out in stiff, cold or angry ways. Grudges develop slowly, when communication continues to fail, and lies, pain, and confusion compound. Many children grow up feeling that their siblings or their parents have grudges against them although "no one ever talked about it" and nothing was ever done that was hurtful enough to prove that a grudge actually existed. Private grudges are also part of the larger web of problem patterns.

Public Grudges

Some grudges become public in ways that are obvious. A least favored or always blamed member of the family may be the subject of a public family grudge. This person often develops private grudges in response and retaliation to family members' grudges against him or

her. Using drugs or engaging in other addictions without telling anyone may be one way of acting out a private grudge. On the other hand,
using drugs despite the fact that "everyone knows about it and disap-
proves" can be a public grudge bearing act. Public grudges are also
part of the larger web of problem patterns.

HURTS

Every member of a problem pattern addicted family is hurt by that
family's network of troubled pattern addictions.

Obvious Hurt

Some of the hurt is visible in the forms of multiple explicit addictions, other health problems, domestic violence, emotional abuse, fro-
zen silence, tears at the table, and so on.

Blatant Hurt-Back

"You hurt me, I'll hurt you back." This is "an eye for an eye," tit-
for-tat, type of hurt. It too is very obvious, but it can last for years
and be extremely destructive.

Buried Hurt

But even more dangerous is hurt that has been buried. Adult children of alcoholics and addicts may go through half their lives before
discovering and learning to express their *buried hurt*. By then, they
have made buried hurt a part of their deep patterning or programming
and must work very hard to transcend it. Too often buried hurt is
directed against oneself before it can be expressed.

Secret Hurt-Back

Many people who have buried hurt express it through *secret
hurt-back*. Private grudges, lies, and more direct but still secret
acts like theft, damage, and gossip—these are all manifestations
of secret hurt-back. But the most secret of hurt-backs is hidden

self-destruction. Families may not notice that one of their members is on a self-destruct path until the destruction has reached a crisis stage. This is often the case with eating disorders and drug addictions.

FAMILIAL CO-ADDICTIONS

Over a period of time, families with problem addiction patterns and webs of these patterns begin to get used to living with lies, broken communications, grudges, and hurts. Some families even become dependent on these patterns, these twisted ways of relating to each other. When this happens the family is experiencing *familial co-addiction*. This addiction is a detrimental and implicit pattern addiction shared by all family members and takes various forms.

Simple Co-Addiction

No form of co-addiction is simple. I use the word *simple* to indicate, not that the relationship is easy to understand, but that the family has only one "identified patient," that is, one person whom the family admits has a problem. The characteristics of simple co-addiction include:

DEPENDENCE: While only one person may be directly dependent on drugs, other family members are dependent on the "fact" that "the addict is the one with the problem, not the rest of us."

ATTENTION: Most all of the family's attention is paid to the person who has the most visible problem—the addicted individual.

TIME: Family time is organized, and more often disorganized, around the addicted member's drug problem.

MONEY: Family money is consumed by the *problem*, either in buying drugs, paying for treatment or medical attention, paying for damages, or spending money as an activity to relieve the family from its stress of addiction

CONFUSED FEELINGS: Family members who depend on the addicted member to have all the problems in the family become confused about *their own* problems and feelings.

Compound Co-Addiction

When more than one member of the family is addicted to drugs or has another unhealthy habit pattern, the family's simple co-addiction is compounded. All of the lies, broken communications, grudges, and hurts are multiplied many times over—and each of the five characteristics of simple co-addiction listed above ever more pronounced.

PRACTICAL DIFFICULTIES AND SIMPLE CATASTROPHES

Over time, a family with a drug problem finds it more and more difficult to function. Practical difficulties compound and lead to simple catastrophes again and again—in a pattern of ongoing difficulties and catastrophes. What does this mean?

Practical Difficulties

The basic function of a family is to provide *protection* (food, clothing, and shelter), *organization* (management of time, money, and the family's living environment), *socialization* and *development* (teaching values and socially acceptable behavior, and preparing members to "learn" in school and "earn" at work), and finally *love* (however intangible that may be). Practical difficulties arising in problem addicted families are (a) problems of *protection*, such as dinner not being served, inadequate nutrition, poorly dressed children, or things around the house falling into a state of disrepair; (b) problems of *organization*, such as a sense that everyone is always late, that there is never enough time for anything, that money is not budgeted, or that the house is messy, chaotic, and eventually dirty; (c) problems of *socialization* and *development*, such as children being poorly mannered, developing behavior problems, and/or falling behind in school.

Problems of Love and Practical Catastrophes

Destruction is the process by which the *structure* of something falls apart. When practical problems compound, they lead to a pattern of practical catastrophes. Family life grinds to a halt. Enough practical catastrophes compounded together will *destroy* a family. In this case, love loses out to chaos.

24
Protecting the Children of Our Patterns

Children and teens (who are also our children) are the innocent inheritors of genetic, societal, family and invidually learned patterning. When a parent is experiencing a drug or other addiction problem, the children suffer from inconsistent and often entirely nonexistent attention to their needs, in addition to many of the practical difficulties just described. At first, addicted parents anguish over the situation, too. But if changes are not made soon, the worst can happen. As all of these difficulties begin to *break* the family down, everyone suffers from a general waning of care and love. Eventually nothing is left but little bits of what was once a real family—nothing but the pattern addictions housed by the family and its individual members. Amidst the rubble are the children trying to grow up.

CARRIERS OF PATTERNS?

Children are the carriers into the future of our values and knowledge. They will likely (and fortunately) want to improve upon their parents' values and expression of these, and their parents' behaviors, and this is good! So much can be done better. These precious people, their parents' offspring, deserve a great deal of caring and intelligent assistance identifying, and recovering from, their exposure to adults' troubled patterns. Problem patterns can be mimicked, learned, acquired, transferred from parents to children. To break the cycle of ongoing problem patterning we must understand and fully admit, not deny, that all of this can spill from generation to generation in some form unless a conscious effort to stop the patterning is made!

It is also important to see that, when adults repeatedly exhibit problem patterns around children, they are including children in these patterns. Any detrimental habits, negative addictions, played out around children brings these children right into these patterns. Compulsive, destructive, cycles include any children on the seeming sidelines. They cannot be unaffected. Nor can be they saved from the roller coaster rides of cycles played out by adults who are likely, in some difficult to explain (to a parent let alone the child) way, addicted to the even the most subtle patterns they have established. No matter how much a parent believes a child is insulated from her or his ongoing involvement in a troubled pattern addiction, there is little protection from this reality for the child. Children see and hear—*and feel*—even the smallest signs of this pattern around them and within their worlds.

TEACHING DENIAL

To pretend to children and teens that there is no problem pattern addiction around them when there is one, is not only absurd but cruel. The young people do perceive something, they feel it, usually also hear and see it or the injuries. When this feeling, hearing and seeing is not validated by the parent, this denial of an actual reality is disturbing, confusing and distressing. Why drive a child into denial-like patterns, teaching that denial of a serious problem pattern addiction is alright? Why add to a child's pain and roller coaster experience lessons in denial?

HARSH AND PAINFUL REALITY

The harsh and painful reality is that these children are dependent upon these adults who are living out problem pattern addictons. They have no way of ending the relationship with these adults, and they have no way of choosing not to need these adults. This dependence upon these problem addicted adults, coupled with the mixed messages that children in these situations typically receive (such as it is bad to use this drug even though you see this happening here at home), can be highly stressful and emotionally disturbing—even crazy-making—for these children.

Riding the roller coaster of high low high low and so on, children absorb elements of troubled addictive cycle patterning. Moreover, they absorb the ride itself—high low high low high low again and again. For some children, especially those who do not know what patterning is, or what is happening to them as child witnesses of problem addictions, these patterns can become deeply buried deep inside them. Many years later, or maybe not so much later, a trigger may fire the pattern into action, and the child is at risk of continuing the cycle. Or the child is at risk of playing out the cycle in another way, via a different addictive drug or addictive activity—an alcohol and drug, or food addiction, or other detrimental and dangerous behavioral patterns.

CHILDREN HAVE A RIGHT TO THIS INFORMATION

Children have a right to know what the risks of being child witnesses of adult's problem patterns might be. We do not mind children seeking information about any family tree disease that they are at risk for, do we? Why would we mind children seeking information about the possible future tendencies to problem addictions they are both at risk of being the victims of, and are also at risk of being the sources of? And how dare we not inform children that the detrimental behavior patterning they have witnessed and live around and within may in itself be addictive—whether played out in the same form or another? It is only right that we inform young people that problem addiction patterning can be contagious. It is only right that we inform young people that they are at risk and can take preventive and protective steps to be aware and be well now?

Children should be told and taught early what it means to see a behavioral cycle, to see problem addiction patterning and behavior, to look closely and see the steps in thinking and feeling that can be changed, redirected, once these are identified. Children can be taught to slow down and GO CONSCIOUS!!! Adults seeking to rewrite the detrimental programming they may have instilled in their children must teach their children the same thing they themselves need to learn: **how to recognize and transcend problem situations and patterns**. (Children and teens are quite good at drawing the trigger charts, and the life patterns and maps, described in Chapters 15, 17 and 21.) Not to teach these children these things out of concern that the material that will be taught is too much for childrens' ears and eyes is illogical. These children have already been exposed to addictions, serious problem addictions in many cases. Now they have a right to a recapturing of this information in a way that prepares them to avoid the same experiences their parents have had.

CONFLICT OF INTERESTS

We all engage in some not seeing of patterns, whether desirable or less than desirable patterns, because instinct tells us to go onto automatic. Now another conflict of instincts looms: the powerful instinct to establish and then to preserve patterns may override the instinct to avoid danger! Basically, when we are receiving two conflicting messages from ourselves, we might let one override the other. Amazingly enough, we can endure exposure to a negative experience better when this negative experience is part of an ongoing pattern. When the negative experience is part of a pattern we have grown used to, we are less shocked by it.

FADING HEART

The drug problem family is no "haven in a heartless world." When its core is eaten away, love fades. The family's soul dies. Even going home for dinner may become a painful of painfully empty prospect. Many family members begin to function automatically, even robotically, as a means of coping with the pain and emptiness. Some family members hurt themselves or others or get physically sick as an expression of their pain. As the heart of the family begins to fade, family members die inside—little by little:

**THE FAMILY IS A SYSTEM
THAT REPRESENTS AND AFFECTS
THE ENCOMPASSING SOCIAL SYSTEM.
AND, THEREFORE, AS THE FAMILY'S HEART FADES,
THE WORLD AROUND IT BECOMES EVEN MORE
HEARTLESS.
FAMILIES WITHOUT HEART LEAD TO SOCIAL
SYSTEMS WITHOUT
HEART,
AND HURT CHILDREN.**

So how do we protect the children? And how do we protect our-selves so that we can protect the children? So how do we affect societal change? Let us begin with the family. No family member is an island. The family is a system. Its whole is greater than the sum of its parts. When any one family member transcends the situation of addiction, other family members must either change or try to stay the same. Those who change break out of the rigid addictive and co-addictive pattern their family is ensnared in. They transcend the Catch 22 (dou-ble bind paradox) of the drug problem family; that is, "We want you well, but we also want you sick, because we *need* you to be well, but we also *need* you to be sick, because the family must change and get well to survive, but the family must stay the same—stay sick to retain its identity. Because if we change, we will never again be *us*—we will be different." Families, just like other organisms and organizations, tend to want to stay the same—*to preserve the status quo*—even if change will be for the better. This is why so many families with prob-lem pattern addictions among them cling to their paradoxical holding patterns. This is why when a problem addicted member of a family attempts to break his or her problem addiction, other members of the family will often (either subconsciously or consciously) do every-thing in their power to sabotage the efforts—just so everyone will *stay the same*. Individuals' quite rigid problem addiction patterns are fre-quently surrounded by the far more rigid problem co-addiction pat-terns of their co-addicts.

When parents and spouses of addicted people claim that they want the problem addicted person to "get well," they must be ready to make the behavioral, nutritional, economic, social, and emotional changes necessary to be a problem pattern addiction free family. They must also be willing to see all that they have done to help create, feed and protect a problem pattern addiction in their family.

Addiction, both positive and negative addiction, is indeed a family affair. And the problem pattern does not end at the family's bounda-ries. All of society is affected. And, in turn, all of society affects the family, creating the environment for the family's problem pattern addictions. The same is true for most pattern addictions, including eating, spending, emotional, and perhaps even some illness patterns. These are all family affairs. And these are all social system affairs.

This means that, just as families must release their members from rigid holding patterns, societies must release their individual members and families from the rigid societal holding patterns that resist Situational Transcendence. Can an entire society transcend the overarching problem pattern addiction situations it faces? Yes. Just remember that even the largest wave is composed of millions and millions of drops of moving water. Social change is built upon the ground swell of personal change.

25

When "Love" or What Appears As Love Is Too Much

No discussion of problem pattern addiction can overlook highly instructive troubled relationships patterns, expecially patterns found in troubled "love" relationships. As the tendency is to shut troubled relationship patterns out of discussions regarding addiction, I am making the space for this important commentary on how we can mimic love relationships in drug and nondrug addictions, yes; but also how we can mimic drug and nondrug addictions in love relationships or relationships where there is an intimate partner, whether or not these are truly "love" relationships.

The truly addictive nature of actual patterns of abuse and violence in relationships remains largely hidden to us, perhaps because we shy away from this understanding. Understanding this could be disturbing, could call far too many behaviors into question. Bottom line: we must admit that PEOPLE CAN BECOME ADDICTED TO BOTH POSITIVE AND PROBLEM RELATIONSHIPS, AND TO SEVERLY TROUBLED RELATIONSHIPS, AND EVEN TO INTIMATE PARTNER VIOLENCE the way they can become addicted to just about any thing else repeated over time—any which has positive and negative sensations associated with it. Even where healthy patterns of relating are experienced on a regular basis, troubled patterns can work their way in, moving from low level almost invisible emotional abuse to higher levels of emotional abuse, even to other levels of other forms of abuse including financial and physical. The general downturning relationship pattern can look something like this:

**emotional abuse → verbal abuse → threats of physical abuse →
physical abuse**

Patterns of troubled relating can develop and carry built-in sensations (such as love, then tension, then fight, then makeup, then relief of built-up tension, then love, and then the cycle begins all over again.). These built-in sensations work like rewards—things that may seem to feel good—positive reinforcements which are typical in addictive patterning. These so-called rewards are easy to reap, in that they are natural parts of the cycle.

A sad example of positive reinforcement of a dangerous habit is the habit of make-up sex after a dangerous level of intimate partner violence has taken place. Couples have even been known to engage in their habit of make-up sex after violence instead of going to the doctor or the hospital for stitches! (And then to return to the violence after the sex!) How very much like the picture we have of severe drug addiction—craving the drug during withdrawals—then using and getting high and using again despite the damage and injury this is causing: Even using while needing to get medical attention for a wound inflicted while high or while desperately seeking the drug. The general script reads like this: undergo suffering, feel relief and or pleasure, undergo suffering, feel relief and or pleasure, undergo suffering, feel relief and or pleasure, and so on.

WHY "LOVE" IS RELEVANT TO DRUG AND OTHER ADDICTIONS—WHICH WE ALSO THINK WE LOVE

People go for rewards for many reasons. When it comes to intimate partner violence, the reward can tie into the addiction to the pattern. First there is a potentially addictive pain-no-pain-pain cycle. Yes, the cycle of abuse and violence often (but not always) ebbs and flows, and when it does, may bring with it the simple reward that there will at least be breaks, whether momentary or hourly or weeks long, from cyclic extremes such as physical violence and possibly from the physical pain it brings (although sometimes it is only after the violence stops that the physical injury and pain it causes is felt). Suddenly, the person abusing stops hurting the person being abused and there is new relief—the beating has ceased. This fleeting so-called relief is a form of reward (albeit a "cheap" reward), a positive reinforcement for this pattern.

Let's be very clear here: there is nothing in these words that says the person being abused likes being abused. Instead, these words say that: even momentary relief from abuse can be looked forward to or longed for; that tolerating abuse from which there seems to be no escape is facilitated by anticipation of even brief relief; that when this situation becomes a pattern, both the person abusing and the person being abused can become habituated or programmed to it.

Second, there is potential addiction to a specific reward. Many relationships' patterns of abuse include what has been called a "hearts and flowers" or "make-up" stage. During this time, no matter how long or short-lived it may be, there can be politeness, or emotional caring, or gift giving, or make-up sex. Each of these stages brings with it not only the positive effect of the respite from the violence, but also the positive experience of the make-up activity.

Third, addiction to the highs and lows themselves—to the very behavioral pattern—is quite natural. Highs and lows are experienced as—in terms occasionally used to describe the experience of drug use and addiction—a roller coaster ride. This ride itself can become addictive, as it can produce biochemical shifts which in themselves produce something similar to cycles of:

Seeking stimulation—then relief by excitement, adrenaline rush;
Tension building—then relief from tension in some form;
Pain building—then relief from pain in some form;

and even a—

Longing for relief from discomfort—then comfort in some form;
Longing for the sense of contact with someone or something—then contact with something or someone in some form.
(Refer to Figures 15.6 and 15.7.)

In a violent relationship, hidden unrecognized habituation of, addiction to, a pattern of highs and lows has distinctly detrimental effects. Prolonged addiction to roller coaster rides of stress and violence increases the probability of more and more damage and more and more severe instances of damage and injury, with the potential of these additional last phases being added onto the general pattern:

physical abuse → physically damaging abuse →
<u>physically disabling abuse</u> → <u>murder</u>

CHECKPOINTS ALONG THE PATH TO VIOLENCE

And somewhere along the line, usually from the very start when attraction and or love is intensely biochemical, we may cross checkpoints on a path which could be traveling from: general interaction, to habitual non-physical abuse, to habitual physical violence, to addiction to the highs and lows of the pattern of relationship abuse and violence. This is not to say that all or even a majority of relationships follow this path. This is to emphasize that everyone in a relationship can benefit by knowing about these paths, warning signs, and checkpoints. To say that anyone has a relationship which should not look at this issue is to say we support a sort of not-seeing or denial of a problem pattern.

TOLERANCE CAN BE DANGEROUS

Sometimes people experiencing relationship violences—whether these be emotional or physical or both—grow numb to the pain. This numbing to pain takes place because the emotional and physical pain is too much to bear. However, this numbing behavior as a coping skill is terribly dangerous. This numbing causes us to not only not see how serious the situation is, but to not feel the intensity of the pain! We humans are supposedly pain averse, pain avoiding, animals, programmed to avoid pain in order to keep ourselves safer. But hah! We sometimes risk our safety by numbing to the very pain that would allow us to sense the true level of danger!

Unfortunately, detrimental habitual behaviors bring with them not only the continuing of the damaging and dangerous behavior patterns, but the potential for numbing to the effects of detrimental behavior itself. Habituation to abuse and violence in relationships does not make it less damaging or dangerous, instead the damage and danger may increase as we grow less and less aware of its severity. When our moral or emotional responses to inflicting or receiving abuse and violence diminish, we have developed a tolerance to the abuse and violence. This tolerance emerges much the way a person addicted to a drug will eventually require more and more of the drug to feel or achieve the same effects, and also much the way a child who has watched thousands of hours of violence on television grows accustomed to witnessing violence and is less and less shocked or morally taken aback by it. This tolerance to abuse and violence is quite similar to the tolerance of abusing oneself (ongoing harm to self) a drug addicted person can develop.

What tolerance can look like in intimate partner abuse and violence is a numbing to the experience of being abused as well as to the experience of abusing. Again, (and yes, again and again), we must remember that numbing to violence does not prevent the damage it causes, rather it can allow the violence, danger and damage to continue and even get worse. And note again that this numbing parallels the numbing, the denial, as well as the tolerance, that a person addicted to drugs can develop. This cannot be emphasized enough.

Consider addiction to a neurostimulant (such as cocaine, methamphetamine, or even caffeine, as discussed in earlier chapters): A person addicted to a drug with stimulating effects will crave the stimulation and energy increase when not "high" on the drug. Over time, when not high, the energy drop will become increasingly low and miserable. Each time the stimulant is taken to relieve the low, brain cells may open more receptor sites which fit the stimulant. Tolerance emerges. These sites eventually "expect" the stimulant, and during phases when there is no stimulant available, the brain cells are hungry for the stimulant, more and more of the stimulant, while the individual is very tired, more and more tired, without it. Tolerance means, again here, that the highs get lower and the lows get lower. The brain cells require more and more of the same stimulant to feel the high. Even with more and more and more of the same drug, the highs eventually get lower.

CONFLICTING EXPERIENCE

If we transfer this thinking to the experience of violence, we might say that while the intensity of the violence may increase, the conscious sensation of "receiving" the violence (or of "giving" the violence) decreases over time. The word conscious is used here as we may turn off to pain consciously, grow more and more numb to it, while suffering immensely deep inside. The suffering is taking place whether or not we allow ourselves to recognize it.

Such conflicting messages we can give ourselves! And, this applies to both persons abusing and persons being abused. Being either the cause of the pain or the recipient of the pain is painful. This does not in any way say that an abuser who on some level suffers as much as the abusee is therefore OK'd to abuse or is off the hook for the damage and injury caused. Accountability is healing, just as is understanding while asking for accountability.

ESTABLISHING AND MAINTAINING HEALTHY PATTERNS

Most relationships can establish a healthy holding pattern, a way of life which stabilizes and promotes not only stability for the relationship but also safety and healthy living for its members, and for the people, including the children, around them. However, some relationships stabilize in holding patterns which on the surface work, but which are laden with risks lingering like time bombs waiting to go off. For example, a "little bit of hitting" or "getting mad and throwing things sometimes" may be alright for partners and may work for quite a while. Still, if there are time bombs lurking it is generally best to detect and diffuse them before they become more damaging and dangerous. It is best to work together to make a conscious and shared decision to:

1. Protect the relationship from deteriorating into problem patterns which once in place are more difficult to change.
2. Try to spot, in the early stages of their formation, patterns which could grow into problems.
3. Weigh the risks of doing nothing preventive about patterns which may eventually become problem patterns.
4. See the risk of certain potentially abusive behaviors and patterns, spotting these before they exacerbate into clear abuse and violence.
5. When spotting abusive behaviors, even very subtle ones, be ready to call them—admit these are—abusive.
6. Understand that even emotional abuse is violence.
7. Direct and change patterns and behaviors in a direction away from potential and or actual abuse and violence.
8. Be highly alert to the process of numbing to pain, and of avoiding (not-seeing and not-feeling) pain.
9. Do not let the relationship tolerate certain levels of violence, as there is no OK level of violence.
10. Recognize that the above-listed efforts can be made along the way, and acknowledge yourselves, as members of a partnership, for choosing the path of conscious relating.

11. Know when one or both members of the relationship choose not to participate in the above-listed efforts, acknowledge this reality; and, consider seeking assistance to participate in the above-listed items—or assistance to plan for exiting each other's company.

12. If exiting each other's company, have a clear plan and agreement about a clear plan for so doing.

13. If a clear plan for so-doing is not possible, the individual member or members of the relationship, and the children if any, whose safety is in question or peril must get away. Seek assistance in exiting the relationship where the safety of the exit process is in question. Exit does not necessarily mean leaving, it may mean that the other individual in the relationship leaves, however, when safety is at stake, exit does mean leaving whenever required for safety's sake.

14. Do not sacrifice personal or children's safety for the preservation of the relationship.

15. Knowing whether, when and how to get away from each other is also conscious relating.

LOVE?

Let's talk further about relationship addiction, a discussion many avoid addressing, may want desperately to avoid, or simply do not know they are avoiding. One reason for avoiding this discussion is that some addicted relationships go beyond the emotional and biochemical addiction to the feeling of love itself to include what some perceive as, or label for want of a better term, physical and or sex addiction. Other intimate partner relationship addictions which may or may not center on sex may include addiction to cycles of complex forms of emotional sadomasochism.

Both emotional and physical interactions between two people can release hormones and other biochemicals in the bodies of those people. Just thinking about certain physical and emotional activities such as sexual attraction and sexual intercourse can cause the body to release certain hormones and biochemicals. Pleasurable sexual experiences, and even the imagination of these, can be habit-forming, even addictive. This is the result of a simple process which involves positive reinforcement, when each time the same or a similar act is performed, the same or a similar pleasure is experienced. Repeated exposure to this pleasurable experience reinforces the internal awareness that this act brings on this pleasure. A hunger for this pleasure is established, and the hunger desires to be fed, and fed and fed. This is the way at least a gentle and harmless addiction is born: of course a person will do repeatedly something she or he likes a lot.

Usually the ongoing desire for contact with, or sex with, the person who was involved in the pleasurable experience is a positive drive. However, there are instances when a positive drive begins to dominate other life activities to the point of negative or even destructive interference. A detrimental pattern addiction is born.

HABITS SNEAK UP ON US

Destructive habits sneak up on us. Because positive patterning is desirable, we do not necessarily screen for negative patterning, something for which all people are at risk. As noted earlier, some people may develop destructive dependencies on certain eating habits or foods, others on sexual behavior, others on the people in their close personal relationships—and some on drugs or alcohol. Destructive dependencies, or negative addictions, are habitually repeated behaviors which are detrimental and dangerous to self or others.

The reality of human existence is that a "little addict person" lurks within all of us, waiting for the opportunity to turn healthy patterning behavior into addictive behavior. This tendency can even affect an intimate partner relationship, resulting in relationship addiction itself, alone or coupled with other addictions such as to drugs.

RUNNING INTO SOMEONE'S ARMS, ANYONE'S

So when that feeling—let me go have sex with someone, anyone— besweeps a very lonely person, there is a deep need driving a pattern of behavior that will not address the deep need. Stepping back from this level of desperation just a bit, we get a picture of loneliness even within an intimate partner relationship being difficult for some persons to cope with. (See Figures 15.6 and 15.7.) Look at the relationships you see around you. Can you find a relationship in which one or both partners are seeking to have met and meet deep needs for something which no other person can give ever really give them?

EMOTIONAL SADOMASOCHISM

And now a word about the sadomasochistic relationship. This is a challenging topic for a number of reasons. Because people tend to assume that sex has to be involved in this sort of relationship, with the person being described as the sadist taking sexual pleasure when causing someone else pain or suffering, and with the person being described as the masochist taking sexual pleasure in suffering or responding to the abuse someone, usually the sadist, is inflicting. Yes, for some purposes, these definitions of physical sadomasochism and masochism are close to accurate. However, there are many variations on what is called sadomasochism in daily life and daily relating, many of these not necessarily linked to sexual pleasure, and more often linked to emotional pain and pleasure.

Therefore, a special discussion of the sadomasochistic relationship is useful at this point in this discussion of emotional and physical abuse. A sadomasochistic relationship may or may not be one which includes the above-referred to sexual sadomasochism but it does include elements of emotional sadism and or masochism. What I call emotional sadomasochism is a relationship pattern that is often hidden although existing right before our very eyes, with major components of the sadomasochistic process themselves invisible, non-physical, emotional, and even non- or pre-emotional (still buried deep enough in the subconsciousness that they are not registering consciously with any emotional or recognizable impact). In fact, these unseen elements play powerful roles, far more than we give them credit for. These hidden patterns are composed of intricate and often quite subtle energy exchange processes.

Emotional sadomasochism may never apply the actual tools oft used in sexual masochism, but the sadomasochistic role parodies, role distortions, and the bondage-like handcuffs and whips are nevertheless metaphorically present. Situations in which emotional pain is inflicted and endured can follow sadomasochistic patterns, or versions of these. We may not want to see this as a reality, in fact not-seeing of patterns of emotional sadomasochism is quite common. Moreover, where there is no emotional sadomasochism, or no detectable emotional sadomasochism, or no admitted emotional sadomasochism, it is clear that relationships between two people can and frequently do play out in their own ways the patterns depicted in Figures 15.6 through 15.13.

Also of significance here is the fact that individuals in relationships (to other people or even to drugs or activites of addiction) may imagine themselves to be involved in particular emotional patterns that the partner or drug or activity of addiction does not experience. Yes, we can ride emotional roller coaster rides all alone. When it comes to intimate partner relationships, what sheer irony it is that all the while we are compromising and trading—interacting in any way—with our intimate partners, we are actually living in our own worlds, even when we are not, we are actually experiencing our own perceptions—not anyone else's—of what is taking place. We are riding our own patterns and their cycles while those around us ride their own, certainly affected by us but never having the exact experience we are.

Hence, we travel through our own personal emotional cycles all alone, even when keeping company with another who may or may not be on the same emotional ride! Take for example the comfort-discomfort cycle depicted in Figure 15.6 and the longing for contact cycle depicted in Figure 15.7. Do you see someone you know in either of those cycles? Do you see two people in either of those cycles? Clearly, an individual can be taking these cyclic rides virtually alone. The longing for contact and discomfort-comfort relationship experiences depicted in Figures 15.6 and 15.7 may not be anything like what the other member of the relationship would know or say is taking place. Yet two different problem pattern addictions can exist here, side by side!

LIKE IS TOO SIMPLE A WORD FOR LOVE OR DRUG ADDICTIONS

Another reason that discussion of sadomasochism is touchy is that, quite rightly, there is a concern that persons who are being abused by their intimate partners like it, and therefore stay. This is not the case. "Like" is too simple a word here. For example, longing for contact is not liking abuse, taking any form of contact as a form of comfort is not liking abuse.

Emotional sadomasochism involves the overlapping of emotional abuse with perceived consent. Permission to hurt me, even to break my heart, to destroy me, seems to have been granted although it has not. Hearing that consent has been given is just thinking that it has, or pretending that it has. This confusion or distortion of reality can become quite perilous. And where the consent is given by the self to the self, the consent saying it is OK to do me harm, to do harm to myself, the confusion is multiplied. Here we have the problem addiction pattern subsuming the SELF, causing the SELF to believe that the problem pattern is the SELF talking and is the SELF giving permission to harm the self, as well as harm others.

WHEN RELATIONSHIPS LIKE DRUGS KILL

The majority of abusive, violent human relationships do not end in death by accident, murder, or suicide. Yet, ultimately, there is always a risk of actual physical harm once an abusive relationship becomes physical. By degrees, some relationships are so out of control that murder is an actual risk, and where it is not, death by accident during violence is. And where severe depression and or other psychological problems result from exposure to violence, there may be risk of suicide.

Face it, being repeatedly beaten repeatedly over time, with the risk of serious injury increasing, involves risk of death. To deny this risk is to not see the problem. To be in a violent relationship where this risk is not acknowledged is to be in a dangerous mix of denial and physical danger. There is no guarantee or prediction regarding when out of control abuse may go too far.

26

Rethinking Recovery As Discovery

We have become familiar with the standard jargon of, and common debates in, addiction treatment. In that jargon, what I call problem addiction, or problem pattern addiction, is simply called addiction. Clearly I have made an effort to reformulate this thinking here. Furthermore, what I explicitly describe as explicit addiction is just generally called addiction. I seek to differentiate between the levels of addiction, hence I have discussed explicit, and implicit pattern addiction, as well as underlying source patterning.

LIMITATIONS IN OUR THINKING

A number of relevant debates have rocked the addiction treatment and research worlds. Where addiction has been described as a moral matter, in some instances even as a sin, the problem addicted person has been viewed as immoral, and even at fault. As we have moved beyond this thinking, and understood the biological and biochemical elements of problem addiction, the medical model label, *disease*, has surfaced and resurfaced. This has allowed us to place emphasis on the role of the biology and even on the genetics in problem addiction, and to begin to remove the stigma from "bad" addictions. Other efforts to rethink addiction along the lines of social and public health models have surfaced: e.g., the individual is part of a troubled system, the problems of the individual are part of those of a troubled system, the system can and must intervene to address and to strive to prevent problem addiction. I would say the discussion herein builds upon both the medical and the social models to expand our thinking about addiction.

Philosophical Limitation: Recovery?

There is another concept and accompanying term that I seek to reformulate or add to: recovery. Recovery is a disease model term: the time spent getting well is called a period of *recovery* from that disease. According to this adaptation of language, once someone has been addicted, she or he will be a life-long *recovering addict.* I have no great qualm with the recovery model. This disease/recovery model has helped many thousands, even millions, of people directly and indirectly confront and then work through their explicit addiction problems. The concept of life-long recovery also helps friends and relatives appreciate the gravity of the problem and the continuing seriousness of addiction long after the addicted person has stopped drinking, drugging, or manifesting any other explicit addictive behavior. But despite its utility, it is important that we recognize the philosophical, social and psychological limitations of the disease/recovery model, and how these limitations affect the addicted person's ability to fully transcend addiction (and perhaps also the "sick" person's ability to stop being "ill").

First, while it is true that the disease/recovery model helps to remove some of the blame from our description of explicitly addicted persons, it does not really remove as much blame as we imagine it does. True, when addiction is viewed as a disease, it follows that it is not the addicted person's fault that she or he is addicted. In a society so eager to label explicit addicts as untouchables, as the dregs of society, the disease/recovery model provides some relief from the moral overtones of a blame-the-victim public outlook. Unfortunately, the model provides only some relief. A diseased person is still very often stigmatized and blamed for the disease in our society. Disease is not a positive image, and recovery from disease, while more positive still suggests disease.

Philosophical Limitation: Problem Focus on Individuals?

Another philosophical limitation stemming from the disease/recovery model is that it allows the focus to remain on the individual rather than on society. The individual is viewed as having the unfortunate disease of addiction in an otherwise "well" society, rather than societies or even the world or the entire species being viewed as being afflicted with the pervasive problem of detrimental pattern addiction and susceptibility to this. For example, during the U.S. so-called "War on Drugs," media campaigns to "Just Say No" addressed the drug crisis as though drugs were only the problem of individuals. At least public funds were used to provide this information, which means that the public was involved in fighting this explicit addiction. But this is far short of what must be done to address the situation: all of society, all of the world, must focus a substantial portion of its attention, energy, and money on owning pattern addiction on a societal and global level. Perhaps an effort on this level could require making Situational Transcendence-oriented training and treatment available to organizations, businesses and governments, as well as to everyone, regardless of whether or not they are explicitly addicted, and regardless of income, age, symptoms, or criminal record—essentially widespread across-the-board social programs with the enrollment of all citizens. It would also mean changing the emphasis of our public announcements from a "Just Say No" focus on the individual to a declaration that we are all part of the problem and are all therefore responsible for addressing problem pattern addiction.

Philosophical Limitation: Disease to Recovery to What?

Yet another limitation of the disease/recovery model is the view that the only positive change away from the "disease" is a state of life-long "recovery." There are no other positive and certain change options. While recovery is an excellent model, and recovery has framed transition out of problem patterns for millions of people, recovery itself has its limitations. Let's step back and see recovery for what it is.

The effect of this model is to limit the scope of behavior and self-definition available to someone who was once in trouble with an addiction. It limits people's concepts of themselves. They are told to think of themselves primarily as "recovering addicts." Yet, as people can be many things before becoming problem addicts, they can be much more than simply "recovering addicts" after treatment. If they were fathers, mothers, lawyers, artists, before their addiction problems, they can continue to be these things after the problems have been addressed. They must be assisted to be fully aware of this, in a powerful way, so that their SELVES can dominate their identities, rather than their problem addictions and recovery from problem addictions (essentially the same pattern, different faces) dominating them. The use of the term *recovery* is limiting in that:

- Recovery, as per the word itself, continues to suggest the medical or disease model of addiction. While this does help to fight the stigma of being labeled the cause of the problem, this is just a first step toward rewiring the identity of problem addicted persons.
- Recovery is for the most part the *only* positive mode of existence being made available to a person who has been addicted.
- Recovery is the *primary* life-challenge posed for the person who has been addicted.
- The nature of recovery, by its very name, is thus convalescence.
- Life-long convalescence imposes severe limits on people in that they are perpetually getting over a "bad thing that once happened."
- Recovery thus invites a social stigma against "recovering addicts" in that they are labeled, for the rest of their lives, as "recovering addicts."
- Recovery, in itself, is not necessarily *growth*, although many people grow psychologically and spiritually during recovery.

Perhaps the greatest limitation of the disease/recovery model is that it limits our ability to think creatively about the nature of addiction. It prevents our addressing addiction from alternative perspectives. The disease model necessitates the use of the term *recovery*, which further justifies the use of the disease model. This model prevents us from even considering the possibility that addiction is anything but individual sickness and its aftermath anything but getting well. We are ensnared in a philosophical conundrum, our minds and hearts trapped by the words we use.

RETHINKING ADDICTION

Instead of viewing problem addiction as an illness that afflicts the individual, let's think of all pattern addiction as a challenge for all of us as a species, a challenge that some of our fellow humans are clearly going through and making visible for all of us. *The explicitly problem addicted and afflicted among us are our pioneers, searching for a way out of the problem of our programming running awry. Explicitly addicted persons are reflecting to all of us our individual, societal, and planetary stress.* They are alerting us to the chemicalization and mechanization of life on earth. They are manifesting our addictive materialism and addictive inadequacy so that we can examine it. They are warning us that our biotechnologies, our bodies and brains, can go wrong. They are exploring the frontiers of the human spirit and psyche, as others have explored uncharted continents on earth and still others will explore our solar system and even reach beyond to unknown regions of space.

SUGGESTING THE DISCOVERY MODEL

When the addicted among us find an answer to their personal dilemmas, no matter how large or small, they have made *discoveries* that bring enlightenment to us all. With this perspective in mind, the addicted individual, instead of being sentenced to a life of *recovery*, has the option of entering into a commitment to life-long *discovery*, what I call the *discovery model*.

The *discovery model* implies that its actors are the vanguard, even the leaders, in the effort of our species to identify its shackles, to see what imprisons it, to recognize the glitch in its coding or programming. Persons who enter life-long discovery seek answers for themselves and for their fellow humans. In the transcendence of the crises of their addictions, these seekers are addressing the question, "How can we as a species transcend the global crises being experienced by our species?"

To some observers, explicit substance and nonsubstance addiction, appears to be a "luxury problem" for people "who have nothing else to be troubled by." Nothing could be further from the truth. We have only to look across socioeconomic lines and into our own and other nations, large and small, rich and poor, to see that drug addiction is an insidious and, indeed, global reality. It affects the homeless on the streets of American cities, the hungry in Somalia or Biafra, and the peasants in the back-country hills of Burma every bit as much as the affluent of Beverly Hills. No matter who encounters the pain of addiction, it is the same. Addiction is the great equalizer.

Problem addiction brings all people to their knees. Problem addiction acquaints everyone with the hazards of the larger war between the human mind-brain (and soul) and the forces that program and automate it. Drug and nondrug problem behavior addicted people are at war with themselves, their struggle explicitly brutal, their carnage physical and spiritual, feeling themselves sucked into the black hole of enslavement to patterning every time they feel the craving—the inner screaming for their chemical switches. If they fight to control the urge to use drugs addictively, or to engage in other addictive activities addictively, they are at war with themselves. This warring takes its toll on both the problem addicted persons and those around them. Death can seem to be the only escape. Some die of overdoses; some kill themselves; some kill others while driving under the influence or while feeling paranoid and crazed from the drugs; some hurt their children so much that the children die inside or turn to problem addictions themselves in order to cope with the pain. But many addicts choose robotic lives over death. They simply allow their own hearts and souls to succumb to automatic, soulless programming. They are what we often call the "living dead," the soul dead. The light literally leaves their eyes, but they refuse to let their programming die. Transcendence of the situation is blocked.

We are all involved in this anguish, this limbo. One way or another, we all feel its effects. Addiction is a world war, a spiritual struggle that alerts us to the global diminishment of human freedom. We must thank problem addiction for teaching us this. Addiction is a strange kind of enemy in that weapons best used against it are awareness and truth, along with understanding, compassion, respect for human dignity, love and even peace. Anyone who has worked with or lived with addicted individuals knows the need for these kinder, gentler weapons. In the field of addiction treatment, we have wandered the battlefields of the mind, body, and soul where this war between life and drugs— between transcendence and soul death—is raging. There are times when the automatic robotic side—the dark side—looks so very overpowering. Standard weapons do not work against it—only a sustained stream of light can drive the dark away.

Many persons who have been explicitly addicted have discovered that the key to moving past addiction is the development of a personal spirituality. Although their versions of spirituality differ, its importance is almost universally agreed upon. Sometimes the friends and family of a person who discovers life beyond addiction can see and feel the glow of this person's newfound spirituality. When they see this glow, they know that somehow, out of his or her suffering, the loved one who has been addicted is coming to terms with what it means to be alive, having somehow developed reverence for life and discovered the great gift of being. Every crisis in such people's lives provides an opportunity for them to be "only human," to struggle and to overcome—to rise above, to see more, to travel to a new level of mastery, of being, of seeing—to *transcend*. These people have committed themselves to discovery, and their discoveries bring enlightenment to all of us.

It is time that we award explicitly addicted persons, and other people who are suffering or have suffered from troubled patterns, our respect, rather than simply setting them aside under the naïve labels of *diseased* and *recovering from disease*. It is time that we understand the fundamental role that the person who has been pattern addicted can fill in our society. It is time that we rename "recovery," *discovery*, and begin calling recovering problem pattern addicts explorers on discovery missions, discovering addicts, because that is what they really are. This is indeed a process of DISCOVERY and must be acknowledged as such.

27

A Note About Synaptic Rights

A word here about rights. As I write, I am aware that this book has come down largely against problem addiction and has even implied ever so slightly a questioning of positive addiction in terms of our freedom to choose what patterns we instill within ourselves. Clearly we are dependent upon and survive as a result of our ability to pattern, so it is difficult to complain about this coding: except of course when this coding runs awry in the form of problem addiction patterning. Still, we must take a moment to ask: Does an individual have a right to the biochemical control of her or his own biology? Does he or she have a right to choose the mental chemistry which dictates his or her thoughts and behaviors? I hope so. But, what does it mean to our individual human minds when we relinquish the right to choose our own mental chemistries to problem pattern addictions? What does it mean to turn over control of our brains' synaptic actions to detrimental patterns?

THE SYNAPSE

Meet the synapse. The synapse is the connection between neurons which are key components of the brain, the spinal cord and the nervous system. (We focus primarily on neurons in the brains of human beings in this discussion.) Synpases are found between neurons and between neurons and brain cells. The human brain contains from 100 to 500 trillion synapses, located among some at least 100 billion neurons, these synapses being essential to just about everything the brain does, such as the biological workings of our perceiving and other thinking. Chemical synpases are junctions through which neurons signal each other and other cells by means of electrochemical signaling. In the brain, the "synapse" (the gap between brain cells) is the site of perhaps greatest importance, the site through which the electrical impulse within a cell triggers the release of a neurotransmitter which triggers electrical activity across the synapse and in the next cell.

Theory holds that when an individual takes a drug—say, a tranquilizer or a stimulant—its metabolite may bind with receptors in the brain and deceive the body by telling it that there is a sufficient or even overabundant amount of its natural (in body) counterpart—interfering with the sending and receiving of natural electrical signals moving across synapses. The natural production of the natural counterpart eventually decreases or ceases. When the artificial drug-induced neurotransmitter is withdrawn, the shortage of natural neurotransmitter is felt, and the withdrawal symptoms appear. It has been suggested that prolonged use of drugs may produce chronic or permanent imbalance in some natural neurotransmitters. It has also been suggested that some problem addicted persons self-medicate with drugs or addictive activities in response to natural, preexisting biochemical deficiencies—and that this deficiency may be the physiological basis of an addictive personality.

MENTAL CHEMISTRY

Your mental chemistry is your own. You can have a say in what it does and when it does what it does. You can have a say in when your mental chemistry brings on happiness and sadness, energy and exhaustion. After all, you are in charge, right? Or are you? What factors control your mental chemistry and why are these generally running on a sub and even unconscious level? Why is it that you do not really know what is going on in your head, not consciously?

So much information is being processed by our mind-brains at all times that were we to try to track it all from moment to moment, we would likely be overwhelmed past the point of being able to stay sane. It is convenient that our brains silently manage the ever flooding inflow of data for us, selecting only a miniscule fraction of a percent of all this data to present to our consciousnesses, while we go about our conscious business, paying little heed to the hard work our brains are doing for us. Yet, in the massive and consciously undetected flow of incoming data can be bits of information that can quietly be organized (or organize themselves) within us to cause and to fuel the formation of problem patterns and problem pattern addictions. Here, in this barrage of incoming data, can even be found the bits, the components of, pattern addictions' triggers—and cues for these triggers—and reinforcements for these cues—and cues for these reinforcements—and so on right down to the bits of informative material attracting and holding onto our attentional biases (see again Chapter 11). Like invisible invaders slipping in behind our backs, we are flooded with all the notes and data bits required to build a pattern on the mental chemistry level and on the overt physical behavioral level.

While being bombarded by input, the brain is also like a scavenger, scouring the flood of data for whatever bits it can use. The patterns the brain builds are scavengers as well, collecting all they need to reinforce themselves, to lure us into replaying the pattern's cycles again and again, to addict us to the patterns (and their cues and triggers) most hungry for our attention. The patterns of the brain build additional patterns and subpatterns, and corresponding patterns. **These patterns want to survive and be fed.** These patterns want us, their hosts, to keep them alive. These patterns want us addicted to these patterns. Wherever possible, hidden and more implicit patterns build explicit patterns for us to get caught in, to be commandeered by, either for our own good, or for the good of the patterns themselves.

And sure, some of these patterns are troubled patterns, problem pattern addictions, from whose grasp we may find it hard to escape or even want to escape. And it is here, within these patterns that the control of the mind-brain's mental chemistry is acquired. Now, instead of working for you, your mental chemistry works for your patterns, and brings about an addiction to these patterns within you, and even within the synapses of your brain, to hold you prisoner.

ADDICTING THE BRAIN

When we say that someone is addicted to a feeling such as stress (recall the old "I eat stress for breakfast" adage), we may be referring to the brain's and body's ability to desire a sensation and then to change its mental chemistry to meet that desire. (The brain can design and construct this desired mental chemistry without the assistance of outside substances, drugs from outside the body, and then become addicted to particular states of mind.) Whatever the individual's motivation for or method of tampering with the synapse, which is the site of the crucial conducting of messages from one brain cell to the next, the synapse remains her or his own. And any social regulation of this very private, molecular, inner transaction may be viewed as an intervention, and where not desired and invasive, as a transgression. The individual should have the freedom of choice between using only her or his internal and natural neurotransmitters and using other external and artificial chemicals—addictive drugs and activites perhaps—to affect action at her or his own synapses. The individual should retain control over her or his own state of mind. At least this might be the argument.

At what point, however, should this individual choice be regulated by outsiders? In the face of harm to self or others? This makes sense, especially in the face of harm to others we say. But, where on the Addictivity, Addictivity Harm, and Addictivity Tolerance Continuums, listed in Figure 2.1 on page 16, do we want external regulation and intervention? Where should the outside world intervene into choices we make for the bioelectrical actions taking place deep inside ourselves, there within our synaptic junctures? Perhaps we want to reply again: In the face of harm to self or others, right there when recognized definition of detrimental addiction itself kicks in? Perhaps we mean to say, only when the welfare of the outsiders is threatened by what we as individuals do deep within our brains, at our synapses.

If this choice should be regulated, how should this choice be regulated by outsiders? We believe we are regulating drug use by making the use of illegal drugs and their related highs and lows illegal. Is this the way we engage in imposing synaptic control on citizens? Or, perhaps we want to label the altering of action at the synapse which in turn can alter consciousness to produce an altered state of consciousness (ASC) as a sacred right, a spiritual privilege?

Certainly in various indigenous settings where this is still done, there are age old traditions that teach and frame and even guide the engagement in achieving altered states. We do not provide such guidance in modernized settings today. Instead, we are confused about our motivations for addictive drug use and addictive activity engagement when we know that altered states can result. And, we do know altered states result, even where these ASCs are simply the relief from pain, anxiety, loneliness, hunger, and or other discomfort. We know that we are seeking ASCs but perhaps for the wrong reasons or from the wrong sources. Perhaps however we also know that we are not allowed to freely seek ASCs, that travel to altered states is generally illegal, that something happens there at the synapse that is not allowed.

We could talk about the importance of having and protecting a fundamental human right to dictate what takes place there at the individual synapse. However, we do not frame the issue this way. Perhaps we are not mature enough as a society, as societies around the planet, and as a species, to have this discussion. You see, we are, and in fact are more and more so, abusing and becoming addicted to altered states, and to at least simple relief from discomfort states. What might indeed be framed and guided into as a sacred experience, or a gateway to important states of consciousness and knowing, is being taken down another road. So long as the privileges of potentially problem addictive drug use and potentially problem addictive activity engagement are abused, and so long as addictions to these run rampant, it is clear we are not able to regulate ourselves from within. Outside regulation is, then, quite sadly for the entire human species, necessary.

THE OTHER FACE

What of the susceptibility to patterning discussed in Parts One and Two of this book, the function necessary to survival that has run so very far awry? What of the tendency we have to become pattern addicted to just about anything we do regularly and enjoy in some way, even if this way is merely seeking relief from discomfort? When we consider taking back control of what takes place at our synapses, we have to know we are going to come face to face with our own coding to become pattern addicted. We have to know that outside government control is not all that might usurp our freedom—our own coding to be patterned, programmed, is doing this to us at least as well.

I do believe that we can learn to internally regulate our patterns and ourselves, and to dominate the functioning of our minds—rather than be dominated by troubled and dangerous pattern addictions. This is why I have written this book, *Rewiring Your Self to Break Addictions and Habits: Overcoming Problem Patterns*, because we **can.**

28

Epilogue: Calling for Complete Overhaul

Answer Problem Addiction with Complete Overhaul

(Illustration by and courtesy of Angela Browne-Miller.)

We humans are such sensitive, feeling organisms, so sensitive we run from the very pain we are able to feel, we seek relief from the very discomfort we are programmed to experience. Patterns of problem addictions offer us a seemingly "safe" refuge from discomfort, the illusion of a hiding place.

We can run, but we cannot hide. Pattern addiction is wired right into us. We are creatures of habit, slaves to our programming, chained to the very coding that makes it possible for us to survive while it also makes it possible for us to exterminate ourselves. How do we break free of this trap, this double bind, this paradox? What would a complete overhaul of our situation look like?

Most afflictions, (including but not limited to troubled addictions), are either the product of, or carry with them, problematic or troubled energy flow patterns. A rebalancing or *correction in the transmission of patterns of neurological energy* throughout the body can reduce and even alleviate many health problems. When this rebalancing is brought about, a *harmful energetic pattern*, the implicit and rigid pattern of the affliction, is broken, or at least made malleable, and can be rewired.

However, concerted effort must be made to effectively eliminate the negative impact of the deeper aspects of this pattern. The pattern must be extinguished or at least profoundly rewritten. Without correcting the underlying and the most implicit pattern addictions, without overriding, overcoming, and then erasing the power of the *programming behind* the troubled psychological behaviors and addictions, the same or similar symptoms can continue, recur, and expand. **The deeper problematic pattern behind the surface problem pattern must go.**

However, surgery will not erase this deeper underlying patterning, nor will pills nor general medical interventions. This inability to permanently eliminate deep patterns is, of course, largely due to the inability of current medical and psychological technology to see the layers of patterning driving a large part of all behavior and disease. Yet, each of us carries internally the gift of ending patterns from the inside: a kind of internal shedding must take place. The knowledge allowing us to do this is already within us. We must travel through the surface patterns down to the implicit patterns, and then down to the source patterns driving them. We know how to will ourselves to undergo a thorough transformation—A COMPLETE OVERHAUL —we just need to be reminded how. All we need to be able to do is travel deep enough, to the place where we can let underlying patterning die.

SUBSTANCE ADDICTION AS AN EXAMPLE

Let's travel back up from source patterning through implicit patterning all the way to the surface, the explicit patterning and addiction which we can see. Drug and alcohol or *substance addiction* offers one of the most tangible examples of explicit patterning. Persons addicted to substances move from "triggers," which bring out in them reflexes, urges and even "cravings" to repeat again and again the behavior of the addiction patterning, which bring out in them the use yet again of the drug to which they are addicted. Until the pattern of this addiction is broken, the person trapped in it remains just this—trapped. A new response will interfere with the patterning, providing at least an insight into an alternative to this pattern, however it will take substantial work to hold that insight and break this deeply burned in pattern. Breaking this pattern would allow the new response to be the new way of life as suggested in Figures 9.1, 17.3, and 17.4 on pages 69, 134, and 135.

THE CHOICEPOINT

We are at a critical choicepoint in human evolution. We squirm with discomfort, in faint recognition of this landmark, and then we look away, denial being so soothing. Population, urbanization, institutionalization, mechanization, globalization, and other modern pressures are bringing about a profound change in the life of the individual. Depersonalization and dehumanization are encroaching upon us. Even if she or he does not see it or believe it, the individual human is receding in the face of the technological collective. More than ever before, we are members of a large species which swarms the globe. We are soldiers, drones in the army of change. We are the new working-class heroes. We each do our part to help build the mirage of progress, to manifest what we believe is the human destiny. We participate, we cooperate, because this gives our lives meaning. We are good at taking orders, especially implicit ones which are difficult to question. As we become increasingly committed to our individual roles in the development of an increasingly global social order, we must be certain to remain highly conscious, to recognize the subtle trade-offs that we are making. Many of the desired outcomes of modernization are beneficial; however, we must ask ourselves if we are willing to pay their price.

It is important to pay attention at all times, to shake off our daze, and never to look away. In this way we will be able to override the specific evolutionary developments which make it increasingly difficult to pay and want to pay attention. Consider some of the undesirable futures depicted by science fiction writers. How close have we already come to these fictionally depicted means of mind and social control? In Yevgeny Ivanovich Zamyatin's book, *We*, workers live in glass houses, have numbers rather than names, wear identical uniforms, eat chemical foods, and have their sex rationed by the government. The "single state" depicted in the anti-Utopian *We* uses an operation resembling a lobotomy on workers to control them. In our culture, we are not subjected to surgical lobotomies; however, we do use drugs, television, and our denial mechanisms to lie to and "control" ourselves and our feelings. In George Orwell's *1984*, torture and brainwashing are relied upon to keep the masses in line. In the nonfictional times of today, the present day, we don't need to use torture on ourselves when we are so adept at cultural brainwashing. Aldous Huxley's *Brave New World* depends upon artificial biological selection and drugs to control the masses. In our real life brave new world, we are virtually able to perform conception in a jar, and genetic engineering is upon us. But, the most shocking is that our government does not need to drug us. We willingly do this ourselves. Social control is most expedient when the subjects participate voluntarily and, better yet, when they do so unbeknownst to themselves.

The atrocities of *Brave New World* are not restricted entirely to fiction. As noted earlier, it was only centuries ago, in the early 1500s, that Spanish conquistadores conquered the Incan empire of what is now called South America. In doing so, they assumed control over the Incas' coca leaves. They changed the use of the coca leaf, which is the source of the modern drug cocaine, from a cherished right to a form of social control. The Spaniards gave coca quite liberally to the Indians in order to enslave them. Under the influence of coca, the Indians were able to work harder, longer, with less food, and with less awareness of their misery. Similar to what happens in fictional accounts of futuristic controlled societies, in this culture of the past, tucked away neatly in history, the Indians were drugged by their "employers" to work, to work hard, and then they were worked to death.

Are we controlled today? I would say yes, although the mechanisms are quite subtle. Take people management—crowd control—for example. The administration of drugs is less expensive and seemingly less immoral than the use of chains, whips, straitjackets. If the people who are being controlled will willingly drug themselves or engage in some activity that dazes their minds, it will not even be necessary to hire the staff to administer the drugs. When we stretch the definition of drugs (as this book has done) just a bit to include drug-like activities such as gambling, shopping, and that all favorite past time, television, we see how common outside controls are—even the voluntarily ingested audiovisual tranquilizer—television.

Although we were once outraged by the fictional *Brave New World* concept of compulsory mass psychoactive medication in a controlled society, we calmly acquiesce to massive self-medication in our free society. We do not merely acquiesce; we insist upon trying to convince ourselves that the "addiction problem" is small—that it affects only a small portion of the population—and that we are not part of it. We tell ourselves that some addictive drugs and some addictive activities are acceptable while others are not. If we are this unclear and this dishonest about alcohol, painkillers, tranquilizers, maybe caffeine, then we are bound to be in a deep state of denial about supposed nondrugs which drug us such as television, computers, work, gambling, shopping, and the biggest and most paradoxical drug of all, the need for and drive to have money itself. We are living in such a daze, such a largely benevolent stupor, that we do not recognize how drugged, how dulled, our minds and our senses are. We do not realize how numb and drone-like, even mechanical, we are becoming. We may not realize this, we may not see ourselves making this adaptaion, but we feel it deeply.

OVERHAUL IS KEY TO HEALING PATTERN AFFLICTION

Breaking troubled pattern addictions can heal a variety of maladies, most likely even diseases. After all, sickness is a problem pattern. These are all **pattern afflictions**. Hitting bottom, crashing into a sort of psychological death, can be utilized in healing afflictions. We need to realize this, to get it. When addicted or ill individuals arrive at any treatment or medical service, program, or facility, they should find themselves at the door to mental, physical, and *spiritual overhaul*. To walk themselves through such a doorway—a doorway into true overhaul—to really do this, is to die a death or, better stated, is to **have the problem pattern die a death**. This problem pattern death is actually a rebirth or survival of the SELF, a movement into greater free will and freedom: free of detrimental patterns which can make us problem addicted and can make us sick, past the death of these patterns. Here is the threshold of transcendence. Here is the opportunity to harvest the death of the negative patterning for the very energy needed to be free from it!

All too often, addicted and otherwise afflicted individuals find themselves standing at a door to anything but health and freedom. Most mental and physical health care services manifest a range of attitudes toward affliction, but they rarely say, "*Welcome. We are fortunate to have you among us, because you are about to lead us in an exploration of the deepest level of self—mind, body and spirit. You are about to meet the challenge of addiction to hidden patterning, to understand the death of one's patterning and in that understanding help to explore the frontiers of healing, of freedom, of human potential, of healing potential, and of the human soul. We are truly fortunate to have you among us.*"

Instead, addicted and even physically ill people are subtly labeled, implicitly stigmatized, treated "like sick people." It is not so much a lack of expertise that is the problem with most mental and physical health care, it is a lack of understanding of what so-called "sick" individuals are all about and a lack of respect for the critical role that they play in the evolution of human health and consciousness. Like canaries going ahead of miners in a cave, testing the air for breatheability, reading the signs of danger, people who fall into problem addictions and other pattern sicknesses give us signs. And people who heal their problem addictions and pattern sicknesses indicate there is a way to survive the cave, to forge a new path out of the cave to a new place. The path is rewiring the SELF.

Bibliography

Acquas, E., Tanda, G., Di Chiara, G., (2002). "Differential Effects of Caffeine on Dopamine and Acetycholine Transmission in Brain Areas of Drug-naïve and Caffeine-pretreated Rats." *Neuropsychopharmacology* 27 (2): 182–193.

Acton, G. S. (2002). "Measurement of Impulsivity in a Hierarchical Model of Personality Traits: Implications for Substance Use." *Substance Use and Misuse* 38, 67–83.

Adinoff, B., Devous, M.D., Cooper, D. B., Best, S. E., Chandler, P., Harris, T., et al. (2003). "Resting Regional Cerebral Blood Flow and Gambling Task Performance in Cocaine-dependent Subjects and Healthy Comparison Subjects." *American Journals of Psychiatry* 160, 1892–1894.

Amen, D. G. (2005). *Making a Good Brain Great.* New York: Harmony Books.

American Academy of Family Physicians. (2006). *Smoking Cessation in Recovering Alcoholics.* Retrieved April 4, 2008, from http://familydoctor.org/online/famocen/home/common/addictions/tobacco/269.printview.

American Psychiatric Association. (1994). *Diagnostic and Statistical Manual of Mental Disorders* (4th ed.). Washington, DC: American Psychiatric Association.

American Psychiatric Association. (2000).*Diagnostic and Statistical Manual of Mental Disorders* (4th ed., text revision). Washington, DC: American Psychiatric Association.

Anderson, C. M. (2001). "The Integrative Role of the Cerebellar Vermis in Cognition and Emotion." *Consciousness and Emotion* 2 (2): 284–299.

Anderson, P., & Baumberg, B. (2006). *Alcohol in Europe.* London: Institute of Alcohol Studies.

Andrews, Z., & Harvath, T. (2008, March). "Tasteless Food Reward." *Neuron* 57, 806–808.

Ardila, A., Rosselli, M., & Strumwasser, S. (1991). "Neuropsychological Deficits in Chronic Cocaine Abusers." *The International Journal of Neuroscience* 57, 73–79.

Aron, A. R., Fletcher, P. C., Bullmore, E. T., Sahakian, B. J., & Robbins, T. W. (2003). "Stop-signal Inhibition Disrupted by Damage to Right Inferior Frontal Gyrus in Humans." *Nature Neuroscience* 6 (2): 115–116.

Atkinson, B. (2005). *Emotional Intelligence in Couples Therapy: Advances from Neurobiology and the Science of Intimate Relationships.* New York: W.W. Norton and Company.

Atkinson, R. M., Green, J. D. (1983). "Personality, Prior Drug Use, and Introspective Experience during Nitrous Oxide Intoxication." *International Journal of Addiction* 18 (5): 717–738.

Attwood, A. S., Higgs, S., Terry, P. (2006). "Differential Responsiveness to Caffeine and Perceived Effects of Caffeine in Moderate and High Regular Caffeine Consumers." *Psychopharmacology* 190, 469–477.

Babin, B. J., Darden, W. R., & Griffin, M. (1994). "Work and/or Fun: Measuring Hedonic and Utilitarian Shopping Value." *Journal of Consumer Research* 20, 644–656.

Babor, T. F., Higgins-Biddle, J. C., Saunders, J. B., & Monteiro, M. G. (2001). *AUDIT, The Alcohol Use Disorders Identification Test: Guidelines for Use in Primary Care* (2nd ed.). Geneva, Switzerland: World Health Organization.

Bailey, W. C., Woodiel, D. K., Turner, M. J., & Young, J. (1998). "The Relationship of Financial Stress to Overall Stress and Satisfaction." *Personal Finances and Worker Productivity* 2, 198–206.

Baird, A. A., Gruber, S. A., Fein D. A., et al. (1999). *Functional Magnetic Resonance Imaging of Facial Affect Recognition in Children and Adolescents.* http://nimh.nih.gov. Retrieved February 22, 2008.

Balster, R. L. (1998). "Neural Basis of Inhalant Abuse." *Drug and Alcohol Dependence* 51, 207–214.

Bandura, A. (1986). *Social Foundations of Thought and Action: A Social Cognitive Theory.* Englewood Cliffs, NJ: Prentice Hall.

Bandura, A. (1997). *Self-efficacy: The Exercise of Control.* New York: Worth Publishers.

Barnes, G., Reifman, A., Farrell, M., & Dintcheff, B. (2000). "The Effects of Parenting on the Development of Adolescent Alcohol Misuse: A Six Wave Latent Growth Model." *Journal of Marriage and the Family* 62, 175–186.

Bartosiewicz, P. (2004, May). "A Quitter's Dilemma: Hooked on the Cure." *New York Times*, Retrieved March 18, 2008, from http://www.nytimes.com/2004/05/02/business/yourmoney/02smok.html?pagewanted=all&position=.

Bass, M. (1970). "Sudden Sniffing Death." *Journal of the American Medical Association* 212 (12): 2075–2079.

Bauer, L. (2001, September). "EEG Shown to Reliably Predict Drug and Alcohol Relapse Potential." *Neuropsychopharmacology* 25 (3): 332–340.

Beard, K. W., & Wolf, E. M. (2001). "Modification in the Proposed Diagnostic Criteria for Internet Addiction." *CyberPsychology & Behavior* 4, 377–383.

Beatty, W. W., Katzung, V. J., Moreland, V. J., & Nixon, S. J. (1995). "Neuropsychological Performance of Recently Abstinent Alcoholics and Cocaine Abusers." *Drug and Alcohol Dependence* 37, 247–253.

Beauvais, F., Jumper-Thurman, P., Plested, B., Helm, H. (2002). "A Survey of Attitudes among Drug User Treatment Providers toward the Treatment of Inhalant Users." *Substance Use & Misuse* 37 (11): 1391–1410.

Bechara, A. (2005). "Decision Making, Impulse Control and Loss of Willpower to Resist Drugs: A Neurocognitive Perspective." *Nature Neuroscience* 8 (11): 1458–1463.

Bechara, A., Dolan, S., Denburg, N., Hindes, A., Anderson, S. W., & Nathan, P. E. (2001). "Decision-making Deficits, Linked to a Dysfunctional VentromedialPrefrontal Cortex, Revealed in Alcohol and Stimulant Abusers." *Neuropsychologia* 39, 376–89.

Beck, A. T., Wright, F. D., Newman, C. F., & Liese, B. S. (1993). *Cognitive Therapy of Substance Abuse*. New York: Guilford Press.

Beckman, N. J., Zacny, J. P., Walker, D. J. (2006). "Within-Subject Comparison of the Subjective and Psychomotor Effects of a Gaseous Anesthetic and Two Volatile Anesthetics in Healthy Volunteers." *Drug and Alcohol Dependence* 81, 89–95.

Beckstead, M. J., Weiner, J. L., Eger, E. I., II, Gong, D. H., Mihic, S. J. (2000). "Glycine and Gamma-Aminobutyric Acid a Receptor Function is Enhanced by Inhaled Drugs of Abuse." *Molecular Pharmacology* 57, 1199–1205.

Begleiter, H., & Porjesz, B. (1988). "Potential Biological Markers in Individuals at High Risk for Developing Alcoholism." *Alcoholism: Clinical and Experimental Research* 12 (4): 488–493.

Beil, L. (2008). "Weighty Evidence: The Link Between Obesity, Metabolic Hormones, and Tumors Brings the Promise of New Targets for Cancer Therapies." *Science News* 173 (7): 104–106.

Benjamin, L. T. Jr., Rogers, A. M., & Rosenbaum, A. (1991). "Coca-Cola, Caffeine, and Mental Deficiency: Harry Hollingworth and the Chattanooga Trial of 1911." *Journal of the History of the Behavioral Sciences* 27 (1): 42–55.

Benson, A. L., & Gengler, M. (2004). "Treating Compulsive Buying." In *Handbook of Addictive Disorders: A Practical Guide to Diagnosis and Treatment*, ed. R.H. Coombs. Hoboken, N.J.: Wiley.

Bickel, W. K., & Marsch, L. A. (2001). "Toward a Behavioral Economic Understanding of Drug Dependence: Delay Discounting Processes." *Addiction* 96 (1): 73–86.

Bickel, W. K., Miller, M. L., Yi, R., Kowal, B. P., Lindquist, D. M., & Pit-
    cock, J. A. (2007). "Behavioral and Neuroeconomics of Drug Addiction:
    Competing Neural Systems and Temporal Discounting Processes."
    Drug and Alcohol Dependence 90 (Suppl. 1): S85–S91.
Black, M. M., & Ricardo, I. B. (1994). "Drug Use, Drug Trafficking, and
    Weapon Carrying among Low-income, African-American, Early Ado-
    lescent Boys." *Pediatrics* 93, 1065–1073.
Blackwell, A. H. (2004). *The Essential Dictionary of Law*. New York: Barnes &
    Noble Books.
Blume, A. W. (2004). "Understanding and Diagnosing Substance Use Dis-
    orders." In *Handbook of Addictive Disorders: A Practical Guide to Diagnosis
    and Treatment*, ed. R.H. Coombs. Hoboken, N.J.: Wiley.
Blume, A. W., Lostutter, T.W., Schmaling, K.B., & Marlatt, G.A. (2003).
    "Beliefs About Drinking Behavior Predict Drinking Consequences."
    Journal of Psychoactive Drugs 35, 395–399.
Blume, S. (1988).*Alcohol/Drug Dependent Women: New Insights into Their
    Special Problems, Treatment and Recovery*. Minneapolis, MN: Johnson
    Institute.
Boettiger, C. A., Mitchell, J. M., Tavares, V. C., Robertson, M., Joslyn, G.,
    D'Esposito, M., et al. (2007). "Immediate Reward Bias in Humans:
    Fronto-Parietal Networks and a Role for the Catechol-O-
    Methyltransferase 158(Val/Val) Genotype." *Journal of Neuroscience*, 27
    (52): 14383–14391.
Boles, S. M., & Miotto, K. (2003). "Substance Abuse and Violence: A Review
    of the Literature." *Aggression and Violent Behavior* 8, 155–174.
Bolla, K., Ernst, M., Kiehl, K., Mouratidis, M., Eldreth, D., Contoreggi, C.,
    et al. (2004). "Prefrontal Cortical Dysfunction in Abstinent Cocaine
    Abusers." *The Journal of Neuropsychiatry and Clinical Neurosciences* 16,
    456–459.
Bolla, K. I., Funderbuk, F. R., & Cadet, J. L. (2000). "Differential Effects of
    Cocaine and Cocaine + Alcohol on Neurocognitive Performance." *Neu-
    rology* 54, 2285–2292.
Bonebright, C. A., Clay, D. L., & Ankenmann, R. D. (2000). "The Relation-
    ship of Workaholism with Work-life Conflict, Life Satisfaction, and
    Purpose in Life." *Journal of Counseling Psychology* 47, 469–477.
Bosch, X. (2000). "Please Don't Pass the Paella: Eating Disorders Upset
    Spain." *JAMA* 283 (11): 1405, 1409–1410.
Bowen, S. E., Mohammadi, M. H., Batis, J. C., Hannigan, J. H. (2007).
    "Gestational Toluene Exposure Effects on Spontaneous and
    Amphetamine-Induced Locomotor Behavior in Rats." *Neurotoxicology
    and Teratology* 29, 236–246.
Bower, B. (2006, May 27). "Burden of Abuse: Violent Partners Take Their
    Toll on Women. *Science News*, 323.

Boyd, S. (1999). *Mothers and Illicit Drugs: Transcending the Myths*. Toronto: University of Toronto Press.

Brady, K. (1997, April 21). "Dropout Rise a Net Result of Computers." *The Buffalo News*, p. A1.

Brass, M., & Haggard, P. (2007). "To Do or Not to Do: The Neural Signature of Self-control." *Journal of Neuroscience* 27 (34): 9141–9145.

Brass, M., Derrfuss, J., Forstmann, B., & von Cramon, D. Y. (2005). "The Role of the Inferior Frontal Junction Area in Cognitive Control." *Trends in Cognitive Sciences* 9 (7): 314–316.

Breiter, H. C., Aharon, I., Kahneman, D., Dale, A., & Shizgal, P. (2001). "Functional Imaging of Neural Responses to Expectancy and Experience of Monetary Gains and Losses." *Neuron* 30 (2): 619–639.

Brett, J. M., & Stroh, L. K. (2003). Working 61 Plus Hours a Week: Why Do Managers Do It? *Journal of Applied Psychology* 88, 67–78.

Briere, J., &. Scott, C. (2006). *Principles of Trauma Therapy: A Guide to Symptoms, Evaluation, and Treatment*. Thousand Oaks, CA: Sage.

Britt, G. C., & McCance-Katz, E. F. (2005). "A Brief Overview of the Clinical Pharmacology of 'Club Drugs.'" *Substance Use & Misuse* 40, 1189–1201.

Brookhaven National Laboratory. (2004). *Exposure to Food Increases Brain Metabolism*. Retrieved September 21, 2004 from http://www.bnl.gov/bnlweb/pubaf/pr/2004/bnlpr041904.htm.

Brouette, T., Anton, R. (2001). "Clinical Review of Inhalants." *The American Journal on Addictions* 10, 79–94.

Brown , T. G., Seraganian, P., & Tremblay, J. (1994). "Alcoholics Also Dependent on Cocaine in Treatment: Do They Differ from 'Pure' Alcoholics?" *Addictive Behaviors* 19, 105–112.

Brown, P. J., Stout, R. L., & Mueller, T. (1996). "Post-traumatic Stress Disorder and Substance Abuse Relapse among Women." *Psychology of Addictive Behavior* 10, 124–128.

Brown, S. A. (1985). "Expectancies Versus Background in the Prediction of College Drinking Patterns." *Journal of Consulting and Clinical Psychology* 53, 123–30.

Brown, S. A., Goldman, M. S., Inn, A., & Anderson, L. (1980). "Expectations of Reinforcement from Alcohol: Their Domain and Relation to Drinking Pattern." *Journal of Consulting and Clinical Psychology* 48, 419–426.

Browne-Miller, A. (2007). *To Have and to Hurt: Seeing, Changing or Escaping Patterns of Abuse in Relationships*. Westport, CT: Praeger.

Browne-Miller, A. (2009). "Troubled IPR Addiction: Habitual Attraction, Abuse, and Violence in Intimate Partner Relationships." In Vol. 4 of *Praeger International Collection on Addictions*, ed. A. Browne-Miller, 123–131.Santa Barbara, CA: Praeger..

Buelmans, M., & Poelmans, S. A. Y. (2004) "Enriching the Spence and Robbins Typology of Workaholism: Demographics, Motivational and

Organizational Correlates." *Journal of Organizational Change Management* 17, 446–458.

Bugarin, A. (2002). *The Prevalence of Domestic Violence in California*. Sacramento: California Research Bureau, California State Library.

Bulik, C. M., et al. (2008, April). "Suicide Attempts in Anorexia Nervosa." *Psychosom Med* 70, 378.

Bureau of Justice Statistics. (2001). "Criminal Offender Statistics." *U.S. Department of Justice: Office of Justice Programs*. Retrieved May 28, 2008, from http://www.ojp.usdoj.gov/bjs/crimoff.htm.

Bureau of Justice Statistics. (2004). "Profile of Jail Inmates, 2002." *U.S. Department of Justice: Office of Justice Programs*. Retrieved May 28, 2008, from http://www.ojp.usdoj.gov/bjs/abstract/pji02.htm.

Burgess, A. W., Hartman, C. R., & Clements Jr., P. T. (1995, March). "Biology of Memory and Childhood Trauma." *Journal of Psychosocial Nursing: Mental Health Services* 33 (3): 16–26.

Burke, R. J. (1999a). "Workaholism in Organizations: Measurement Validation and Replication." *International Journal of Stress Management* 6, 45–55.

Burke, R. J. (1999b). "Workaholism in Organizations: The Role of Personal Beliefs and Fears." *Anxiety, Stress and Coping* 14, 1–12.

Burke, R. J. (1999c). "Workaholism in Organizations: The Role of Organizational Values." *Personnel Review* 30, 637–645.

Burke, R. J. (1999d). "Are Workaholics Job Satisfied and Successful in Their Careers?" *Career Development International* 26, 149–158.

Burke, R. J. (1999e). "It's Not How Hard You Work But How You Work Hard: Evaluating Workaholism Components." *International Journal of Stress Management* 6, 225–239.

Burke, R. J., Richardsen, A. M., & Mortinussen, M. (2004). "Workaholism among Norwegian Senior Managers: New Research Directions." *International Journal of Management* 21, 415–426.

Burroughs, J., & Rindfleisch, A. (2002). "Materialism and Well-being: A Conflicting Values Perspective." *Journal of Consumer Research* 29, 348–370.

Burwell, R., & Chen, C. P. (2008). "Positive Psychology for Work-life Balance: A New Approach in Treating Workaholism." In *The Long Workhours Culture: Causes, Consequences and Choices*, ed. R. J. Burke & C. L. Cooper.. London: Elsevier.

Campbell, W. K., Rudich, E., & Sedikides, C. (2002). "Narcissism, Self-esteem, and the Positivity of Self-views: Two Portraits of Self-love." *Personality and Social Psychology Bulletin* 28, 358–368.

Caplan, S. E. (2002). "Problematic Internet Use and Psychosocial Well-being: Development of a Theory-based Cognitive-behavioral Measurement Instrument." *Computers in Human Behavior* 18, 553–575.

Carlson, N. R. (2007). *Physiology of behavior*. Boston: Allyn and Bacon.

Carvey, P. M. (1998). *Drug Action in the Central Nervous System.* New York: Oxford University Press.

Chanon, V., & Hopfinger, J. (2007). "Memory's Grip on Attention: The Influence of Item Memory on the Allocation of Attention." *Visual Cognition* 16 (2 & 3): 325–340.

Chanon, V., and Boettiger, C. (2009). "Addiction and Cognitive Control." In Vol. 2 of *Praeger International Collection on Addictions*, ed. A. Browne-Miller, ., , 273–286. Santa Barbara, CA: Praeger.

Chawla, J., & Suleman, A. (2006). "Neurologic Effects of Caffeine." *eMedicine*, Retrieved May 05, 2008, from http://www.emedicine.com/neuro/topic666.htm.

Chen, C. (2006). "Improving Work-life Balance: REBT for Workaholic Treatment." In *Research Companion to Working Time and Work Addiction*, ed. R.J. Burke, 310–329. UK: Edward Elgar..

Chen, J. P., van Praag, H. M., Gardner, E. L. (1991). "Activation of 5-HT3 Receptor by 1-phenylbiguanide Increases Dopamine Release in the Rat Nucleus Accumbens." *Brain Research* 543: 354–357.

Chin, R. L., Sporer, K. A., Cullison, B., Dyer, J. E., & Wu, T. D. (1998). "Clinical Course of Gamma-hydroxybutyrate Overdose." *Ann Emerg Med* 31: 716–722.

Christenson, G. A., Faber, R. J., de Zwaan, M., Raymond, N. C., Specker, S. M., & Ekern, M. D. (1994). "Compulsive Buying: Descriptive Characteristics and Psychiatric Comorbidity." *Journal of Clinical Psychiatry* 55: 5–11.

Christopher, G., Sutherland, D., Smith, A. (2005). "Effects of Caffeine in Non-withdrawn Volunteers." *Human Psychopharmacology: Clinical & Experimental* 20: 47–53.

Chu, K. (2006, May 8). "Many Marriages Today Are 'Til Debt Do Us Part: Managing Your Money." *USA Today*. Retrieved March 14, 2007, from usatoday.com/money/perfi/basics/2006–04–27-couples-cash-series_x.htm.

Clark, L., & Robbins, T. (2002). "Decision-making Deficits in Drug Addiction." *Trends in Cognitive Sciences* 6 (9): 361–363.

Clark-Lempers, D. S., Lempers, J. D., & Netusil, A. J. (1990). "Family Financial Stress, Parental Support, and Young Adolescents' Academic Achievement and Aepressive Symptoms." *Journal of Early Adolescence* 10: 21–36.

Cocozza, J. J., Jackson, E. W., Hennigan, K., Morrissey, J. P., Reed, B. G., & Fallot, R., et al. (2005). "Outcomes for Women with Co-occurring Disorders and Trauma: Program-level Effects." *Journal of Substance Abuse Treatment* 28 (2): 109–120.

Coker, A. L., Smith, P. H., McKeown, R. E., & King, M. J. (2000). "Frequency and Correlates of Intimate Partner Violence by Type: Physical,

Sexual, and Psychological Battering. *American Journal of Public Health* 90: 553–559.

Collins, R. L. (2005). "Relapse Prevention for Eating Disorders and Obesity." In *Relapse Prevention: Maintenance Strategies in the Treatment of Addictive Behaviors*, eds. G.A. Marlatt & D.M. Donovan. New York: Guilford.

Collins, R .L., & Ricciardelli, L.A. (2005). "Assessment of Eating Disorders." In *Assessment of Addictive Behaviors*, eds. D.M. Donovan & G.A. Marlatt. New York: Guilford.

Committee on Substance Abuse and Committee on Native American Child Health (1996). "Inhalant Abuse." *Pediatrics* 97 (3): 1996.

Compton, W. M., Cottler, L. B., Dinwiddie, S. H., Mager, D. E., Asmus, G. (1994). "Inhalant Use: Characteristics and Predictors." *American Journal on Addiction* 3 (3): 263–272.

Coombs, R. H. (Ed.). (2004). *Handbook of Addictive Disorders: A Practical Guide to Diagnosis and Treatment*. Hoboken, N.J.: Wiley.

Coombs, R. H., & Howatt, W.A. (2005). *The Addiction Counselor's Desk Reference*. Hoboken, N.J.: Wiley.

Coon, G. M., Pena, D., & Illich, P. A. (1998). "Self-efficacy and Substance Abuse Assessment Using a Brief Phone Interview. *Journal of Substance Abuse Treatment*15: 385–391.

Cooper, A., & Sportolari, L. (1997). "Romance in Cyberspace: Understanding Online Attraction." *Journal of Sex Education and Therapy* 22 (1): 7–14.

Cooper, A., Putnam, D. E., Planchon, L. A., & Boies, S.C. (1999). "Online Sexual Compulsivity: Getting Tangled in the Net: Sexual Addiction & Compulsivity." *The Journal of Treatment and Prevention* 6 (2): 79–104.

Cooper, A., Scherer, C., Boies, S. C., & Gordon, B. (1999). "Sexuality on the Internet: From Sexual Exploration to Pathological Expression. *Professional Psychology: Research and Practice* 30 (2): 154–164.

Copeland, A. L., Brandon, T. H., & Quinn, E. P. (1995). "The Smoking Consequences Questionnaire—Adult: Measurement of Smoking Outcome Expectancies of Experienced Smokers." *Psychological Assessment*7: 484–494.

Corbett, S. (2007, March 18). "The Women's War." *New York Times Magazine*, section 6, 41–55, 62, 71–72.

Corbetta, M., & Shulman, G. L. (2002). "Control of Goal-directed and Stimulus-driven Attention in the Brain." *Nature Reviews Neuroscience* 3 (3): 201–215.

Corcoran, K. J., & Segrist, D. J. (1993). "Personal Expectancies and Group Influences Affect Alcoholic Beverage Selection: The Interaction of Personal and Situational Variables." *Addictive Behaviors* 18: 577–582.

Cota, D., Tschöp, M., Horvath, T., & Levine, A. (2006). "Cannabinoids, Opioids and Eating Behavior: The Molecular Face of Hedonism?" *Brain Res Rev* 51 (1): 85–107.

Covey, C., (2009). "What is Methamphetamine and How and Why Is it Used?" In Vol. 4 of *Prager International Collection on Addictions*, ed. A. Browne-Miller, 141–164. Santa Barbara, CA: Praeger.

Cox, A. D., Cox, D., & Anderson, R. D. (2005). "Reassessing the Pleasures of Store Shopping." *Journal of Business Research* 58: 250–259.

Cozolino, L. (2006). *The Neuroscience of Human Relationships: Attachment and the Developing Social Brain*. New York: W. W. Norton and Company.

Crano, W. D., Siegel, J. T., Alvaro, E. M., Patel, N. M. (2007). "Overcoming Adolescents' Resistance to Anti-inhalant Appeals." *Psychology of Addictive Behaviors* 21 (4): 516–524.

Csikszentmihalyi, M. (1990). *Flow: The Psychology of Optimal Experience*. New York: Harper Collins.

Cummings, C., Gordon, J., & Marlatt, G. (1980). "Relapse Strategies of Prevention and Prediction." In *The Addictive Disorders: Treatment of Alcoholism, Drug Abuse, Smoking, and Obesity*, ed. W.R. Miller. New York: Pergamon.

d'Astous, A. (1990). "An Inquiry into the Compulsive Side of Normal Consumers." *Journal of Consumer Policy* 13: 15–31.

Daaleman, T., & Kaufman, J. (2006). "Spirituality and Depressive Symptoms in Primary Care Outpatients." *Southern Medical Journal* 99 (12): 1340–1345.

Dahlberg, L. L., & Krug, E. G. (2002). "Violence—A Global Public Health Problem." In *World Report on Violence and Health*, eds. E. G. Krug, L. L. Dahlberg, J. A. Mercy, A. B. Zwi, & R. Lozano, 3–21. Geneva, Switzerland: World Health Organization.

Dapice, A., Cobb, L., Hutchins, E. B., & Siegel, G. (1988). "Teaching and Learning Values." *Educational Horizons* 66 (3): 107–110.

Dapice, A., Inkanish, C., Martin, B., & Montalvo, E. (2001, June). "Killing Us Slowly: The Relationship between Type II Diabetes and Alcoholism." *Native American Times*. Retrieved May 25, 2004 from http://vltakaliseji.tripod.com/Vtlakaliseji/id20.html.

Davis, R. A. (2001). "A Cognitive Behavioral Model of Pathological Internet Use." *Computers in Human Behavior* 17: 187–195.

Dawson, D. A. (1998). "Beyond Black, White and Hispanic: Race, Ethnic Origin and Drinking Patterns in the United States." *Journal of Substance Abuse* 10: 321–339.

De Araujo, I., Oliveira-Maia, A., Sotrikova, T., Gainetdinov, R., Caron, M., Nicolelis, M., et al. (2008, March). "Food Reward in the Absence of Taste Receptor Signaling." *Neuron* 57: 930–941.

Dean, L. R., Carroll, J. S., & Yang, C. (2007). "Materialism, Perceived Financial Problems, and Marital Satisfaction." *Family and Consumer Sciences Research Journal* 35: 260–281.

Deci, E. L., & Ryan, R. M. (1985). *Intrinsic Motivation and Self-Determination in Human Behavior*. New York: Plenum.

Deci, E. L., & Ryan, R. M. (2000). "The 'What' and 'why' of Goal Pursuits: Human Needs and the Self-determination of Behavior." *Psychological Inquiry* 11: 227–268.

Declerck, C. H., Boone, C., & De Brabander, B. (2006). "On Feeling in Control: A Biological Theory for Individual Differences in Control Perception." *Brain and Cognition* 62 (2): 143–176.

Dews, P. B. (Ed.). (1987). *Caffeine: Perspectives from Recent Research*. Berlin: Springer.

Dholakia, U. M. (2000). "Temptation and Resistance: An Integrated Model of Consumption Impulse Formation and Enactment." *Psychology and Marketing* 17: 955–982.

Di Sclafani, V., Tolou-Shams, M., Price, L. J. & Fein, G. (2002). "Neuropsychological Performance of Individuals Dependent on Crack-cocaine, or Crack-cocaine and Alcohol, at 6 Weeks and 6 Months of Abstinence." *Drug and Alcohol Dependence* 66: 161–171.

DiClemente, C. C., Carbonari, J. P., Montgomery, R. P. G., & Hughes, S. O. (1994). "The Alcohol Abstinence Self-efficacy Scale." *Journal of Studies on Alcohol* 55: 141–148.

DiClemente, C. C., Prochaska, J. O., Fairhurst, S., Velicer, W. F., Rossi, J. S., & Valesquez, M. (1991). "The Process of Smoking Cessation: An Analysis of Precontemplation, Contemplation, and Contemplation/ Action." *Journal of Consulting and Clinical Psychology* 59: 295–304.

Dingfelder, S.F. (2007, February). "The Love Drug: More Than a Feeling." *Monitor on Psychology* 38 (2): 40–41.

Dinwiddie, S. H. (1994). "Abuse of Inhalants: A Review." *Addiction* 89: 925–939.

Dittmar, H. (2004). "Understanding and Diagnosing Compulsive Buying." In *Handbook of Addictive Disorders: A Practical Guide to Diagnosis and Treatment*, ed. R. Coombs, 411–450. Hoboken, N.J.: Wiley.

Dittmar, H. (2005). "Compulsive Buying—a Growing Concern? An Examination of Gender, Age, and Endorsement of Materialistic Values as Predictors." *British Journal of Psychology* 96: 467–491.

Drentea, P. (2000). "Age, Debt and Anxiety." *Journal of Health and Social Behavior* 41: 437–50.

Drentea, P., & Lavrakas, P. J. (2000). "Over the Limit: The Association among Health, Race and Debt." *Social Science and Medicine* 50: 517–529.

Duke University. (2004). *Prenatal Nicotine Primes Adolescent Brain for Addiction*. Retrieved March 5, 2008, from http://www.sciencedaily.com/releases/2004/04/040420214434.htm.

Duncan, J., & Owen, A. M. (2000). "Common Regions of the Human Frontal Lobe Recruited by Diverse Cognitive Demands." *Trends in Neurosciences* 23 (10): 475–483.

Dunn, C., Hungerford, D., Field, C., & McCann, B. (2005, September). "The Stages of Change: When Are Trauma Patients Truly Ready to

Change?" *Journal of Trauma Injury, Infection, and Critical Care* 59 (3): S27–S31.

Edwards, E. A. (1993). "Development of a New Scale for Measuring Compulsive Buying Behavior." *Financial Counseling and Planning* 4: 67–85.

Ernst, D., Miller, W., & Rollnick, S. (2007). "Treating Substance Abuse in Primary Care: A Demonstration Project." *International Journal of Integrated Care* 7 (10): 1–8.

Ernst, T., Chang, L., Leonido-Yee, M., & Speck, O. (2000). "Evidence for Long-term Neurotoxicity Associated with Methamphetamine Abuse: A 1H MRS Study." *Neurology* 54: 1344–1349.

Evans, S. M., Griffiths, R. R. (1999). "Caffeine Withdrawal: A Parametric Analysis of Caffeine Dosing Conditions." *Journal of Pharmacology and Experimental Therapeutics* 289: 285–294.

Evenden, J., & Ko, T. (2007). "The Effects of Anorexic Drugs on Free-fed Rats Responding under a Second-order FI15-min (FR10:S) Schedule for High Incentive Foods." *Behav Pharmacol* 18 (1): 61–69.

Everitt, B. J., & Robbins, T. W. (2005). "Neural Systems of Reinforcement for Drug Addiction: From Actions to Habits to Compulsion." *Nature Neuroscience* 8 (11): 1481–1489.

Everitt, B. J., Hutcheson, D. M., Ersche, K. D., Pelloux, Y., Dalley, J. W., & Robbins, T. W. (2007). "The Orbital Prefrontal Cortex and Drug Addiction in Laboratory Animals and Humans." *Annals of the New York Academy of Sciences* 1121: 576–597.

Faber, R. J. (2004). "Self-control and Compulsive Buying." In *Psychology and Consumer Culture: The Struggle for a Good Life in a Materialistic World*, eds. T. Kasser & A. D. Kanner, 169–188. Washington DC: American Psychological Association.

Faber, R. J., & O'Guinn, T. C. (1988). "Compulsive Consumption and Credit Abuse." *Journal of Consumer Policy* 11: 97–109.

Faber, R. J., & O'Guinn, T. C. (1992). "A Clinical Screener for Compulsive Buying." *Journal of Consumer Research* 19: 459–469.

Fassel, D. (1990). *Working Ourselves to Death: The High Costs of Workaholism, the Rewards of Recovery.* San Francisco, CA: Harper Collins.

Feinberg, J. (1987). "Psychological Egoism." In *Moral Philosophy*, ed. G. Sher, 5–15. San Diego, CA: Harcourt, Brace, Jovanovich.

Feldman, R. S., Meyer, J. S., & Quenzer, L. F. (1997). *Principles of Neuropsychopharmacology.* Sunderland, MA: Sinauer Associates, Inc.

Ferrara, S. D., Tedeschi, L., Frison, G., & Rossi, A. (1995). "Fatality Due to Gamma-hydroxybutyric Acid (GHB) and Heroin Intoxication." *Journal of Forensic Science* 40: 501–504.

Ferris, J. (2001). "Social Ramifications of Excessive Internet Use among College-age Males." *Journal of Technology and Culture* 20 (1): 44–53.

Fisher, H. (2004). *Why We Love: The Nature and Chemistry of Romantic Love.* New York: Henry Holt.

Fisher, L., & Feldman, S. (1998). "Familial Antecedents of Young Adult Health Risk Behaviors: A Longitudinal Study." *Journal of Family Psychology* 12: 66–80.

Flanagan, R. J., Ruprah, M., Meredith, T. J., Ramsey, J. D. (1990). "An Introduction to the Clinical Toxicology of Volatile Substances." *Drug Safety* 5: 359–383.

Fleming, M. F. & Maxwell, L. B. (1999). "Brief Intervention in Primary Care Settings: A Primary Treatment Method for At-risk, Problem, and Dependent Drinkers." *Alcohol Research and Health* 23 (2): 128–138.

Flier, J., & Maratos-Flier, E. (2007, September). "What Fuels Fat." *Scientific American* 297 (3): 72.

Ford, C. P., Mark, G. P., & Williams, J. T. (2006). "Properties and Opioid Inhibition of Mesolimbic Dopamine Neurons Vary According to Target Location." *The Journal of Neuroscience* 26: 2788–2797.

Fornazzari, L. (1988). "Clinical Recognition and Management of Solvent Abusers." *Internal Medicine for the Specialist* 9 (6): 2–7.

Fornazzari, L., Wilkinson, D. A., Kapur, B. M., Carlen, P. L. (1983). "Cerebellar Cortical and Functional Impairment in Toluene Abusers." *Acta Neurologica Scandinavica* 67: 319–329.

Foulds, J., Gandhi, K., Steinberg, M., Richardson, D., Williams, J., Burke, M., et al. (2006). "Factors Associated with Quitting Smoking at a Tobacco Dependence Treatment Clinic." *American Journal of Health Behavior* 30 (4): 400–412.

Frank, M. J., Scheres, A., & Sherman, S. J. (2007). "Understanding Decision-making Deficits in Neurological Conditions: Insights from Models of Natural Action Selection." *Philosophical Transactions of the Royal Society of London B: Biological Sciences* 362 (1485): 1641–1654.

Fredlund, E. V., Spence, R. T., Maxwell, J. C. (1989). "Substance Use among Students in Texas Secondary Schools, 1988." *Austin: Texas Commission on Alcohol and Drug Abuse.*

Fredrickson, B. L. (1998). "What Good Are Positive Emotions?" *Review of General Psychology* 2: 300–319.

Fredrickson, B. L. (2001). "The Role of Positive Emotions in Positive Psychology: The Broaden-and-build Theory of Positive Emotions." *American Psychologist* 56: 218–226.

Friedman, J., Westlake, R., & Furman, M. (1996). " 'Greivous Bodily Harm': Gamma Hydroxybutyrate Abuse Leading to the Wernicke-Korsakoff Syndrome." *Neurology* 46: 469–471.

Friedman, S. D., Christensen, P., & DeGroot, J. (1998). "Work and Life: The End of the Zero-sum Game." *Harvard Business Review* 76: 119–129.

Friedmann, P., Zhang, Z., Hendrickson, J., Stein, M., & Gerstein, D. (2003). "Effect of Primary Medical Care on Addiction and Medical Severity in

Substance Abuse Treatment Programs." *Journal of General Internal Medicine* 18: 1–8.

Fromme, K., Stroot, E., & Kaplan, D. (1993). "Comprehensive Effects of Alcohol: Development and Psychometric Assessment of a New Expectancy Questionnaire." *Psychological Assessment* 5: 19–26.

Gable, R. S. (2004). "Acute Toxic Effects of Club Drugs." *Journal of Psychoactive Drugs* 36: 303–313.

Gaher, R. M., & Simmons, J. S. (2007). "Evaluations and Expectancies of Alcohol and Marijuana Problems among College Students." *Psychology of Addictive Behaviors* 21: 545–554.

Gallimberti, L., Schifano, F., Forza, G., & Miconi, L. (1994). "Clinical Efficacy of Gamma-hydroxybutyric Acid in Treatment of Opiate Withdrawal." *European Archives of Psychiatry and Clinical Neuroscience* 244: 113–114.

Galloway, G. P., Frederick, S. L., Staggers, F. E., Gonzales, M., Stalcup, S. A., & Smith, D. E. (1997). "Gamma-hydroxybutyrate: An Emerging Drug of Abuse That Causes Physical Dependence." *Addiction* 92: 89–96.

Gardner, B., Rose, J., Mason, O., Tyler, P., & Cushway, D. (2005). "CognitiveTherapy and Behavioural Coping in the Management of Work-related Stress: An Intervention Study." *Work and Stress* 19 (2): 137–152.

Garrett, B. E., Griffiths, R. R. (1997). "The Role of Dopamine in the Behavioral Effects of Caffeine in Animals and Humans." *Pharmacology Biochemistry and Behavior* 57 (3): 533–541.

Gatley, S., Volkow, N., Wang, G., Fowler, J., Logan, J., Ding, Y., et al. (2005). "PET Imaging in Clinical Drug Abuse Research." *Curr Pharm Des* 11 (25): 3203–3219.

Genazzani, A. R., Nappi, G., Facchinetti, F., Mazzella, G. L., Parrini, D., Sinforiani, E., et al. (1982). "Central Deficiency of $-endophin in Alcohol Addicts." *Journal of Clinical Endocrinology and Metabolism* 55: 583–586.

Gilbert, D. G., Sharpe, J. P., Ramanaiah, N. V., Detwiler, F. R. J., & Anderson, A. E. (2000). "Development of a Situation x Trait Adaptive Response (STAR) Model-based Smoking Motivation Questionnaire." *Personality and Individual Differences* 29: 65–84.

Goldman, M. S., Del Boca, F. K., & Darkes, J. (1999). "Alcohol Expectancy Theory: The Application of Cognitive Neuroscience." In *Psychological Theories of Drinking and Alcoholism*, eds. K. E. Leonard & H. T. Blane. New York: Guilford.

Gillen, R. W., Kranzler, H. R., Bauer, L. B., Burleson, J. A., Samarel, D.& Morrison, D. J. (1998). "Neuropsychological Findings in Cocaine-dependent Outpatients." *Progress in Neuro-Psychopharmacology & Biological Psychiatry* 22: 1061–1076.

Gillis, A. (1993). "Determinants of a Health-promoting Lifestyle: An Integrative review." *Journal of Advanced Nursing* 18: 345–353.

Gillman, M.A., Lichtigfeld, F. J. (1998). "Clinical Role and Mechanisms of Action of Analgesic Nitrous Oxide." *International Journal of Neuroscience* 93 (1-2): 55–62.

Glasper, A., McDonough, M., & Bearn, J. (2005). "Within-patient Variability in Clinical Presentation of Gamma-hydroxybutyrate Withdrawal: A Case Report." *European Addiction Research* 11: 152–154.

Gold, M. S., & Jacobs, W. S. (2005). "Cocaine and Crack: Clinical Aspects." In *Substance Abuse: A Comprehensive Textbook*, eds. J. H. Lowinson, P. Ruiz, R. B. Millman, J. G. Langrod, 218–251. Philadelphia: Lippincott Williams & Wilkins.

Goldstein, R. Z., & Volkow, N. D. (2002). "Drug Addiction and Its Underlying Neurobiological Basis: Neuroimaging Evidence for the Involvement of the Frontal Cortex." *American Journal of Psychiatry* 159 (10): 1642–1652.

Gonzalez, A., & Nutt, D. J. (2005). "Gamma Hydroxyl Butyrate Abuse and Dependency." *Journal of Psychopharmacology* 19: 195–204.

Goode, E., Troiden, R. R. (1979). "Amyl Nitrite Use among Homosexual Men." *American Journal of Psychiatry* 136: 1067–1069.

Goodman, A. (1990). "Addiction: Definition and Implications." *British Journal of the Addictions* 85: 1403–1408.

Gorman, C. (2007, January 29). "A User's Guide to the Brain: Six Lessons for Handling Stress." *Time*, 80–85.

Gorman, J. (2002, July 20). "The Original Cocoa Treat: Chemistry Pushes Back First Use of the Drink." *Science News* 162 (3): 38.

Graham, A. W., Schultz, T. K., Mayo-Smith, M. F., Ries, R. K., Wilford, B. B. (Eds.). (2003). *Principles of Addiction Medicine* (3rd Ed.). Chevy Chase, MD: American Society of Addiction.

Grant, J. E., & Potenza, M. N. (2005). "Pathological Gambling and Other 'Behavioral' Addictions." In *Clinical Textbook of Addictive Disorders*, eds. R. J. Frances, S. I. Miller, & A. H. Mack. New York: Guilford.

Graves, L., Ruderman, M., & Ohlott, P J. (2006, August). "Effect of Workaholism on Managerial Performance: Help or Hindrance" Paper presented at the Academy of Management. Atlanta.

Greenberg, J. A., Dunbar, C. C., Schnoll, R., Kokolis, S., Kassotis, J. (2007). "Caffeinated Beverage Intake and the Risk of Heart Disease Mortality in the Elderly: A Protective Analysis." *American Journal of Clinical Nutrition* 85: 392–398.

Greenfield, D. (1999). *Virtual Addiction: Help for Netheads, Cyberfreaks, and Those Who Love Them*. Oakland, CA: New Harbinger Publication.

Griffiths, M. (1996). "Technological Addictions." *Clinical Psychology Forum* 76: 14–19.

Griffiths, M. (1990). "The Cognitive Psychology of Gambling." *Journal of Gambling Studies* 6: 31–42.

Gunzerath, L., Faden, V., Zakhari, S., & Warren, K. (2004). "Alcoholism: Clinical and Experimental Research." National Institute on Alcohol Abuse and Alcoholism Report on moderate drinking.

Hammer, H., Finkelhor, D., & Sedlak, A. J. (2002, October). "Children Abducted by Family Members: National Estimates and Characteristics." *National Incidence Studies of Missing, Abducted, Runaway, and Thrownaway Children.* U.S. Department of Justice. Retrieved from http://www.ncjrs.gov/pdffiles1/ojjdp/196466.pdf.

Hansen, S. (2002). "Excessive Internet Usage or 'Internet Addiction'? Diagnostic Categories for Student Users." *Journal of Computer Assisted Learning* 18 (2): 235–239.

Hucker, S.J. (2004). "Disorders of Impulse Control." In *Forensic Psychology*, eds. W. O'Donohue and E. Levensky. New York: Academic Press.

Harvard Mental Health Letter. (2004). *The Addicted Brain.* Retrieved March 1, 2008, from http://www.health.harvard.edu/newsweek/The_addicted_brain.htm.

Hatcher, S. (1994). "Debt and Deliberate Self-poisoning." *British Journal of Psychiatry* 164: 111–114.

Haverkos, H. W., Kopstein, A. N., Wilson, H., Drotman, P. (1994). "Nitrite Inhalants: History, Epidemiology, and Possible Links to AIDS." *Environmental Health Perspective* 102: 858–861.

He, X., & Baker, D. (2004). "Body Mass Index, Physical Activity, and the Risk of Decline in Overall Health and Physical Functioning in Late Middle Age." *Am J Public Health* 94 (9): 1567–1573.

HealthCentral.com. (2000). *WHO Accuses Tobacco Companies.* Retrieved March 10, 2008, from http://medicalnewstoday.com/articles/9706.php.

Hernandez, M., McDaniel, C. H., Costanza, C. D., & Hernandez, O. J. (1998). "GHB-induced Delirium: A Case Report and Review of the Literature on Gamma Hydroxybutyric Acid." *American Journal of Alcohol Abuse* 24: 179–183.

Hewlett, P., Smith, A. (2007). "Effects of Repeated Doses of Caffeine on Performance and Alertness: New Data and Secondary Analysis." *Human Psychopharmacology: Clinical & Experimental* 22: 339–350.

Hewlett, S. A., & Luce, C. B. (2006, December) "Extreme Jobs: The Dangerous Allure of the 70-hour Work Week." *Harvard Business Review*, 49–59.

Holbrook, M. B., & Hirschman, E. C. (1982). "The Experiential Aspects of Consumption: Consumer Fantasies, Feelings and Fun." *Journal of Consumer Research* 9: 132–140.

Holden, C. (2001). " 'Behavioral' Addictions: Do They Exist?" *Science* 294: 980–982.

Horner, M.D. (1997). "Cognitive Functioning in Alcoholic Patients with and without Cocaine Dependence." *Archives of Clinical Neuropsychology* 12: 667–676.

Hylton, H. (2008). *A Drug to End Drug Addiction*. Retrieved April 12, 2008, from http://www.time.com/time/health/article/0,8599,1701864,00.html.

Interlandi, J. (2008, March 3). "What Addicts Need." *Newsweek*, 36–43.

Jackson, S. A. & Marsh, H. W. (1996). "Development and Validation of a Scale to Measure Optimal Experience: The Flow State Scale." *Journal of Sport and Exercise Psychology* 18: 17–35.

Jackson, T. (2006). "Relationships between Perceived Close Social Support and Health Practices within Community Samples of American Women and Men." *Journal of Psychology* 140 (3): 229–246.

Jacobs, D.F. (1986). "A General Theory of Addictions: A New Theoretical Model." *Journal of Gambling Behavior* 2: 15–31.

James, G., Gold, M., & Liu, Y. (2004). "Interaction of Satiety and Reward Response to Food Stimulation. *J Addict Dis* 23 (3): 23–37.

James, G., Guo, W., & Liu, Y. (2001). "Imaging in vivo Brain-hormone Interaction in the Control of Eating and Obesity." *Diabetes Technol Ther* 3 (4): 617–622.

James, J. E. (2005). "Caffeine-induced Enhancement of Cognitive Performance: Confounding Due to Reversal of Withdrawal Effects." *Australian Journal of Psychology* 57 (3): 197–200.

Jang, K. L., Lively, W. J., & Vernon, P. A. (1996). "Heritability of the Big Five Personality Dimensions and Their Facets: A Twin Study." *Journal of Personality* 64: 577–591.

Jayanthi, L. D., & Ramamoorthy, S. (2005). "Regulation of Monoamine Transporters: Influence of Psychostimulants and Therapeutic Antidepressants." *The AAPS Journal* 27: 728–738.

Johnson, B. A., Dawes, M. A., Roache, J. D., Wells, L. T., Ait-Daoud, N., Mauldin, J. B., et al. (2005). "Acute Intravenous Low- and High-dose Cocaine Reduce Quantitative Global and Regional Cerebral Blood Flow in Recently Abstinent Subjects with Cocaine Use Disorder." *Journal of Cerebral Blood Flow & Metabolism* 25: 928–936.

Johnston, L. D., O'Malley, P. M., Bachman, J. G., Schulenberg, J. E. (2006). "Monitoring the Future National Results on Adolescent Drug Use: Overview of Key Findings." NIH, National Institute on Drug Abuse, Bethesda, MD.

Johnstone, A., & Johnston, L. (2005) "The Relationship between Organizational Climate, Occupational Type and Workaholism." *New Zealand Journal of Psychology* 34: 181–188.

Jones, B. T., & McMahon, J. (1994). "Negative and Positive Alcohol Expectancies and Predictors of Abstinence after Discharge from a Residential Treatment Program: A One-month and Three-month Follow-up Study in Men." *Journal of Studies on Alcohol* 55: 543–548.

Jones, E., Knutson, D., & Haines, D. (2003). "Common Problems in Patients Recovering from Chemical Dependency. *American Family Physician* 68 (10): 1971–1978.

Jordan, C. H., Spencer, S. J., Zanna, M. P., Hoshino-Browne, E., & Correll, J. (2003). "Secure and Defensive High Self-esteem." *Journal of Personality and Social Psychology* 85: 969–978.

Juliano, L. M., Griffiths, R. R. (2004). "A Critical Review of Caffeine Withdrawal: Empirical Validation of Symptoms and Signs, Incidence, Severity, and Associated Features." *Psychopharmacology* 176: 1–29.

Julien, R. M. (2005). *A Primer of Drug Action: A Comprehensive Guide to the Actions, Uses, and Side Effects of Psychoactive Drugs* (10th Edition). New York: Worth Publishers.

Kalechstein, A. D., Newton, T. F., & Green, M. (2003). "Methamphetamine Dependence Is Associated with Neurocognitive Impairment in the Initial Phases of Abstinence." *The Journal of Neuropsychiatry and Clinical Neurosciences* 15: 215–220.

Kanai, A., Wakabayashi, M., & Fling, S. (1996). "Workaholism among Employees in Japanese Corporations: An Examination Based on the Japanese Version of the Workaholism Scales." *Japanese Psychological Research* 38: 192–203.

Kawabata, T., Cross, D., Nishioka, N., & Shimai, S. (1999). "Relationship between Self-esteem and Smoking Behavior among Japanese Early Adolescents: Initial Results from a Three-year Study." *Journal of School Health* 69 (7): 280–284.

Keath J. R., Iacoviello M. P., Barrett L. E., Mansvelder H .D., & McGehee D. S. (2007). "Differential Modulation by Nicotine of Substantia Nigra Versus Ventral Tegmental Area Dopamine Neurons." *Journal of Neurophysiology* 98: 3388–3396.

Keepers, G. A. (1990). "Pathological Preoccupation with Video Games." *Journal of the American Academy of Child and Adolescent Psychiatry* 29 (1): 49–50.

Kemmel, V., Taleb, O., Perard, A., Andriamampandry, C., Siffert, J. C., Mark, J., & Maitre, M. (1998). "Neurochemical and Electrophysiological Evidence for the Existence of a Functional Gamma-hydroxybutyrate System in NCB-20 Neurons." *Neuroscience* 86: 989–1000.

Kessler, R., Nelson, C., McGonagle, K., Edlund, M., Frank, R., & Leaf, P. (1996). "The Epidemiology of Co-occurring Addictive and Mental Disorders: Implications for Prevention and Service Utilization." *Annuals of Orthopsychiatry* 66: 17–31.

Killinger, B. (1991). *Workaholics: The Respectable Addicts*. New York: Simon & Schuster.

Kim, J., & Garman, E. T. (2003). "Financial Stress and Absenteeism: An Empirically Derived Model." *Financial Counseling and Planning* 14: 31–42.

Knight, A. (1995). *Long Hours Culture*. London: Austin Knight.

Knutson, B., Rick, S., Wimmer, G. E., Prelec, D., & Loewenstein, G. (2007). "Neural Predictors of Purchases." *Neuron* 53: 147–156.

Knutson, B., Wimmer, G. E., Kuhnen, C., & Winkelman, P. (2008, March). "Nucleus Accumbens Activation Mediates the Influence of Reward Cues on Financial Risk Taking." *NeuroReport* 19 (5): 509–513.

Kohlberg, L. (1984). *The Psychology of Moral Development: Essays on Moral Development* (Vol. 2). San Francisco: Harper and Row.

Kohlberg, L., & Candee, D. (1981, December 17–19). *The Relationship of Moral Judgment to Moral Action*. Paper presented at the Florida International University conference on Morality and Moral Development, Miami Beach.

Konrad, K., Neufang, S., Thiel, C. M., Specht, K., Hanisch, C., Fan, J., et al. (2005). "Development of Attentional Networks: An fMRI Study with Children and Adults." *Neuroimage* 28 (2): 429–439.

Koob, G. H., Ahmed, S. H., Boutrel, B., Chen, S. A., Kenny, P. J, Markou, A., et al. (2004). "Neurobiological Mechanisms in the Transition from Drug Use to Drug Dependence." *Neuroscience and Biobehavioral Reviews* 27: 739–749.

Koran, L. M., Faber, R. J., Aboujaoude, E., Large, M. D., & Serpe, R. T. (2006). "Estimated Prevalence of Compulsive Buying Behavior in the United States." *American Journal of Psychiatry* 163: 1806–1812.

Kosten, T. (2005). "What are America's Opportunities for Harm Reduction Strategies in Opiate Dependence?" *American Journal of Addictions* 14: 307–310.

Kruger, A. (1996). "Chronic Psychiatric Patients' Use of Caffeine: Pharmacological Effects and Mechanisms." *Psychological Reports* 78: 915–923.

Kubey, R., (2009). "Adddiction to Pornography: Its Psychological and Behavioral Implications." In Vol. 4 of *Praeger International Collection on Addictions*, ed. A. Browne-Miller, 183–216. Santa Barbara, CA: Praeger.

Kyrios, M., Frost, R. O., & Steketee, G. (2004). "Cognitions in Compulsive Buying and Acquisition." *Cognitive Therapy and Research* 28: 241–258.

Ladd, G., & Petry, N. M. (2002). "Gender Differences among Pathological Gamblers Seeking Treatment." *Experimental and Clinical Psychopharmacology* 10: 302–309.

Laforge, R. G., Maddock, J.E., & Rossi, J. S. (1998). "Comparison of Five Stage Methods for Alcohol Abuse among College Students." *Annals of Behavioral Medicine* 20: 170 (Abstract).

Larimer, M. E., Palmer, R. S., & Marlatt, G. A. (1999). "Relapse Prevention: An Overview of Marlatt's Cognitive-behavioral Model." *Alcohol Research & Health* 23: 151–160.

Lejoyeux, M., Mathieu, K., Embouazza, H., Huet, F., & Lequen, V. (2007). "Prevalence of Compulsive Buying among Customers of a Parisian General Store." *Comprehensive Psychiatry* 48: 42–46.

Leonard, K. (2000). "Domestic Violence and Alcohol—What is Known and What Do We Need to Know to Encourage Environmental Interventions." In commissioned papers, Alcohol Policy XII Conference: Alcohol and Crime, Research and Practice for Prevention, 69–91. Washington, DC: National Crime Prevention Council.

Lesieur, H. R., & Blume, S. B. (1993). "Pathological Gambling, Eating Disorders, and the Psychoactive Substance Use Disorders." *Comorbidity of Addictive and Psychiatric Disorders*, 89–102.

Levinthal, C. F. (2006). *Drugs, Behavior, and Modern Society*. Boston: Allyn and Bacon.

Levy, S. (1997, Dec.30/Jan. 6). "Breathing is Also Addictive." *Newsweek*, 52–53.

Lezak, M.D. (1995). "Alcohol Related Disorders." *Neuropsychological Assessment* (3rd Ed.), 246–258.

Liu, N., Li, B., Sun, N., & Ma, Y. (2008). "Effects of Addiction-associated and Affective Stimuli on the Attentional Blink in a Sample of Abstinent Opiate Dependent Patients." *Journal of Psychopharmacology* 22 (1): 64–70.

Lopreato, G. F., Phelan, R., Borghese, C. M., Beckstead, M. J., Mihic, S. J. (2003). "Inhaled Drugs of Abuse Enhance Serotonin-3 Receptor Function." *Drug and Alcohol Dependence* 70: 11–15.

Loring, M. T. (1998). *Emotional Abuse: The Trauma and Treatment*. San Francisco: Jossey Bass.

Mandel, H. G. (2002). "Update on Caffeine Consumption, Disposition and Action." *Food and Toxicology* 40: 1231–1234.

Lubman, D. I., Yucel, M., & Pantelis, C. (2004). "Addiction, a Condition of Compulsive Behaviour? Neuroimaging and Neuropsychological Evidence of Inhibitory Dysregulation." *Addiction* 99 (12): 1491–1502.

Lyubormirsky, S. L., King, L., & Diener, E. (2005). "The Benefits of Frequent Positive Affect: Does Happiness Lead to Success?" *Psychological Bulletin* 131: 803–855.

Machlowitz, M. (1980). *Workaholics: Living with Them, Working with Them*. Reading, MA: Addison-Wesley.

MacLeod, C. M. (1991). "Half a Century of Research on the Stroop Effect: An Integrative Review." *Psychological Bulletin* 109 (2): 163–203.

Margolis, E. B., Lock, H., Chefer, V. I., Shippenberg, T. S., Hjelmstad, G. O., & Fields, H. L. (2006). "Kappa Opioids Selectively Control Dopaminergic Neurons Projecting to the Prefrontal Cortex." *Proceedings of the National Academy of Sciences of the United States of America* 103: 2938–2942.

Martinelli, A. (1999). "An Explanatory Model of Variables Influencing Health Promotion Behaviors in Smoking and Nonsmoking College Students." *Public Health Nursing* 16 (4): 263–269.

Marlatt, G. A., & Donovan, D. M. (Eds.). (2005). *Relapse Prevention: Maintenance Strategies in the Treatment of Addictive Behaviors* (2nd Ed.). New York: Guilford.

Mathews-Larson, J. (1991). *Seven Weeks to Sobriety*. New York: Villard Books.

McClure, S. M., Ericson, K. M., Laibson, D. I., Loewenstein, G., & Cohen, J. D. (2007). "Time Discounting for Primary Rewards." *Journal of Neuroscience* 27 (21): 5796–5804.

McClure, S. M., Laibson, D. I., Loewenstein, G., & Cohen, J. D. (2004). "Separate Neural Systems Value Immediate and Delayed Monetary Rewards." *Science* 306 (5695): 503–507.

McDonough, M., Kennedy, N., Glasper, A., & Bearn, J. (2004). "Clinical Features and Management of Gamma-hydroxybutyrate (GHB) Withdrawal: A Review." *Drug and Alcohol Dependence* 75: 3–9.

McHugh, M. J. (1987). "The Abuse of Volatile Substances." *Pediatric Clinics of North America* 34: 333–340.

McMillan, L. H. W., & O'Driscoll, M.P. (2007). "Exploring New Frontiers to Generate an Integrated Definition of Workaholism." In *Research Companion to Working Hours and Work Addiction*, ed. R.J. Burke, 89–107. Cheltenham: Edward Elgar.

McMillan, L. H. W., O'Driscoll, M.P., & Burke, R. J. (2003). "Workaholism in Organizations: A Review of Theory, Research and Future Directions." In *International Review of Industrial and Organizational Psychology*, eds. C. L. Cooper & I. T. Robertson, 167–190. New York: John Wiley.

McMillan, L. W. H., O'Driscoll, M. P., Marsh, N. V., & Brady, E. C. (2001). "Understanding Workaholism: Data synthesis, Theoretical Critique, and Future Design Strategies." *International Journal of Stress Management* 8: 69–92.

Meadows, R., Verghese, A. (1996). "Medical Complications of Glue Sniffing." *Southern Medical Journal* 89 (5): 455–462.

Meyers, Hannah. (2005, March 7). "Suave Molecules of Mocha: Coffee, Chemistry, and Civilization." *New Partiisan*. Retrieved May 7, 2008, from http://www.newpartisan.com/home/suave-molecules-of-mocha-coffee-chemistry-and-civilization.html.

Miller, E. K., & Cohen, J. D. (2001). "An Integrative Theory of Prefrontal Cortex Function." *Annual Review of Neuroscience* 24: 167–202.

Miller, N. S., & Gold, M. S. (1988). "The Human Sexual Response and Alcohol and Drugs." *Journal of Substance Abuse Treatment* 5: 171–177.

Mills, R. J., Grasmick, H. G., Morgan, C. S. & Wenk, D. (1992). "The Effects of Gender, Family Satisfaction, and Economic Strain on Psychological Well-being." *Family Relations* 41: 440–445.

Mitchell, J. M., Tavares, V. C., Fields, H. L., D'Esposito, M., & Boettiger, C. A. (2007). "Endogenous Opioid Blockade and Impulsive Responding in Alcoholics and Healthy Controls." *Neuropsychopharmacology*, 32 (2): 439–449.

Moos, R. H., Fenn, C. B., Billings, A. G., & Moos, B. S. (1989). "Assessing Life Stressors and Social Resources: Applications for Alcoholic Patients." *Journal of Substance Abuse* 1: 135–152.

Morabia, A., & Costanza, M. (2004). "Does Walking 15 Minutes Per Day Keep the Obesity Epidemic Away? Simulation of the Efficacy of a Populationwide Campaign." *Am J Public Health* 94 (3): 437–440.

Munafò, M., & Albery, I. P. (Eds.). (2006). *Cognition Addiction*. Oxford, UK: Oxford University Press.

Muralidharan, K., Rajkumar, R. P., Mulla, U., Kayak, R. B., Benegal, V. (2008). "Baclofen in the Management of Inhalant Withdrawal: A Case Series." *Primary Care Companion Journal of Clinical Psychiatry* 10 (1): 48–51.

Murphey, B. (1996, June). "Computer Addictions Entangle Students." *The APA Monitor*, p. 38.

Nace, E. P. (2007). *Patients with Substance Abuse Problems: Effective Identification, Diagnosis, and Treatment*. New York: W.W. Norton and Company.

Nash, L., Stevenson, H. (2004). *Just Enough: Tools for Creating Success in Your Work and Life*. New York: John Wiley.

National Institute of Mental Health. (2006). "NIMH, the Numbers Count." National Institutes of Health. Retrieved March 4, 2007, from http://nimh.nih.gov/publicat/numbers.cfm.

National Institute on Drug Abuse. (1999). *InfoFacts—Workplace Trends*. Retrieved January 6, 2007, from www.nida.nih.gov/infofacts/work place.html.

Naughton, T. J. (1987). "A Conceptual View of Workaholism and Implications for Career Counseling and Research." *Career Development Quarterly* 14: 180–187.

Ng, T. W. H., Sorensen, K. L., Feldman, D. C. (2007). "Dimensions, Antecedents, and Consequences of Workaholism: A Conceptual Integration and Extension." *Journal of Organizational Behavior* 28: 111–136.

Nestler, E. J. (2005, December). "The Neurobiology of Cocaine Addiction." *Science & Practice Perspectives*, 4–11.

Neuner, M., Raab, G., & Reisch, L. A. (2005). "Compulsive Buying in Maturing Consumer Societies: An Empirical Re-inquiry." *Journal of Economic Psychology* 26: 509–522.

Newell, G. R., Spitz, M. R., Wilson, M. B. (1988). "Nitrite Inhalants: Historical Perspective." *National Institute on Drug Abuse Research Monogram Series* 83: 1–14.

Nicholson, K. L., & Balster, R. L. (2001). GHB: "A New and Novel Drug of Abuse." *Drug and Alcohol Dependence* 63: 1–22.

Nigg, C. R., Burbank, P., Padula, C., Dufresne, R., Rossi, J. S., Velicer, W. F., Laforge, R. G., & Prochaska, J. O. (1999). "Stages of Change across Ten Health Risk Behaviors for Older Adults." *The Gerontologist* 39: 473–482.

Nordahl, T. E., Salo, R., & Leamon, M. (2003). "Neuropsychological Effects of Chronic Methamphetamine Use on Neurotransmitters and Cognition: A Review." *The Journal of Neuropsychiatry and Clinical Neurosciences* 15: 317–325.

Nordahl, T. E., Salo, R., Natsuaki, Y., Galloway, G. P., Watres, C., & Moore, C. D. (2005). "Methamphetamine Users in Sustained Abstinence: A Proton Magnetic Resonance Spectroscopy Study." *Archives of General Psychiatry* 62: 444–452.

O'Guinn, T. C., & Faber, R. J. (1989). "Compulsive Buying: A Phenomenological Exploration." *Journal of Consumer Research* 16: 147–157.

O'Neill, B., Sorhaindo, B., Xiao, J. J., & Garman, E. T. (2005). "Financially Distressed Consumers: Their Financial Practices, Financial Well-being, and Health." *Financial Counseling and Planning* 16: 73–87.

Orzack, M. (1999). "Computer Addiction: Is It Real or Is It Virtual?" *Harvard Mental Health Letter* 15 (7): 8.

Ostlund, S. B., & Balleine, B. W. (2007). "The Contribution of Orbitofrontal Cortex to Action Selection." *Annals of the New York Academy of Sciences* 1121: 174–192.

Padilla, E. R., Padilla, A. M., Morales, A., Olmedo, E. L., Ramirez, R. (1979). "Inhalant, Marijuana, and Alcohol Abuse among Barrio Children and Adolescents." *International Journal of the Addictions* 14 (7): 945–964.

Parazzini, F., Chiaffarino, F., Chatenoud, L., Tozzi, L., Cipriani, S., Chiantera, V., & Fedele, L. (2005). "Maternal Coffee Drinking in Pregnancy and Risk of Small for Gestational Age Birth." *European Journal of Clinical Nutrition* 59: 299–301.

Parsons, O. A. (1996). "Alcohol Abuse and Alcoholism." *Neuropsychoology for Clinical Practice; Etiology, Assessment and Treatment of Common Neurological Disorders* 6: 175–184.

Paton, C., & Beer, D. (2001). "Caffeine: The Forgotten Variable." *International Journal of Psychiatry in Clinical Practice* 5: 231–236.

Peele, S. (1995). *Diseasing of America: How We Allowed Recovery Zealots and the Treatment Industry to Convince Us We Are Out of Control.* New York: Jossey-Bass.

Peele, S., & Brodsky, A. (1979). *Love and Addiction*, p. 72. Scarborough, Ontario: New American Library of Canada.

Pelchat, M., Johnson, A., Chan, R., Valdez, J., & Ragland, J. (2004). "Images of Desire: Food-craving Activation during fMRI." *Neuroimage* 23 (4): 1486–1493.

Perkins, H. W. (2003). "The Emergence and Evolution of the Social Norms Approach to Substance Abuse Prevention." In *The Social Norms Approach* to *Preventing School and College Age Substance Abuse: A Handbook for Educators, Counselors, and Clinicans*, ed. H. W. Perkins. San Francisco: Wiley.

Perkins, H. W., Haines, M. P., & Rice, R. (2005). "Misperceiving the College Drinking Norm and Related Problems: A Nationwide Study of Exposure to Prevention Information, Perceived Norms, and Student Alcohol Misuse." *Journal of Studies on Alcohol* 66: 470–478.

Perkins, H. W., Meilman, P. W., Leichliter, J. S., Cashin, J. R., & Presley, C.A. (1999). "Misperceptions of the Norms for Frequency of Alcohol and Other Drug Use on College Campuses." *Journal of American College Health*47: 253–258.

Petry, N. (2006). "Internet Gambling: An Emerging Concern in Family Practice Medicine?" *Family Practice* 23 (4): 421–426.

Petry, N. M. (2005). "Stages of Change in Treatment-seeking Pathological Gamblers." *Journal of Consulting and Clinical Psychology* 73: 312–322.

Pineles, S. L., Street, A. E., & Koenen, K. C. (2006). "The Differential Relationships of Shame-proneness and Guilt-proneness to Psychological and Somatization Symptoms." *Journal of Social and Clinical Psychology* 25: 688–704.

Porter, G. (1996). "Organizational Impact of Workaholism: Suggestions for Researching the Negative Outcomes of Excessive Work." *Journal of Occupational Health Psychology* 1: 70–84.

Prochaska, J.O., Velcier, W.F., Rossi, J.S., et al. (1994). "Stages of Change and Decisional Balance for Twelve Problem Behaviors." *Health Psychology* 13: 39–46.

Prochaska, J. O., & Norcross, J. C. (2007). *Systems of Psychotherapy: A Transtheoretical Analysis*. Belmont, CA: Thomson Brooks/Cole.

Prochaska, J. O., DiClemente, C. C., & Norcross, J. C. (1992). "In Search of How People Change: Applications to Addictive Behaviors." *American Psychologist*47: 1102–1114.

Prochaska, J. O., Velicer, W. F., Rossi, J. S., Goldstein, M. G., Marcus, B. H., Rakowski, W., et al. (1994). "Stages of Change and Decisional Balance for 12 Problem Behaviors." *Health Psychology*13: 39–46.

Rachlin, H. (1990). "Why Do People Gamble and Keep Gambling Despite Heavy Losses?" *Psychological Science*1: 294–297.

Raylu, N., & Oei, T. P. S. (2004). "The Gambling Related Cognitions Scale (GRCS): Development, Confirmatory Factor Validation and Psychometric Properties." *Addiction* 99: 757–769.

Reidel, S., Hebert, T., Bird, P. (1995). "Inhalant Abuse: Confronting the Growing Challenge." In *Treating Alcohol and Other Drug Abusers in Rural and Frontier Areas; Technical Assistance Publication Series #17*. Center for Substance Abuse Treatment: Rockville, MD.

Rennison, C. M., & Welchans, S. (2000, May). *Intimate Partner Violence. Bureau of Justice Statistics Special Report* NCJ 178247. Washington, DC: U.S. Department of Justice.

Reynolds, B. (2006). "A Review of Delay-discounting Research with Humans: Relations to Drug Use and Gambling." *Behavioral Pharmacology* 17 (8): 651–667.

Rindfleisch, A., Burroughs, J. E., & Denton, F. (1997). "Family Structure, Materialism, and Compulsive Consumption." *Journal of Consumer Research* 23: 312–325.

Rippeth, D. J., Heaton, K. R., Carey, L. C., Marcotte, D. T., Moore J. D., González R., et al. (2004). "Methamphetamine Dependence Increases Risk of Neuropsychological Imparment in HIV Infected Persons." *Journal of the International Neuropsychological Society: JINS* 10: 1–14.

Rivara, F. P., Mueller, B. A., Somes, G., Mendoza , C. T., Rushforth, N. B., & Kellerman, A. L. (1997). "Alcohol and Illicit Drug Abuse and the Risk of Violent Death in the Home." *Journal of the American Medical Association* 278: 569–575.

Robinson, B. E. (1998). *Chained to the Desk: A Guidebook for Workaholics, Their Partners and Children and the Clinicians Who Treat Them*. New York: New York University Press.

Robinson, T. E., & Berridge, K. C. (2003). "Addiction." *Annual Review of Psychology* 54: 25–53.

Roffman, R. A., & Stephens, R. S. (2005). "Relapse Prevention for Cannabis Abuse and Dependence." In *Relapse Prevention: Maintenance Strategies in the Treatment of Addictive Behaviors*, eds. G. A. Marlatt & D. M. Donovan. New York: Guilford.

Rogers, P. J., Martin, J., Smith, C., Heatherley, S. V., Smit, H. J. (2003). "Absence of Reinforcing, Mood and Psychomotor Performance Effects of Caffeine in Habitual Non-consumers of Caffeine." *Psychopharmacology* (Berlin) 167: 54–62.

Rogers, P. J., Smith, J. E., Heatherley, S. V., Pleydell-Pearce, C. W. (2008). "Time for Tea: Mood, Blood Pressure and Cognitive Performance Effects of Caffeine and Theanine Administered Alone and Together." *Psychopharmacology* 195: 569–577.

Rogers, R. D., Everitt, B. J., Baldacchino, A., Blackshaw, A. J., Swainson, R., Wynne, K., et al. (1999). "Dissociable Deficits in the Decision-making Cognition of Chronic Amphetamine Abusers, Opiate Abusers, Patients with Focal Damage to Prefrontal Cortex, and Tryptophan-depleted Normal Volunteers: Evidence for Monoaminergic Mechanisms." *Neuropsychopharmacology* 20 (4): 322339.

Rogers, R. D., & Robbins, T. W. (2001). "Investigating the Neurocognitive Deficits Associated with Chronic Drug Misuse." *Current Opinion in Neurobiology* 11: 250–257.

Ron, M. A. (1986). "Volatile Substance Abuse: A Review of Possible Long-Term Neurological, Intellectual, and Psychiatric Sequelae." *British Journal of Psychiatry* 148: 235–246.

Rook, D. W. (1987). "The Buying Impulse." *Journal of Consumer Research* 14: 189–199.

Rook, D. W., & Fisher, R. J. (1995). "Normative Influences on Impulsive Buying Behavior." *Journal of Consumer Research* 22: 305–313.

Rose, P. & DeJesus, S. (2007). "A Model of Motivated Cognition to Account for the Link between Self-monitoring and Materialism." *Psychology and Marketing* 24: 93–115.

Rose, P. (2002). "The Happy and Unhappy Faces of Narcissism." *Personality and Individual Differences* 33: 379–392.

Rose, P. (2007). "Mediators of the Association between Narcissism and Compulsive Buying: The Roles of Materialism and Impulse Control." *Psychology of Addictive Behaviors* 21: 576–581.

Rose, P. and Segrist, D. "Excessive Buying as a Genuine Addictive Behavior." In Vol. 4 of *Praeger International Collection on Addictions*, ed. A. Browne-Miller, 81–96. Santa Barbara, CA: Praeger..

Rosenthal, R. N., & Solhkhah, R. (2005). "Club Drugs." In *Clinical Manual of Addiction Psychopharmacology*, eds. D. A. Ciraulo, & H. R. Kranzler, 243–267. Washington DC: American Psychological Publishing.

Rosselli, M., & Ardilla, A. (1996). "Cognitive Effects of Cocaine and Polydrug Abuse." *Journal of Clinical and Experimental Neuropsychology* 18: 122–135.

Rosselli, M., Ardila, A., Lubomski, M., Murray, S., & King, K. (2001). "Personality Profile and Neuropsychological Test Performance in Chronic Cocaine-abusers." *The International Journal of Neuroscience* 110: 55–72.

Rotter, J. B. (1966). "Generalized Expectancies for Internal Versus External Control of Reinforcement." *Psychological Monographs* 80 (1): 1–28.

Ruiz, A., Barrera, H., Jackson, N. "Craving Pizza? This is Your Brain on Drugs: Eating Disorders as Addiction." In Vol. 4 of *Praeger International Collection on Addictions*, ed. A. Browne-Miller, 163–164. Santa Barbara, CA: Praeger.

SAMSHA. (2007). "The Surgeon General's Call to Action to Prevent and Reduce Underage Drinking." *Surgeongeneral.gov*. Retrieved on February 27, 2008.

Savitz, D. A., Chan, R. L., Herring, A. H., Howards, P. P., Hartmann, K. E. (2008). "Caffeine and Miscarriage Risk." *Epidemiology*. 19 (1): 55–62.

Sawnock, J. (1995). "Pharmacological Rationale for the Clinical Use of Caffeine." *Drugs* 49: 37–50.

Scaer, R. (2005). *The Trauma Spectrum: Hidden Wounds and Human Resiliency*. New York: W.W. Norton and Company.

Schafer, J., & Brown, S.A. (1991). "Marijuana and Cocaine Effect Expectancies and Drug Use Patterns." *Journal of Consulting and Clinical Psychology* 59: 558–565.

Schaufeli, W. B., Taris, T. W., & Bakker, A. B. (2008). "It Takes Two to Tango: Workaholism is Working Excessively and Working

Compulsively." In *The Long Work Hours Culture: Causes, Consequences and Choices*, eds. R. J. Burke & C. L. Cooper. . London: Elsevier.

Schaufeli, W. B., Taris, T. W., & Bakker, A. B. (2007). "Dr. Jekyll or Mr. Hyde: On the Difference between Work engagement and Workaholism." In *Research Companion to Working Time and Work Addiction*, ed. R. J. Burke, 193–220. Cheltenham, UK: Edward Elgar.

Scherhorn. G., Reisch, L. A., & Raab, G. (1990). "Addictive Buying in West Germany: An Empirical Study." *Journal of Consumer Policy* 13: 355–387.

Schuckit, M. A. (2000). *Drug Alcohol Abuse. A Clinical Guide to Diagnosis and Treatment*. New York: Kluwer Academic/Plenum Publishers.

Schuman, A., Christian, M., Rumpf, H.J., Hanover, W., Hapke, U., & John, U. (2005). "Stages of Change Transitions and Processes of Change, Decisional Balance, and Self-efficacy in Smokers: A Transtheoretical Model Validation Using Longitudinal Data." *Psychology of Addictive Behaviors* 19: 3–9.

Schweighofer, N., Bertin, M., Shishida, K., Okamoto, Y., Tanaka, S. C., Yamawaki, S., et al. (2008). "Low-Serotonin Levels Increase Delayed Reward Discounting in Humans." *Journal of Neuroscience* 28 (17): 4528–4532.

Scott, K. S., Moore, K. S., & Miceli, M. P. (1997). "An Exploration of the Meaning and Consequences of Workaholism."*Human Relations* 50: 287–314.

Sekine, Y., Minabe, Y., Ouchi, Y., Takei, N., Iyo, M., Nakamura, K., et al. (2003). "Association of Dopamine Transporter Loss in the Orbitofrontal and Dorsolateral Prefrontal Cortices with Methamphetamine-related Psychiatric Symptoms." *The American Journal of Psychiatry* 160: 1699–701.

Serper, M. R., Bergman, A., Copersino, M. L., Chou, J. C. Y., Richarme, D. & Cancro, R. (2000). "Learning and Memory Impairment in Cocaine-dependent and Comorbid Schizophrenic Patients." *Psychiatric Research* 93: 21–32.

Shaffer, H. J. (1996). "Understanding the Means and Objects of Addiction: Technology, the Internet, and Gambling." *Journal of Gambling Studies* 12: 461–469.

Shaffer, H. J., & Freed, C. R. (2005). "Assessment of Gambling-related Disorders." In *Assessment of Addictive Behaviors*, eds. G. A. Marlatt & D. M. Donovan. New York: Guilford.

Shaffer, H. J., & LaPlante, D.A. (2005). "Treatment of Gambling Disorders." In *Relapse Prevention: Maintenance Strategies in the Treatment of Addictive Behaviors*, eds. G. A. Marlatt & D. M. Donovan. New York: Guilford.

Shah, R., Vankar, G. K., Upadhyaya, H. P. (1999). "Phenomenology of Gasoline Intoxication and Withdrawal Symptoms among Adolescents in India: A Case Series." *The American Journal on Addictions* 8: 254–257.

Shapira, N. A., Lessig, M. C., Goldsmith, T. D., Szabo, S. T., Lazoritz, M., Gold, M. S., & Stein, D. J. (2003). "Problematic Internet Use: Proposed Classification and Diagnostic Criteria." *Depression and Anxiety* 17: 207–216.

Sharp, C. W., Rosenberg, N. L. (1997). *Substance Abuse: A Comprehensive Textbook*. Baltimore, MD: Williams & Wilkins.

Shen, Y. (2007). "Treatment of Inhalant Dependence with Lamotrigine." *Progress in Neuro-Psychopharmacology & Biological Psychiatry* 31: 769–771.

Shizgal, P., & Arvanitogiannis, A. (2003). "Gambling on Dopamine." *Science* 299: 1856–1858.

Shotton, M. (1991). "The Costs and Benefits of 'Computer Addiction'" *Behaviour and Information Technology* 10 (3): 219–230.

Siahpush, M., Borland, R., & Scollo, M. (2003). "Smoking and Financial Stress." *Tobacco Control* 12: 60–66.

Simon, L. (2003). *Psychology, Psychotherapy, Psychoanalysis, and the Politics of Human Relationships*. Portsmouth, NH: Praeger.

Simon, S. L., Domier, C., Carnell, J., Brethen, P., Rawson, R., & Ling, W. (2000). "Cognitive Impairment in Individuals Currently Using Methamphetamine." *The American Journal on Addictions* 9: 222–231.

Smith, A., Sutherland, D., Christopher, G. (2005). "Effects of Repeated Doses of Caffeine on Mood and Performance of Alert and Fatigued Volunteers." *Journal of Psychopharmacology* 19: 620–626.

Smith, G. T., & Goldman, M. S. (1994). "Alcohol Expectancy Theory and the Identification of High-risk Adolescents." *Journal of Research on Adolescence* 4: 229–247.

Soderberg, L. S., Chang, L. W., Barnett, J. B. (1996). "Elevated TNF-alpha and Inducible Nitric Oxide Production by Alveolar Macrophages after Exposure to a Nitrite nhalant." *Journal of Leukocyte Biology* 60 (4): 459–464.

Spence, J. T., & Robbins, A. S. (1992). "Workaholism: Definition, Measurement, and Preliminary Results." *Journal of Personality Assessment* 58: 160–178.

Spiegel, A., Nabel, E., Volkow, N., Landis, S., & Li, T. (2005). "Obesity on the Brain." *Nat Neurosci* 8 (5): 552–553.

Spinella, M. (2004). "Neurobehavioral Correlates of Impulsivity: Evidence of Prefrontal Involvement." *International Journal of Neuroscience* 114: 95–104.

Srivastava, A., Locke, E. A., & Bartol, K M. (2001). "Money and Subjective Well-being: It's Not the money, It's the Motives." *Journal of Personality and Social Psychology* 80: 959–971.

Steffensen, S. C., Stobbs, S. H., Colago, E. E., Lee, R. S., Koob, G. F., Gallegos, R. A., et al. (2006). "Contingent and Non-contingent Effects of Heroin on Mu-opioid Receptor-containing Ventral Tegmental Area GABA Neurons." *Experimental Neurology* 202: 139–151.

Stone, J. C. I. (2002). "Compulsive Buying: Review and Relevance to Consumer Debt Management." *Dissertation Abstracts International: Section B: The Sciences and Engineering* 62: 3839. Abstract obtained from PsycINFO, 2003.

Strickland, T. L., Mena, I., Villanueva-Meyer, J., Miller, B. L., Cummings, J., Mehringer, C. M., et al. (1993). "Cerebral Perfusion and Neuropsychological Consequences of Chronic Cocaine Use." *The Journal of Neuropsychiatry and Clinical Neurosciences* 5: 419–427.

Stroop, J. (1935). "Studies of Interference in Serial Verbal Reactions." *Journal of Experimental Psychology* 18 (6): 643–662.

Swan-Kremeier, L. A., Mitchell, J. E., & Faber, R. J. (2005). "Compulsive Buying: A Disorder of Compulsivity or Impulsivity?" In *Concepts and Controversies in Obsessive-Compulsive Disorder*, eds. J. S. Abramowitz, & A. C. Houts, 185–190. New York: Springer.

Swartzwelder, H. S. (2004). Certain Components of the Brain's Executive Functions Are Compromised Early in Abstinence. Medicalnewstoday.com. Retrieved December 30, 2007.

Takeuchi, D. T., Williams, D. R., & Adair, R. K. (1991). "Economic Stress in the Family and Children's Emotional and Behavioral Problems." *Journal of Marriage and the Family* 53: 1031–1041.

Tangney, J. P., & Fischer, K. W. (1995). *Self-Conscious Emotions: Shame, Guilt, Embarrassment and Pride*. New York: Guilford.

Tangney, J. P., Wagner, P., & Gramzow, R. (1992). "Proneness to Shame, Proneness to Guilt, and Psychopathology." *Journal of Abnormal Psychology* 101: 469–478.

Thom, B. (1986). "Sex Differences in Help Seeking for Alcohol Problems." *British Journal of Addiction* 81: 777–788.

Tenenbein, M., Casiro, O. G., Seshia, M. M. (1996). "Neonatal Withdrawal from Maternal Volatile Substance Abuse." *Archives of Disease in Childhood —Fetal and Neonatal Edition* 74 (3): F204–F207.

Thompson, P. M., Hayashi, K. M., Simon, S. L., Geaga, J. A., Hong, M. S., Sui, Y., et al. (2004). "Structural Abnormalities in the Brains of Human Subjects Who Use Methamphetamine." *Journal of Neurosciences* 24: 6028–6036.

Tinley, E. M., Yeomans, M. R., Durlach, P. J. (2003). "Caffeine Reinforces Flavour Preference in Caffeine-dependent, But Not Long-term Withdrawn, Caffeine Consumers." *Psychopharmacology (Berlin)* 166: 416–423.

Toomey, R., Lyons, M. J., Eisen, S. A., Xian, H., Chantarujipakong, S., Seidman, L.J., et al. (2003). "A Twin Study of the Neuropsychological Consequences of Stimulant Abuse." *Archives of General Psychiatry* 3: 303–310.

Troisi, J. D., Christopher, A. N., & Marek, P. (2006). "Materialism and Money Spending Disposition As Predictors of Economic and Personality Variables." *North American Journal of Psychology* 8: 421–436.

Tsushima, W. T., Towne, W. S. (1977). "Effects of Paint Sniffing on Neuropsychological Test Performance." *Journal of Abnormal Psychology* 86: 402–407.

Turkle, S. (1995). *Life Behind the Screen: Identity in the Age of the Internet.* New York: Simon & Schuster.

Twerski, A. (1990). *Addictive Thinking: Understanding Self-deception.* New York: HarperCollins.

U.S. Department of Health and Human Services, Public Health Service (USDHHS), National Institutes of Health. (1999). *A Report of the Task Force on the NIH Women's Health Research Agenda for the 21st Century,* Vol. 6. *Differences Among Populations of Women.* Bethesda, MD: NIH Publication No. 99-4390.

U.S. Department of Health and Human Services. (2004). *Health Effects of Cigarette Smoking.* Retrieved June 25, 2006, from http://www.cec.gov /tobacco/factsheets/HelathEffectsofCigaretteSmoking_Factsheet.htm.

U.S. Department of Health and Human Services. (2004). *Progress Review: Substance Abuse.* Retrieved June 19, 2006, from http://www.healthy people.gov/data/2010prog/focus26/.

UNICEF (United Nations Children's Fund). (2000, May). "Domestic Violence Against Women and Girls." *Innocenti Digest* No. 6 (Preliminary Edition). Florence, Italy: Innocenti Research Center.

Valence, G., d'Astous, A., and Fortier, L. (1988). "Compulsive Buying: Concept and Measurement." *Journal of Consumer Policy* 11: 419–433.

van der Kolk, B. A. (1989, June). "The Compulsion to Repeat the Trauma. Re-enactment, Revictimization, and Masochism." *Psychiatr Clin North Am* 12 (2): 389–411.

Velicer, W. F., Fava, J. L., Prochaska, J. O., Abrams, D. B., Emmons, K. M., & Pierce, J. (1995). "Distribution of Smokers by Stage in Three Representative Samples." *Preventive Medicine* 24: 401–411.

Verdejo-García, A., & Pérez-García, M. (2007). "Profile of Executive Deficits in Cocaine and Heroin Polysubstance Users: Common and Differential Effects on Separate Executive Components." *Psychopharmacology* 190: 517–530.

Verdejo-Garcia, A., Bechara, A., Recknor, E. C., & Perez-Garcia, M. (2006). "Executive Dysfunction in Substance Dependent Individuals during Drug Use and Abstinence: An Examination of the Behavioral, Cognitive and Emotional Correlates of Addiction." *Journal of the International Neuropsychological Society* 12 (3): 405–415.

Verdejo-García, A., López-Torrecillas, F., Giménez, C. O. & Pérez-García, M. (2004). "Clinical Implications and Methodological Challenges in the Study of the Neuropsychological Correlates of Cannabis, Stimulant, and Opioid Abuse." *Neuropsychology Review* 14: 1–41.

Verheul, R. (2001). "Comorbidity of Personality Disorders in Individuals with Substance Use Disorders. *European Psychiatry* 16: 274–282.

Verplanken, B., & Herabadi, A. (2001). "Individual Differences in Impulse Buying Tendency: Feeling and No Thinking." *European Journal of Personality* 15: 71–83.

Virick, M., & Baruch, Y. (2007). *Factors Determining Workaholism, Its Postive and Negative Consequences.* Paper presented at the Academy of Management, Philadelphia, August.

Volkow, N. (2007). "This Is Your Brain on Food. Interview by Kristin Leutwyler-Ozelli." *Sci Am* 297 (3): 84–85.

Volkow, N., & O'Brien, C. (2007). "Issues for DSM-V: Should Obesity Be Included As a Brain Disorder?" *Am J Psychiatry* 164 (5): 708–710.

Volkow, N., & Wise, R. (2005). "How Can Drug Addiction Help Us Understand Obesity?" *Nat Neurosci* 8 (5): 555–560.

Volkow, N. D. (2006). "Altered Pathways: Drug Abuse and Age of Onset." *Addiction Professional* 25–29.

Volkow, N. D., Chang, L., Wang, G., Fowler, J. S., Franceschi, D., Sedler, M. J., et al. (2001). "Higher Cortical and Lower Subcortical Metabolism in Detoxified Methamphetamine Abusers." *The American Journal of Psychiatry* 158: 383–389.

Volkow, N. D., Fowler, J. S., Wang, G. J., Hitzemann, R., Logan, J., Shlyer, D. J., et al. (1993). "Decreased Dopamine D2 Receptor Availanility Is Associated with Reduced Frontal Metabolism in Cocaine Abusers." *Synapse* 14: 169–177.

Volkow, N. D., Wang, G-J., Ma, Y., Fowler, J. S., Wong, Ch., Ding, Y-Sh., et al. (2005). "Activation of Orbitofrontal and Medial Prefrontal Cortex by Methylphenidate in Cocaine-addicted Subjects But Not in Controls: Relevance to Addiction." *The Journal of Neurociences* 25: 3932–3939.

Wakefield, K. L., & Baker, J. (1998). "Excitement at the Mall: Determinants and Effects on Shopping Response" *Journal of Retailing* 74: 515–539.

Walker, D. D., Roffman, R. A., Stephens, R. S., Berghuis, J., & Kim, W. (2006). "Motivational Enhancement Therapy for Adolescent Marijuana Users: A Preliminary Randomized Controlled Trial." *Journal of Consulting and Clinical Psychology* 74: 628–632.

Walker, M. B. (1989). "Some Problems with the Concept of 'gambling addiction': Should Theories of Addiction Be Generalized to Include Excessive Gambling?" *Journal of Gambling Behavior* 5: 179–200.

Walters, G. D. (1992). "Drug-seeking behavior: Disease or lifestyle?" *Professional Psychology: Research and Practice* 23 (2): 139–145.

Walters, S. T., & Baer, J. S. (2006). *Talking with College Students About Alcohol: Motivational Strategies for Reducing Abuse.* New York: Guilford.

Walton, M., Reischl, T., & Ramanthan, C. (1995). "Social Settings and Addiction Relapse." *Journal of Substance Abuse* 7 (2): 223–233.

Wang, G., Yang, J., Volkow, N., Telang, F., Ma, Y., Zhu, W., et al. (2006). "Gastric Stimulation in Obese Subjects Activates the Hippocampus and Other Regions Involved in Brain Reward Circuitry." *Proc Natl Acad Sci U S A* 103 (42): 15641–15645.

Watson, D., Clark, L. A., & Tellegen A. (1988). "Development and Validation of Brief Measures of Positive and Negative Affect: The PANAS Scales." *Journal of Personality and Social Psychology* 54: 1063–1070.

Weinberg, B. A., & Bealer, B. K. (2002). *World of Caffeine: The Science and Culture of the World's Most Popular Drug*. New York: Routledge.

Weitsman, Susan. (2000). *Not to People like Us: Hidden Abuse in Upscale Marriages*. New York: Basic Books.

Wellman, N., Kamp, B., Kirk-Sanchez, N., & Johnson, P. (2007). "Eat Better & Move More: A Community-based Program Designed to Improve Diets and Increase Physical Activity among Older Americans." *Am J Public Health* 97 (4): 710–717.

Weun, S., Jones, M. A., & Beatty, S. E. (1997, August). "A Parsimonious Scale to Measure Impulse Buying Tendency." Paper presented at the American Marketing Association Educators' Summer Conference, Chicago, IL.

Wheeler, J. G., George, W. H., & Stephens, K. A. (2005). "Assessment of Sexual Offenders: A Model for Integrating Dynamic Risk Assessment and Relapse Prevention Approaches." In *Assessment of Addictive Behaviors*, eds. G. A. Marlatt & D. M. Donovan. New York: Guilford.

Whelan, C. T. (1992). "The Role of Income, Life-style Deprivation and Financial Strain in Mediating the Impact of Unemployment on Psychological Distress: Evidence from the Republic of Ireland." *Journal of Occupational and Organizational Psychology* 65: 331–344.

Whelan, J. P., Steenbergh, T. A., & Meyers, A. W. (2007). *Problem and Pathological Gambling*. Cambridge, MA: Hogrefe & Huber.

Wiggins, J. S., & Trapnell, P. (1997). "Personality Structure: The Return of the Big Five." In *Handbook of Personality Psychology*, eds. R. Hogan, J. Johnson, & S. Briggs, 737–765. New York: Academic Press.

Wikipedia. (2008). *History of Coffee*. Retrieved May 19, 2008, from http://en.wikipedia.org/wiki/History_of_coffee.

Winn, M. (1977). *The Plug-in Drug*. New York: Viking Penguin, Inc.

Wisborg, K., Kesmodel, U., Hammer Bech, B., Hedegaard, M., Brink Henriksen, T. (2003). "Maternal Consumption of Coffee during Pregnancy and Stillbirth and Infant Death in First Year of Life: Prospective Study." *British Medical Journal* 326: 420.

World Health Organization. (1999, April). "The Newly Defined Burden of Mental Problems." Fact sheet No. 217, p.3. Geneva, Switzerland.

World Health Organization (WHO). (2004). "Preventing Violence: A Guide to Implementing the Recommendations of the 'World Report on Violence and Health'." Geneva, Switzerland, pp. 1–92. Retrieved December 1, 2008, from http://whqlibdoc.who.int/publications/2004/9241592079.pdf.

World Health Organization (WHO). (2005). "WHO Multi-country Study on Women's Health and Domestic Violence against Women: Initial Results On Prevalence, Health Outcomes And Women's Responses." Geneva, Switzerland, pp. 1–38. Retrieved July 15, 2008, from http://www.who.int/gender/violence/who_multicountry_study/ summary_report/summary_report_English2.pdf. Retrieved via: http:// www.who.int/gender/violence/who_multicountry_study/summary _report/en/index.html.

World Health Organization (WHO). (1990). *International Classification for Diseases.* Geneva, Switzerland: World Health Organization.

World Health Organization. (WHO). (1992). *The ICD-10 Classification of Mental and Behavioural Disorders: Clinical Descriptions and Diagnostic Guidelines.* Geneva, Switzerland: World Health Organization.

Wu, L., Howard, M. O. (2007). "Psychiatric Disorders in Inhalant Users: Results from The National Epidemiologic Survey on Alcohol and Related Conditions." *Drug and Alcohol Dependence* 88: 146–155.

Wyshak, C. (2000). "Violence, Mental Health and Substance Abuse—Problems for Women Worldwide." *Health Care of Women International* 21: 631–639.

Yamakura, T., Harris, R. A. (2000). "Effects of Gaseous Anesthetics Nitrous Oxide and Xenon on Ligand-gated Ion Channels." *Anesthesiology* 93: 1095–1101.

Young K., & Klausing, P. (2007). *Breaking Free of the Web: Catholics and Internet Addiction.* Cincinnati, OH: St. Anthony's Messenger Press.

Young, K. S. (1998). "Internet Addiction: The Emergence of a New Clinical Disorder." *CyberPsychology and Behavior* 1: 237–244.

Young, K. S. (2001). *Tangled in the Web; Understanding Cybersex from Fantasy to Addiction.* Bloomington, IN: Authorhouse.

Young, K. S. (2004). "Internet Addiction: The Consequences of a New Clinical Phenomena." In *Psychology and the New Media*, ed. K. Doyle, 1–14. Thousand Oaks, CA: Am. Behavioral Scientist.

Young, K. S. (1998). *Caught in the Net: How to Recognize the Signs of Internet Addiction and a Winning Strategy for Recovery.* New York: Wiley.

Young, K. S. (1999). "The Evaluation and Treatment of Internet Addiction." In *Innovations in Clinical Practice: A Source Book*, eds. L. Vande-Creek & T. Jackson, 17: 19–31. Sarasota, FL: Professional Resource Press.

Yurchisin, J., & Johnson, K. P. P. (2004). "Compulsive Buying Behavior and Its Relationship to Perceived Social Status Associated with Buying, Materialism, Self-esteem, and Apparel-product Involvement." *Family and Consumer Sciences Research Journal* 32: 291–314.

Zhdanova, L., Allison, L. K., Pui, S. Y., & Clark, M. A. (2006, May). *A Meta-analysis of Workaholism Antecedents and Outcomes.* SIOP conference. Dallas, Texas.

Index

abstinence, 42, 81
abstract, 41, 145, 155, 240
accessibility, 1
accountability, 208
activity, 30, 43–44, 47, 53, 57–59, 81,
    108–112, 155–157, 169, 172, 186, 194,
    199, 226, 227; of addiction, 60, 98,
    121, 211; addictive, 17, 24, 43, 89;
    brain-chemistry-altering, 24; high, 81;
    of inactivity, 152; make-up, 205; non-
    drug, 36
adaptation, 73–74
addiction-prone, 17
addiction treatment, 1, 215, 220, 269
addictivity, 16, 226
adolescent, 84, 187, 192
adverse, 31, 84–85, 100
advertise, 16, 187; advertising, 32
affliction, 11, 32, 169, 230, 233, 234
alcohol, 2, 8, 18, 24, 25, 29, 30, 34, 40,
    57, 77, 84, 97, 99, 100, 105–107, 140,
    148, 152–153, 156–157, 163, 169, 174,
    185–188, 190, 192–193, 199, 201, 231,
    233; abuse, 41; alcohol-related stand-
    point, 31; and beta-endorphin craving,
    40; consumption, 17, 40; cues, 81;
    prior to birth, 9; use, 28; use disorders,
    11; users, 11
altered state(s), 14, 82, 226–227

amphetamine, 12, 34, 42, 70, 84, 207
anxiety, 20, 154, 192, 226
arousal, 21, 44, 156,
ASC (altered state of consciousness), 13–
    14, 68, 82, 226–227
association, 29, 77, 82, 89, 153, 162;
    association-driven learning, 89;
    between triggers, 82; brain is under-
    going, forming, 77–81; learned, 81, 82;
    random, 163; through learning, 65;
    with dealers, 156
ATP (amphetamine-type stimulant), 12,
    34, 35, 42, 70, 84, 207
attention, 13, 30, 50, 78, 117–118,
    121–122, 124, 126–127, 147–149, 151,
    172, 177–178, 181, 190, 194, 197, 232;
    attention-activating, 65; paying atten-
    tion, 21
attentional, 50, 79; bias, 3, 7–78, 81, 88,
    99, 130, 225
automatic, 21, 27, 53, 56, 67, 79, 82, 101,
    122, 133, 146–148, 152–153, 163, 170,
    174, 200, 220

behavioral change, 1, 74
belief system, 50
beta-endorphin, 40
bias, 3, 77–82, 88, 98–99, 130, 225
biochemical, 12, 28, 29, 40, 47, 58, 65,

89, 94, 100, 185, 206, 209, 215, 224;
    control, 223; mechanisms, 85; shift,
    24, 205
blame-the-victim, 216
blink, 80, 254
bond, 110–112, 139, 211
brain scan, 68, 74–75, 246
brainwashing, 66
break out, 132, 140, 148, 201
built-in, 39, 204

caffeine, 15–16, 42–45, 80, 157, 163, 174,
    186, 207
capacity, 3, 80
casual, 13, 98–101
CBD (cannabinol), 13, 35
chart, 37, 56, 103–104, 106–107, 121,
    159–166, 178, 199, 219; trigger chart,
    103–104, 106, 159–166, 178
chemical, 40, 42, 50, 58, 65, 155, 157,
    161, 167, 226, 227, 232;
    chemicalization, 19, 50, 188, 218;
    chemically dependent, 131;
    dependence, 186; level, 174, 180;
    man-made, 19; society, 187; struc-
    tures, 42; switches, 21, 219; trigger,
    151, 163
chemically dependent, 132, 187
child, 9, 14, 30, 52, 54–55, 68–70, 81,
    131, 138, 155, 185–188, 190, 192, 195,
    197–201, 208–209
chocolate, 44
clarity, 119, 123
co-addicted, 1, 69
cocaine, 9, 12, 30, 42, 58, 80, 103, 157,
    162–163, 186–187, 207, 232; crack, 12,
    34, 58
code, 2–3, 21, 33–34, 60, 67, 74–75, 97,
    157
coding, 3, 21, 39, 46, 63, 67, 70, 73–75,
    77, 87, 97, 101, 186, 219, 223, 227,
    230
cognitive control, 87–88
command, 68, 87, 94, 120
commitment, 118–122, 124, 126–127,
    141, 149, 167, 176, 178, 181, 219
commodity, 43
communication, 1, 117, 185, 188, 191–

192, 194–195; communication
    process, 1
conflict, 7, 67, 200, 207, 238, 240
consciousness, 14, 20, 54, 66, 123, 127,
    159, 161, 211, 224, 226–227
consequence, 12, 31, 56, 74, 84–85, 89,
    131
consistency, 119
consume, 8, 13, 15, 30, 41, 57–59, 155,
    186, 194; consumer, 13, 15, 57;
    consumption, 17, 30–31, 40–41, 45,
    57–61, 101, 171, 187
coping, 7, 24–25, 200, 206; mechanisms,
    7, 12, 24–25, 28, 46, 66, 77, 84, 85,
    200, 206, 232
cost, 11–12, 15, 47, 75
crave, 24, 32, 67, 147, 207; craving, 32,
    40, 42, 61, 81–82, 125, 130, 149, 162–
    163, 171, 174, 180, 187, 192, 204, 219,
    231
creature, 3, 15, 27, 29, 31, 33, 35, 37, 39,
    41, 43, 45, 47, 77, 101, 230
cues, 65, 78–83, 94, 225
cycle, 23, 40, 50, 59–60, 68–69, 75, 89,
    98, 113–115, 136, 141, 153–154, 161,
    168, 174, 197–199, 204–205, 209, 212,
    225; of addiction, 30, 42, 77, 94;
    addictive, 52, 65, 69, 149; of addictive
    patterning, 149; of detrimental
    patterning, 160; of discomfort-
    comfort, 108; of longing for contact,
    109; of pleasure-pain, 113–115

damage, 15, 41, 55, 189, 194, 204–208
death, 13, 15, 28, 45, 213, 220, 232
decision, 49–56, 83–85, 87–90, 98–99,
    118–120, 175, 208decision-making,
    49–50, 53–56, 83, 85, 88, 98
deficiency, 40, 224
denial, 75, 117, 131, 190, 198, 206–207,
    213, 231–233
dependence, 19–20, 25, 94, 131–132,
    160, 186, 194, 198
descent, 50, 101
desire, 8, 14, 24, 29, 42–43, 47, 67, 88,
    97, 118, 155, 164, 179, 187, 190, 209–
    210, 225–226, 231
destroy, 195, 212; destruction, 194–195

detrimental habits, 2, 28, 145, 198
development, 9, 13–14, 30, 43, 51–52, 74, 99, 126, 141, 145, 176, 188, 192, 195, 220, 231–232
dialoging, 1
dietary, 173, 186–187
diminishing, 42, 43, 65
directive, 2–3, 82
disability, 15, 29
discomfort, 31, 40–42, 47, 108, 205, 212, 226–227, 230–231
discounting, 84–85, 238, 254, 261; delay discounting, 84
discovery, 14, 140, 215, 217, 219, 221
disease, 2, 15, 30, 199, 215–218, 221, 230; disease model, 216, 218
disturbing, 9, 41, 74–75, 198
domestic violence, 193
dopamine, 31, 40, 85
dose, 29, 41, 43–45, 220; dosage, 44, 45
double bind, 131–132, 230
drink, 15, 24, 40–41, 43–44, 68, 74, 77, 81, 89, 99, 147–148, 156, 160, 163, 172–173, 186–189, 192, 216
drug categories, 34–35

economic, 8, 12, 23, 31–32, 59, 120–121, 219
elevate, 45, 262; elevation, 117, 129, 133–135, 138, 140, 145, 179, 181
empower, 56, 96
energetic, 68, 70, 93, 132–133, 147, 164, 167, 178, 181, 230
enslavement, 77, 219
environment, 7–9, 21, 23, 27, 58, 73–74, 80. 153, 157–158, 161–162, 167, 174–175, 180, 186, 195; environmental, 23, 58, 153, 157, 161, 167, 174–175, 180
epidemic, 11–13, 15, 41
equal, 8, 46, 121, 219
equalizer, 219
erotic, 74–75
escape, 20, 24, 33, 50, 68, 77, 94, 96–97, 115, 131–132, 205, 220, 225
evolve, 7, 66, 74; evolving, 7; evolved, 7, 66, 74
excessive, 30, 41, 46–47, 57, 59–61, 81

excuses, 190
executive functions, 52
exercise, 23, 52, 119–126, 156, 169–172, 178–179
exit, 21, 60, 68, 94–95, 117, 209
explicit, 25, 57, 68–71, 97, 99–100, 102, 140, 145, 151, 153, 157–160, 162–164, 174, 178, 185, 188–189, 193, 215–221, 225, 231
exposure, 12, 17, 46–47, 58–59, 197, 200, 209
externally-driven, 58–59

faith, 118, 125–127, 132, 178, 181
family, 13, 41, 49–50, 69–70, 124, 130, 162, 175, 177, 180–185, 187–195, 197, 199–201, 220; families, 3, 11, 31, 73, 100, 185, 188–189, 191–192, 194–195, 200–201
fault, 23, 97, 216
feedback, 7
financial, 31, 74, 94, 120, 245, 171
food, 2, 8, 17, 19–20, 23–24, 30–31, 36, 46–47, 49, 57, 59, 78, 80, 101, 121, 123, 130, 140, 153, 157, 163, 171, 173–174, 186–187, 195, 199, 210, 232
fortitude, 118, 124–127, 178, 181

gambling, 2, 8, 11, 17–18, 24, 29–30, 36, 46, 49, 74–75, 80, 88, 100, 140, 155, 233, 235
gaming, 2, 11, 29, 36, 46, 269
genetic, 21, 23, 27, 65–67, 74, 186, 197, 215, 232
glitch, 219
glue, 9, 30, 255
gratification, 8, 31
greater good, 55
grudge, 185, 188, 192–195

habitual, 27–29, 31, 33, 35, 37, 65, 78, 153, 160, 206, 210, 240, 259
habituation, 66, 206
hallucinogen, 28–29, 35
harm, 14, 16, 32, 39, 47, 56, 58, 66, 145, 207, 210, 212–213, 226, 230
heart, 2–3, 42, 45, 75, 83, 121, 171, 177, 187–188, 200, 205, 212, 218, 220

highs and lows, 33, 129–130, 187,
    205–206
history, 13, 28, 40–41, 101, 177
hit, 24, 58–59, 69, 174, 187, 208, 233
holding pattern, 67, 132, 201, 208
hook, 46, 208
hunger, 9, 30–32, 156, 209, 226
hurt, 185, 188, 191–195, 200, 204, 212,
    220
hypersensitive, 81

identify, 2, 20, 52, 54, 95, 140, 151, 159–
    161, 177–178, 197, 219; dis-identify,
    54; identified, 2, 70, 149, 153, 159,
    167, 194, 199
identity, 23, 65, 155, 201, 218; identities,
    3, 20, 217
illegal, 11–12, 14, 16–17, 157, 187,
    226–227
illness, 124, 201, 218
illusion, 24, 98, 115, 230
impairment, 13, 29, 83
implicit, 57, 68–71, 93, 99–100, 133, 151,
    153, 156, 158, 160–164, 174, 176, 178,
    185, 187, 190, 194, 215, 225, 230–231
impulse, 46, 53, 67, 147, 160, 224
inadequacy, 23–25, 219
indigenous, 32, 226
inhaling, 12
inhibit, 82–85, 88–89, 119; inhibitory,
    83, 254; inhibition, 85, 89, 119, 246
injecting, 12
insight, 93, 129, 133–136, 138, 140, 161,
    179, 181, 231
internal map, 165
internally-driven, 58–59
intimate partner, 203, 204, 207,
    209–212
intimate partner violence, 203, 204
investment, 17–18, 43, 85

journey, 91, 124, 164, 178
judgment, 47–53, 55–56

legal, 11–12, 14–17, 28, 146, 157, 187,
    226–227
lie, 3, 8–9, 11, 14, 24, 29, 31, 40–42, 45,
    50–51, 53–59, 65–67, 73, 81, 96–97,

    100, 117, 124–125, 131, 139, 148, 156,
    164, 176, 185, 188–192, 194–195, 198,
    200–201, 204–205, 207, 210, 212, 216,
    219, 223, 226–227, 230–232; lying, 66,
    69–71, 73–75, 97, 99–101, 149, 189–
    190, 215, 230
life pattern, 2, 136, 138, 145–146, 199
light, 2–3, 44, 67, 75, 80–81, 101, 122,
    219–221, 223
limitation, 215–218
love, 12, 32, 43, 45, 80, 98, 102, 195, 197,
    200, 203–207, 209, 211–213, 220

macro levels, 1
management, 121, 145–148, 150, 167–
    181, 195, 232
map, 117–118, 136–138, 140, 159–161,
    163–166, 178, 199
mapping, 117–118, 155, 159–160, 164,
    166; pattern mapping, 159
marijuana, 13–14, 16, 29, 35, 70, 157,
    163
masochism, 209–212
materialism, 23–25, 50, 218
maturity, 52, 55
mechanisms, 12, 24, 28, 46, 66, 77, 84–
    85, 101, 149, 232mechanisms of
    substance, 1
messages, 3, 87, 188, 198, 207, 226
metabolize, 41
meth (methamphetamine), 2, 9, 12, 16,
    24, 28, 31, 34–35, 42, 45, 49, 51–52,
    56, 58–59, 65, 70, 77, 93, 97, 118, 121,
    125, 131, 133–134, 139, 147–149, 162,
    164, 167–168, 186, 189, 195, 198, 203,
    205, 207, 210, 226–227
mind, 1, 3, 11, 19–20, 23–25, 55, 61, 67,
    78, 81–82, 84, 87–88, 93, 96, 100, 118–
    123, 125–127, 133–134, 151, 153,
    157–158, 161–163, 177, 183, 185, 192,
    199, 218–220, 223–224, 226–227, 230,
    232–233; mind-brain, 1, 3, 55, 93, 96,
    219, 224
model, 13, 42, 52, 59, 73, 83, 97, 102,
    136, 215–219
moment, 1–2, 30, 53, 58, 73, 78, 81, 83–
    84, 118, 120, 123, 133, 140, 170, 179,
    204–205, 223–224

money, 32, 53, 83–84, 121, 152–153, 170, 175, 179–180, 194–195, 217, 233
moral, 50–56, 130, 206–207, 215–216, 233; morality, 50, 52, 130
mutilation, 37

narcotic, 34
neonatal, 12, 264
nervous system, 27–28, 42, 146, 148
neuron, 39, 41, 223–224
neurostimulants, 207
neutral, 74, 79–80
new response, 149, 174, 180, 231
nicotine, 15, 45–46, 157, 163, 174, 186
no-exit, 94
nondrug, 11, 17, 19, 24, 28–30, 33, 36, 46, 57, 79–81, 85, 93, 98, 185, 203, 219, 233
numb, 20, 28, 40, 121, 159, 206–208, 210, 215, 232–233; numbing, 206–208
nutrition, 31, 47, 94, 121, 156–157, 161–162, 169, 172–173, 175, 178, 180, 187, 195

obstacles, 124, 139, 148–149
on-ground, 2, 36, 46
opioid, 12–13, 40–42
opportunity, 8–9, 53, 93, 124–125, 140, 177, 181, 210, 220, 234
organize, 1, 82, 145–147, 162, 168, 170, 174, 179, 194, 225
outcome, 54–56, 75, 89, 125, 231
overcome, 2, 59, 90, 119, 121, 141, 143, 175; overcoming, 1–4, 28, 81, 117, 139, 145, 149, 169, 227, 230
overdose, 45, 220
overeating, 25, 36, 68, 156–157, 160, 164, 169, 173
overspending, 25

pain, 7, 9, 20–21, 24, 30, 31–32, 41–42, 44, 46–47, 67, 75, 104, 107, 113–115, 124, 131–133, 140, 156, 160, 176–177, 181, 192, 198, 200, 204–208, 211, 219–220, 226, 230, 233
pain killer, 107
paradox, 20–21, 59–60, 65–67, 69, 94–

95, 129, 131–133, 135–136, 138, 140, 146, 179, 181, 201, 230, 233
pathway, 30–31, 39, 46, 67, 78, 94, 97, 102, 130, 146–147
pattern addiction, 3, 5, 21, 24–25, 32–33, 43, 66, 69–71, 79, 81–82, 85, 87, 99–100, 117, 139–140, 149, 156, 167, 172, 177, 185, 187, 189, 193–194, 198, 210–202, 210, 212, 215, 217–218, 225, 227, 230, 233
pattern for change, 165
patterns of thought, 101
perception, 2, 20, 65, 90, 122, 132–133, 135, 149, 212
personal, 7, 11, 14, 51, 54–55, 97, 119, 131, 141, 145, 147–148, 172, 178, 185, 192, 202, 209–210, 212, 220, 224
physical, 20, 23–24, 28–30, 46, 49, 68, 101, 121, 146, 148, 156, 160–162, 167, 169, 171–172, 174–175, 177, 179, 200, 203–204, 206, 209, 211, 213, 219, 225, 233–234
pictures, 74–75, 79, 80, 83, 130
pioneer, 218
pleasure, 8–9, 15, 30–32, 39, 41–43, 45–47, 67, 97, 113–115, 170, 204, 209, 211
pornography, 18, 29, 26, 46, 57
pot, 8, 12–14, 30, 46–47, 58, 75, 89, 93, 97, 140, 160, 162, 172, 189, 204–206, 208, 227, 234
potential-laden, 93
practical, 151–152, 155, 161, 167–168, 179, 195, 197
pregnant, 186
prescription drug abuse, 16
prescription, 16–17, 157, 174
preserve, 66, 87, 188, 200
pressure, 3, 15, 24, 32, 42, 50–51, 58, 74, 141, 155–156, 160, 163, 176, 181, 186–188
prisoner, 93, 101, 225
progression, 97–99, 101, 103, 105, 107, 109–113, 115, 137
protection, 14, 195, 198
psyche, 19–20, 24, 57, 120, 219
psychoactive, 11, 13–14, 17, 44, 186, 233

pull, 19, 23, 42, 49, 52, 54–56, 67–68, 81–82, 94, 130, 163, 176

realization, 60, 93, 133
receptors, 45–46, 224
record, 27, 40, 89, 163, 169, 173, 176, 179–180, 217
recovery, 3, 60–61, 169, 177, 215–219, 221
redefine, 78
reflexes, 9, 67, 231
regular, 13, 15, 24–25, 45, 98–101, 157, 168–169, 171–173, 175, 178, 180, 187, 227
regulate, 7–9, 13, 226–227
reinforcement, 9, 23, 204–205, 209, 225
relapse, 81–82
relate, 11, 13, 30–31, 44, 67, 74, 78–81, 83–84, 89, 121, 139, 152, 162, 175, 180, 226; relating, 97–98, 194, 204, 208–209, 211
relationship, 2, 17, 23–24, 29–30, 36, 80, 97, 102, 108–111, 130, 133, 139–140, 145–146, 151, 163, 185, 194, 198, 203, 206, 208–213
relief, 8–9, 31, 40–42, 67, 97, 117, 204–205, 216, 226, 227, 230
repatterning, 23
resistance, 89, 149
resources, 9, 33, 39, 80–81, 94
revolutionary, 117
rewards, 9, 31, 74, 83–84, 88, 97, 126, 155, 204–205
rights, 14, 223, 225, 227; rights, 14
roller coaster, 30, 198–199, 211

sadomasochism, 209–212
scavenger, 225
school, 191, 195
science fiction, 232
selves, 2–3, 12, 15, 17, 20–21, 23, 25, 27, 31–33, 39, 44, 49–51, 54–55, 59–60, 66–67, 73–74, 78, 80, 82, 85, 93, 99–101, 118–119, 130–132, 135, 149, 154, 185, 187, 188, 200–201, 205–208, 211, 217, 219–221, 223, 225–227, 230–234
sensation, 8, 24, 40, 68, 104, 119, 146, 156, 203–204, 207

sex, 2, 11, 17, 21, 24, 29, 36, 46–47, 49, 57, 68, 74, 80, 101, 113–114, 140, 156, 204–205, 209–211, 232, 242–243
shopping, 2, 17–18, 23–24, 29, 31–33, 46, 57, 59, 80, 84, 171, 233
sickness, 2, 234
signals, 93, 224
situation-appropriate, 88
situational transcendence, 3, 90, 93, 95–96, 118–125, 127, 129, 131–133, 135–139, 141, 179, 202
slave, 39, 60, 77, 79–82, 187, 219, 230, 232
smoking, 12, 15, 45, 157
sniffing, 12, 157, 237
social drinker, 81
social, 12, 24–16, 20, 23, 31, 45, 51–52, 81, 121, 147, 151, 155–156, 160–161, 167, 176–177, 181, 185, 187–189, 191, 193, 195, 200–202, 215–218, 225, 231–232
societal excess, 58–59
societal tolerance, 16
society, 16, 24–25, 81, 187, 201–202, 216–217, 221, 227, 233; societies, 3, 16, 27, 100, 201, 227, 232
soul, 121, 200, 219–220, 234
spending, 2, 8, 18, 25, 29, 31–32, 46, 80, 140, 151, 156, 169–171, 194, 201
spiritual, 14, 118–119, 125, 134–135, 155, 161, 167, 176, 178–179, 181, 188, 218–220, 226, 233
stabilize, 208
steroids, 29, 35
stigma, 216, 218, 234
stimulant, 12, 28, 42, 45, 105, 162, 186, 207, 224
stimulus, 42, 79–81, 243; stimuli, 79–81, 83, 88
strength, 119, 124–127, 178
stress, 21, 25, 30, 132–133, 145, 152, 154, 163, 176–178, 181, 194, 198, 218, 225
Stroop Effect, 79
structure, 42, 95, 99, 155, 195, 259, 267
struggle, 19, 88, 125, 129–131, 135–136, 148, 140, 179, 181, 187, 219–220
sub-cycles, 78

subconscious, 16, 40, 75, 78, 81–83, 85, 102, 119, 125, 130, 148, 201, 211

substance, 2, 8–9, 11, 13–17, 20, 24, 28–31, 24, 29, 46, 57–59, 79, 84, 88–89, 98, 149, 153, 219, 225, 231

sugar, 8, 157, 162, 173, 186–187

surfacing, 69

surgery, 143, 145, 147, 149–150, 168, 230

survival, 7–9, 32–33, 39, 47, 66–67, 73–75, 81, 87–88, 101, 227, 234; counter-survival, 7, 9, 66

susceptibility, 14, 58, 66, 227; susceptibilities, 3, 27

switch, 20–21, 219

symptoms, 29, 42, 44–45, 57, 68, 177, 188, 192, 217, 224, 230

synapse, 223–227

teach, 17, 49, 51, 61, 81, 96, 177, 195, 198–199, 220, 226, 244; teaching, 51, 61, 96, 195, 198, 220

teen, 14, 51, 69, 147, 187–188, 197–199

television, 17, 37, 51, 53, 57–58, 147, 154, 207, 232–233

temporal, 39, 152, 161

THC (tetrahydrocannabinol), 13

thinking process, 3

tolerance, 16, 29, 42–43, 47, 206–207, 226

tradition, 15, 31, 66, 74, 226; traditional, 15, 31

tranquilizer, 233

transcendence, 3, 28, 90–91, 93, 95–96, 117–127, 129–133, 135–141, 145, 177–179, 188, 202, 217, 219–220, 234

transfer, 139, 153, 185, 197, 207

trap, 20–21, 59–60, 68, 94–96, 107, 129, 131–132, 136, 218, 230–231, 267

treatment, 1, 13–14, 46, 194, 215, 217, 220, 233

trend, 19, 41, 50, 239, 242, 245

trigger, 3, 21, 23, 30, 65, 68, 74, 77–82, 89, 93–94, 96, 103–107, 119, 147–149, 151–169, 169–170, 172, 175, 178, 180, 199, 224–225, 231

troubled, 2, 19, 28, 31, 46–47, 50, 57, 67, 81–82, 85, 93, 97–100, 102, 108–109, 111, 117, 139, 145, 187, 192–193, 198–199, 203–204, 215, 219, 221, 225, 227, 230, 233

Twelve Step, 118

underlying, 66, 69–71, 73, 75, 97, 99–101, 140, 215, 230

urge, 30, 53, 68, 143, 145, 147, 149–150, 160–161, 167–169, 174, 220, 230–231

value, 8, 43, 50, 53–56, 75, 93, 155, 172–173, 180, 195, 197

violence, 21, 29, 37, 203–204, 206–207, 213

web, 78, 160–161, 190, 193–194

well-being, 44, 47, 171, 240, 255

wired, 12, 40, 65, 70, 78, 96, 230

withdrawal, 29, 42, 44, 47, 81, 192, 204, 224

witnessing, 207

working, 3, 17, 21, 23, 31–33, 43, 48, 50, 52, 55, 57, 59, 77, 84–85, 88–89, 90, 100, 102, 117, 119–120, 123–124, 133, 163, 170, 185, 224–225

yes/no, 83

**Rewiring your self to break addictions
and habits : overcoming problem
patterns / Angela Browne-Miller.**

DATE DUE